AMERICAN LITERARY NATURALISM,
A DIVIDED STREAM

Library of Congress Cataloging in Publication Data

Walcutt, Charles Child, 1908–
    American literary naturalism, a divided stream.

    Reprint of the ed. published by the University
of Minnesota Press, Minneapolis.
    Includes bibliographical references.
    1. American fiction—20th century—History and
criticism. 2. American fiction—19th century—
History and criticism. 3. Naturalism in literature.
I. Title.
[PS379.W28 1973]   813'.03   73-10584
ISBN 0-8371-7017-6

Charles Child Walcutt

AMERICAN LITERARY NATURALISM, A DIVIDED STREAM

GREENWOOD PRESS, PUBLISHERS
WESTPORT, CONNECTICUT

FOR
SUE, MARGARET, AND PHIL

Preface

A STUDY of the naturalistic novel should perform two tasks. It should describe the body of theory that is designated by the term *naturalistic*; and it should show in some detail what this body of theory does to the novels in which it appears. The undertaking would be simpler if the theory actually controlled the "naturalistic" novel, but it does not; it merely affects it in a variety of ways. The body of theory involves philosophy, biology, sociology, psychology, physiology, and economics, loosely, of course, and in terms that change from one decade and writer to the next. What this theory does to particular novels, as well as where and how it is to be found in them, can be shown only through a close examination of a number of works that have been called naturalistic. We are dealing with an element and a tendency that takes as many forms as Proteus but never in itself accounts for the total aesthetic reality of a work of fiction.

My thesis is that naturalism is the offspring of transcendentalism. American transcendentalism asserts the unity of Spirit and Nature and affirms that intuition (by which the mind discovers its affiliation with Spirit) and scientific investigation (by which it masters Nature, the symbol of Spirit) are equally rewarding and valid approaches to reality. When this mainstream of transcendentalism divides, as it does toward the end of the nineteenth century, it produces two rivers of thought. One, the approach to Spirit through intuition, nourishes idealism, progressivism, and social radicalism. The other, the approach to Nature through science, plunges into the dark canyon of mechanistic determinism. The one is rebellious, the other pessimistic; the one ardent, the other fatal; the one acknowledges will, the other denies it. Thus "naturalism," flowing in both streams, is partly defying Nature and partly submitting to it; and it is in this area of tension that my investigation lies, its immediate subject being the forms which the novel assumes as one stream or the other, and sometimes both, flow through it. The problem, as will appear, is an epitome of the central problem of twentieth-century thought.

I am indebted to the following periodicals for kind permission to use materials which have appeared, in somewhat different form, in their pages: *PMLA*, the *Quarterly Review of Literature*, *Accent*, the *University of Kansas City Review*, *Papers of the Michigan Academy of Science, Arts, and Letters*, the *Sewanee Review*, and the *Arizona Quarterly*. I wish to thank the University of Minnesota Press for permission to reprint part of a chapter on Frank Norris which appeared in *Forms of Modern Fiction*, edited by William Van O'Connor, 1948; the University of Michigan Press for the same courtesy with regard to a monograph on Winston Churchill published as Number 18 of *Contributions in Modern Philology*, 1951; and the University of Indiana Press for permission to reprint, with substantial modification, "Theodore Dreiser and the Divided Stream," from *The Stature of Theodore Dreiser*, edited by Alfred Kazin and Charles Shapiro, 1955.

It is a great pleasure to acknowledge my indebtedness and my gratitude to friends who have been generous with suggestions and counsel that make this work much less imperfect than it would otherwise have been — to Warner G. Rice for penetrating criticism and kind encouragement since the inception of the project; to Frederic I. Carpenter for criticizing several of the chapters and for many suggestions that have contributed greatly to the formulation of my central thesis; to Howard Mumford Jones for guidance throughout the undertaking; to Eugene S. McCartney, who persuaded me to take a second and often a third look at certain irresponsible metaphors (but who is not to be blamed for any that remain); to George Arms for reading the entire manuscript in an earlier form and making many valuable suggestions; to Ray B. West, Jr., for very helpful suggestions on the first two chapters; to Harry Kurz for improving some of my translations from Zola; to James H. Case, Jr., for assistance in preparing the manuscript and for much personal stimulation; to Edwin M. Moseley for many enlightening discussions of modern literature; to James E. Tobin, for generous help with the index; to Jeanne Sinnen, of the University of Minnesota Press, for most sympathetic and intelligent help with the manuscript in its final stages and for catching a variety of small errors; and especially to my wife for invaluable assistance at all stages of my work.

C. C. W.

September 1956
Queens College
Flushing, New York

Contents

AMERICAN LITERARY NATURALISM,
A DIVIDED STREAM

I

New Ideas in the Novel

Something extraordinary happened to the American novel about 1890, when what is called the Naturalistic Movement began to gather momentum. It was a wonder, a scandal, and a major force. Its effects appear everywhere today, both in fiction and in popular attitudes, for it reflects at once our faith in science and our doubts about the modern "scientific" world. And perhaps because the effects of science have been so disturbing and ambiguous, the true character of naturalism has not been determined. In one form it appears a shaggy, apelike monster; in another it appears a godlike giant. Shocking, bestial, scientific, messianic — no sooner does its outline seem to grow clear than, like Proteus, it slips through the fingers and reappears in another shape. The critics reflect its elusiveness. Whereas one authority describes it as an extreme form of romanticism, another counters that it is the rigorous application of scientific method to the novel. When others say it is desperate, pessimistic determinism, they are answered by those who insist that it is an optimistic affirmation of man's freedom and progress.

These authorities are not all mistaken. On the contrary, they are all correct. But each has reached his conclusion by looking at different aspects of naturalism, at different times between 1890 and about 1940, and having committed himself to a confining definition he has found it difficult to consider other areas and aspects of the subject. The Beast, which cannot be named until it is caught, is indeed of a Protean slipperiness. But if it may not be caught and

3

held in a single form, it may be observed in enough of its forms so that we can finally mark the varieties and the limits of its changes. Only in this way can naturalism be explained and defined. Seeing it in perspective involves a considerable step backward through the centuries; but it can be taken quickly.

THE EMERGENCE OF NATURALISM

All literature is founded on some concept of the nature of man. When a major new literary trend appears it either assumes or defines some new concept of man and therefore of his place in the world. Such a new image takes its shape against the background from which it has emerged and against which it has in some way reacted. Naturalism has its roots in the Renaissance, its backgrounds in the Middle Ages. The medieval idea of man (which lived on, indeed, through the nineteenth century) was of a fallen creature in a dualistic universe. This dual universe was divided into heaven and earth, God and Satan, eternal and temporal, and, in man, soul and body. Its values pointed always toward the eternal, toward salvation and God — away from the temporal, the worldly, and the natural; for nature was under God's curse. Man too, by his own Fall, was under God's curse. Having both body and soul, he was torn in the eternal battle between good and evil. Man's physical nature — his desires and instincts — was, by and large, the Devil's playground; it had contributed to the original Fall and it continued to corrupt his will and his reason. Nonhuman nature was not only under God's curse; it was also unpredictable because of the workings upon it of fiends and the occasional miraculous intervention of God or a saint.

Reliable truth came from God to man through particular miraculous revelations and through the permanent miraculous authority of the Scriptures, which were interpreted and systematized by the Church. The Church was ordained by God; its head, the Pope, was divinely inspired. Emphasis on authority prevailed: in matters of dogma the Church Fathers of the fourth and fifth centuries were consulted; religious practices and personal morality were rigidly prescribed by the wisdom of the past, for neither man's impulses

4

nor his reason could be trusted; the sovereign, divinely appointed, was not subject to popular mandate; and for the final word on nature men turned not to experiment but to books — to the antique wisdom of Aristotle, Pliny, or Isadore of Seville. Authority dominated then, as reason and observation do today. Science, called "natural philosophy," was not an end in itself; it was "the handmaid of theology," pursued for the glory of God.

This subordination of nature and its dualistic separation from spiritual matters began to vanish during the Renaissance, as a new concept of the nature of man took shape. The change began with astronomy, the science furthest from man and society, but it got to man very rapidly, in a series of great intellectual strides that may be reviewed briefly by reference to the thinkers who made them.

Late in the seventeenth century, Sir Isaac Newton formulated mechanical laws that explained the movements of the planets in our solar system. He calculated their masses, velocities, and gravitational attractions; suggested that the energy and matter in the universe were constant and indestructible; and speculated that the universe was composed of billions of minute particles in ceaseless motion. The work of many astronomers and philosophers — Copernicus, Kepler, Galileo, Descartes — had already pointed this way, but Newton's system seemed mathematically perfect and irrefutable (even Einstein has only modified it). It dignified nature and implied that its laws were not subject to God's miraculous intervention. This system did not consider the problems of form and growth, because according to it all forms were reducible to the same particles and hence the varying forms themselves were not within the scope of mechanical science. In other words, it dealt with phenomena in terms of ultimate constituents, and so it had no tools for the consideration of complex forms like life. The problems of mind and will were not considered, although God and the soul were not denied. But even though not carried to its logical conclusions, the system itself was essentially materialistic and supplied both the method and the direction for later thought. Applied to the individual, the Newtonian system would produce determinism; it would subject man to natural law.

5

Oddly enough, the outlines of a popular philosophy called deism, which anticipated the social and moral consequences of Newton's theories, were set forth some twenty years before the publication of his *Principia Mathematica* (1687). The deists appealed to man's nature as evidence against the orthodox belief that he was fallen. They said that man was innately and instinctively good; they doubted creeds and authority; and during the following century they put increasing emphasis on the worship of nature as God's only revelation. In this latter respect, a popular theology was drawing on science; yet its actual import — and certainly its literary expression — appeared in the belief that the essence of God, nature, and man was to be found in the noble principle of reason. By the end of the eighteenth century, deism's corollary, the philosophy of naturalism (so called because it joined man and God through nature's law of reason), was widely influential; but because science had not yet adequately implemented it with biological data, it was not rigorously applied to man, the works of "necessitarians" like Bentham and Godwin exercising the fascination of rhetorical novelty rather than basically altering the popular belief in the existence of the soul and in man's freedom to sin and be eternally punished therefor. It was in the nineteenth century that scientific method, deistic faith, and biological discoveries began seriously to converge upon man and to suggest not only that his nature was good but also that his natural self was his ultimate self. This trend was soon to be tremendously accelerated by the positivism of Auguste Comte and the Darwinian theory of evolution.

Positivism was presented as an empirical, naturalistic method of finding truth. It stresses accuracy and objectivity and affirms that the only significant reality is the content of experience. The function of science is to observe facts and formulate laws which explain those facts. But positivism was much more than a method. It was a torch to burn the dark rubbish of the past and to light the way into the future. Living in the period following the French Revolution, Comte was impelled by a desire to establish society and its institutions on a more solid foundation. To that end he sought a new faith that would use the intellectual advantages of the age to unite men in a common purpose. In his *Cours de Philosophie Positive* (1830) he devised his famous law of the three stages of thought as it progresses toward maturity. They are the theological, the metaphysical, and the scientific, to which he applied the very prejudiced terms *fictitious* (i.e., mythical), *abstract*, and *positive*, respectively, the last being the triumphant stage at which mankind will for the first time in history enjoy a reliable basis for progress. In this final stage science is descriptive rather than — as philosophy had attempted to be — explanatory. Comte rejects the pursuit of first causes and absolute truths; he wants "effective" causes from which useful laws may be deduced, and he firmly asserts that all phenomena are subject to physical laws. Here is a sweeping rejection of the authority and supernaturalism of the past.

Comte went on to classify the sciences in the order of their complexity, dependency, and perfectibility. He arrived at the conclusion that sociology was the last in each of these categories: it was the most complex; it required the pre-existence of the other sciences; and it would be the last to attain the perfection of positive method. Sociology thus became the unifying discipline of human thought and its purpose the perfect organization of human society. A religion of progress was offered to replace the darkness of antique superstition.

Darwin's *Origin of Species* (1859) was a culmination in the field of biology of the naturalistic temper of the period, presenting a hypothesis toward which many streams of thought and investigation had been converging. A hundred years earlier Montesquieu (*Esprit des Lois*, 1748) had proclaimed the influence of environment in all human affairs. Malthus had written (*Essay on the Principle of Population*, 1798) on the over-fecundity of nature. Wallace, unknown to Darwin, worked in the same area toward the same conclusions. Darwin employed the positive method to show how natural selection operated to produce new species. His theory challenged the prevailing belief of biologists in the immutability of species; it challenged the teleological concepts of "purpose" and "design" in the universe, for it attributed the physical changes of

7

evolution to millions of accidents, innumerable false starts, and the pitiless waste of individuals and even of whole species. Studying man in the perspective of his biological development, it inevitably emphasized his animal nature. To the horror of the pious, it appeared to destroy the foundations of religion and (consequently) of morality. Scientists and the scientifically minded, on the contrary, did not consider it immoral to know the truth; and though some of them said that truth could not damage religion, others were eager to jettison unwieldly dogma and sail with clear fact into the hopeful future.

The works of Comte and Darwin — who are only illustrious figures in a great movement — brought the promise of Newton's mathematics home to man and society. They did not abolish dualism and dispose of the supernatural once and for all, but they made it possible to believe that man could be completely accounted for by physical, psychological, and social facts. When this program won a limited assent, naturalistic fiction could be conceived and attempted.

Herbert Spencer converted Darwin's biological hypothesis into a cosmic generalization. With Comte, he considered that sociology was the end of science; and, like Ernst Haeckel after him, he was deeply impressed by the theory of the conservation of energy, a theory that was implicit in the Newtonian system but was not actually expounded until the nineteenth century. From 1860 to 1902 he labored over the volumes of his famous *Synthetic Philosophy* which attempted to assemble all the special sciences into a whole whose unifying principle was evolution. Just as the sidereal universe had evolved from a gaseous nebula, he maintained, so complex species developed from simple cells and the human will out of elementary sensations and reflexes. From this broad conviction it was only a step to moral and social implications of great significance. For example: Pleasure and good are identified with adaptability. Evolution moves society toward the good life. Ethics are improved as society evolves. Perfection is the final outcome of change. Human nature improves with its improving environment. Evolution toward more complex forms is nature's ultimate law.

The early effect of these beliefs was to affirm the idea of progress and provide a powerful impetus to scientific investigation, although the Darwinian hypothesis could have been — and later was — interpreted as defining a condition of endless and hopeless flux, in which improvement and decay alternated with no discernible purpose. But Spencer affirmed that once society had evolved to perfection it could maintain itself in that state indefinitely.

These naturalistic patterns exclude and indeed frequently assail the supernatural. About the human will, which is by definition "uncaused" and therefore not a material phenomenon, they are not so consistent. Spencer recognized the individual will as an element in natural processes, but he deplored as unnatural the social or collective will. He believed that the "natural" working of economic process included the individual wills and motives of intelligently selfish men — so that social evolution was guided by this trustworthy ingredient. Political and economic *laissez faire* brought about the survival of the socially fittest and thus contributed to evolution's majestic movement toward perfection. But Spencer placed so much importance on the "struggle for existence" and the "survival of the fittest" (this was his phrase, not Darwin's) that he could not look with approval on any organized exercise of the social will that might in any way protect the unfit. He condemned as "unnatural" everything from labor unions to pure food and drug laws. Contrariwise, Marx, on the left wing, interpreting this same "struggle for existence" in terms of class warfare, found the bourgeoisie, which produced for profit, guilty of interfering with the working man's "natural" instinct to produce well and abundantly. So the liquidation of the capitalists was to aid the survival of the more productive and therefore more "fit" workers.

Both Spencer and Marx invoked natural law, which they asserted would inevitably produce certain results; both stressed the power of the human will; and both with similar illogic became morally indignant at those who would presume to interfere with the "inevitable" natural processes. If this mixture, on both sides, of fervid exhortation with concepts of majestic inevitableness evokes a smile today, it also serves to remind us that naturalistic theory

9

was never able to free itself from human passion. All the critical problems ultimately derive from this conflict.

THE DIVIDED STREAM

The zeal of these researchers and theorists shows that the restoration of nature to importance does not, even when carried to the conclusion that all truth is to be found in her provinces, satisfy man's doubts or answer his emotional needs. Naturalistic philosophers since the Renaissance have been motivated by wonder and passion and fear. Just as deism leaped to worship reason long before it could prove that the cosmos was reasonable, so the assault on orthodox dualism sprang from need for a faith that could be united with fact — for a binding principle, an explanation that would unite the scientific and the spiritual domains. The answer came as transcendentalism, a philosophy which in its popular American form converted the formalized and somewhat arid faith of the deists into a dynamic and emotional creed. Deism sustained the wonderful reasonableness of the Founding Fathers; transcendentalism became the spirit of American expansion, the statement of the American Dream of individual opportunity, freedom, and greatness. Transcendentalism rises through the belief that knowledge brings liberty, to its apotheosis of making man equivalent to God.

The essence of transcendentalism is to be found in Emerson's repeated statement that Nature is a symbol of Spirit. This means that what is ideal or absolute as spirit is translated into physical laws and perfectly embodied (incarnated) as nature. It is a monistic philosophy which attempts to draw together the nature-spirit poles of orthodox dualism until they are touching, until, indeed, they are one. The relationship of spirit and nature in this monism can be simply represented as identical to the relation which relativity physicists have discovered between energy and matter: they are two forms of the same one. What seems ultimately to be an electric charge expresses itself as all the forms of the physical universe; taking a metaphysical step, one can infer that all the forms of the universe are latent or *ideal* in that charge. Give energy a moral quality, and you have Spirit. When a modern physicist like Sir James Jeans says that reality seems ultimately to correspond to a thought in a logical mind, he is expressing a version of transcendentalism. If, as Emerson says, "Every natural fact is a symbol of a spiritual fact [i.e., an idea]," it follows that the physical is a form of the divine. "The axioms of physics translate the laws of ethics," and nothing in the world fails to have spiritual significance.

In Emerson's system, man's mind is an aspect of spirit, his body a fact of nature. Thus through the mind, by what the transcendentalists called reason or intuition, man can directly experience truth — or call it the Absolute — because he is that Absolute. He can also approach truth through science, because every natural fact is a symbol of a spiritual fact and when penetrated by the mind will give up its ultimate or spiritual meanings. The mind's contemplation of itself and the study of nature are equally spiritual quests. The system stresses responsibility but not authority: every man is as great as he makes himself; truth is his if he will seek it; no church or power is its special custodian.

Henry Thoreau's successful quest for peace through intuition was achieved by a devoted examination of nature: "God himself culminates in the present moment, and will never be more divine in the lapse of all the ages," he says in *Walden*, and he continues that "we are enabled to apprehend at all what is sublime and noble only by the perpetual instilling and drenching of [ourselves by] the reality that surrounds us." Whitman's early delight in the phenomenal world conveys the same idea of unity:

> You have waited, you always wait, you dumb, beautiful
>   ministers [i.e., phenomena]
> We receive you with free sense at last, and are insatiate
>   henceforward . . .
>   "Crossing Brooklyn Ferry," 1856

Emerson left the ministry because he could not be bound by a doctrine of special or limited access to the divine:

> The word unto the prophet spoken . . .
> Still floats upon the morning wind,
> Still whispers to the willing mind.   "The Problem," 1839

The transcendental ideal of freedom through knowledge expresses America's belief in science and in physical progress as an image of spiritual progress. It unites the practical world and the spiritual world, in a spiritual quest for perfection through mastery of nature. Reason and instinct, fact and faith, join in the image of a perfectible present, a physical world whose conquest would be not only a symbol but also an embodiment of spiritual conquest.

This idea, which is the American Dream, stands somewhere between medieval otherworldliness and the skepticism of the twentieth century. In the Middle Ages revelation was the source of spiritual truth. Natural truth was both unimportant and unreliable. Today we are very skeptical of any ultimate design in nature, for we are apt to believe that the human species is about to prove the absence of design by destroying itself — leaving the world to the next species, as the dinosaurs left it to us. Between these extremes, in the nineteenth century man believed in a divine plan that was to be found in nature. Nature was the physical expression of divine reason, and in its laws revealed the forms and purposes of God. The scientific penetration of nature became a spiritual quest, therefore, into absolute Being. The philosophical basis of this quest is *monistic*: spirit and nature, soul and body, are various expressions of one unified reality. There can be no basic separation of them, as there was in the medieval view of the cosmos.

This monism was the dream that glowed behind naturalism in American thought. But the monist sea (a favorite nineteenth-century symbol of unity) did not stay one. Just as the language of analysis divided it with the words spirit and nature, showing how difficult it is to think a monism, so time and experience divided it into streams of optimism and pessimism, freedom and determinism, will and fate, social reformism and mechanistic despair. When the Nature which was assumed to be a symbol and version of God and of man's spirit grew under scientific analysis into a force which first controlled man's will and presently made it seem an illusion, then it became alien and terrifying; and man's nature too revealed, upon further exploration, depths that were repellent rather than godlike.

The American Dream was a theory, an abstraction, that never completely dispelled old taboos or eliminated the traditional distrust of emotion and impulse. The struggle against authority, which brought in the Renaissance, liberated reason first and emotion a slow second. Indeed, reason had a long head start. Even in the Middle Ages it was the delight of all thoughtful people, though "officially" distrusted. The Puritans likewise were indefatigable rationalists and disputants, always happy to match wits with the benighted. But man's emotions had been distrusted for so many centuries that they could not easily win free from the taint of sin. It was popular during the eighteenth century to say that man's impulses were humane and beautiful; but in America the Puritan tradition kept the flesh a disgrace. Our leading transcendentalist thinkers — Emerson, Thoreau, Alcott — were proper and inhibited to an extreme. Emerson recognized a disciple in Whitman but urged him to suppress physical details in *Leaves of Grass*. When naturalistic writings ignored sexual taboos, they offended other people than Emerson and impelled them back toward the old dualist position that the flesh was, indeed, vile. Monist theory that the instincts were divine could not remove old attitudes. It became easy to denounce frankness as sensationalism, as morbid, as a rejection of American optimism.

Freedom from the taboos of conservative taste and propriety could be a means to a host of desirable ends — ends of truth, freedom, and candor. But when such freedom turned into sensationalism, which seemed to be an end in itself, the reaction toward propriety and conservatism was understandable. The reaction, furthermore, isolated the sensationalism from the more acceptable theoretical expressions of the American Dream. Nor was this entirely a conservative reaction; it is possible for the most liberal reader to find the naturalists' exploration of the dark alleys of human experience obsessive. Sensationalism as a means, pursued thus obsessively, becomes an end. This metamorphosis of means into ends occurs in other areas. It is interesting to turn back to the treatises of Adam Smith or John Stuart Mill and see how completely they subordinated economic activity and democratic process

13

to the ideal of personal freedom and enrichment which they held always before them as the true reward of productive efficiency or progress in democracy. Today, by a metamorphosis that helps to explain this other debasement of idealism into sensationalism, productive efficiency has become an end in itself. The old goal of personal fulfillment deteriorates as the economic means have become ends. In the same way, we have seen scientists abdicate social responsibility, even while they have been rediscovering transcendental unity through relativity physics. The escape from taboo, like the expansion of economic process, can become obsessive and defeat its own ideal ends.

Recent "science fiction" reveals exactly the same processes. Writers like Ray Bradbury, A. A. Van Vogt, Henry Kutter, and a host of others (Orwell's *1984* is in the same class) have been exploring the social and human prospects of a future in which first the machine and then the techniques of mass manipulation have taken charge of man. Society depends upon technological powers to the point where individual freedom cannot be tolerated. The little man must be oriented and organized to the machine. As he becomes more dependent upon it and as its complexities multiply, society itself becomes part of a mechanism.

These dire prophesies of brain-wash and total propaganda come from writers who are devoted to the ideal of human freedom. Their exploration of the ways in which the human spirit may be suppressed has some of the obsessive quality of Swift's fascination with what he found repulsive in man. But their exploration of this horror has had the effect of domesticating it. Being described again and again, often with great imagination, it acquires the fascination of the abomination. It comes to constitute, through repetition and imaginative identification, the only possible future. Youthful readers of science fiction abound who do not suspect the moral implications of these tales and who regard the coming of brain-wash and thought-police as among the inevitable corollaries of space travel.

And thus it would be possible, if not just, to accuse these writers of promoting the very horror they set out to expose. They might be denounced by social "idealists" — whom they in turn would accuse of being the very ostriches who by their willful blindness to what is happening today make the horror of the future probable. This was the situation, early in this century, of the naturalists and their various indignant critics. Both sides believed in Man. Both were moral in intention. Yet each saw the other as the enemy of the Dream. If it is true that science fiction conditions us to expect the Total State, it may be true that naturalistic fiction was an influence in the movement toward pessimism, materialism, and despair. However confidently and happily it was undertaken, the demonstration that social forces operate to control human lives communicated grim pictures of physical deprivation, thwarted hopes, and human frustration. The conviction grew that man could not control the giant forces about him.

There are many other manifestations of this divided stream of transcendentalism. The transcendentalist union of reason and instinct has since deteriorated, on the one hand, into the popular notion that the educated don't have horse sense, that instinct is killed by cultivation, that "nature" is good but knowledge and reason are bad. On the other hand, when human and physical nature becomes unpleasant or unmanageable, it requires only the smallest step to separate good from evil by denouncing the refractory as essentially bad and falling back on authority for standards by which to exhort or chastise rebellious nature. We have still not adjusted the cultural lag that made emotion and instinct suspect. The idea of a whole which embraces nature, spirit, and the sum of human qualities, in perfect harmony, has been easier to define than to maintain.

Still another example of this divided stream has to do with scientific theory on the highest level — the level for which mathematics is the only accurate language — where the emotions of some of the world's leading physicists have become characteristically involved. The aim of Max Planck's quantum theory is, so far as a layman can trust the language, to determine the smallest possible unit of matter or energy. And it seems that the apparent continuous flow or continuity of matter and energy can be reduced, ultimately, to a succession of separate "jumps" by separate "particles." This smallest quantity Planck labeled a *quantum*. It further appears that these particles are known only by the jumps they take — and that the jumps are so quick that it is impossible to determine the position of a particle at any instant during the almost infinitely short time of its jump. Two conclusions have emerged from these investigations: first, that "matter" and "energy" are separate names for things that cannot be separated, since the "particle" and its "jump" are known only in terms of each other, and the particle in effect does not exist except when it is jumping, although its place at any point within the jump cannot be determined; second, that in measurements there is a final irreducible minimum of error which is due to the fact that the tiny "jump" of the "particle" is so quick that it is impossible for human measurement to determine where the particle is at any moment of its jump. (Our language, say the physicists, breaks down here, in this use of "jump" and "particles," but it is the best we can do.) Planck's great contribution was to formulate a theory (called the Indeterminancy Principle) and an equation which would account for this irreducible minimum of error.

It would occasion no surprise if laymen misinterpreted Planck's findings. According to the physicists it is impossible really to understand the quantum theory in any language but mathematics. But what are we to think when certain very eminent physicists seize upon Planck's concept of this irreducible area of ignorance and build upon it whole volumes devoted to re-introducing an element of "freedom" or "will" or "uncaused effects" into the realms of material causation? This is what Arthur Eddington in *The Nature of the Physical Universe* (1928) and James Jeans in *The Universe Around Us* (1929) have done. These volumes were received enthusiastically by those who found in them an attack on the chain of physical causation with which science had for more than a generation been fettering the human spirit.

The reader need not accept the word of a layman on this matter, for Max Planck himself published a volume (*Where Is Science Going?* 1932) in which he sought to combat these writings of Eddington and Jeans by reaffirming that man's inability to measure certain phenomena did not prove that they were "uncaused" and hence evidence of "freedom." In a colloquium appended to this volume, Albert Einstein explained that Eddington and Jeans were moved by the British literary tradition, a tradition that is rich indeed in its affirmation of the human spirit, to write volumes that went counter to what they as scientists must have known about the proper application of Planck's theory.

These literary physicists are in effect transcendentalists: they want to fuse mind or spirit with matter and thus to give nature a moral drive. But their use of Planck's equation to justify a reaffirmation of freedom shows that they do not really see the cosmos as one, for they reveal themselves as trying to widen a crack in the wall of physical law through which they can let freedom wiggle in — rather than seeing the whole range of physical law as an expression of spirit and therefore a *projection* of man's freedom throughout nature. Their hearts are not satisfied by their new monism, and they seek to temper the rigidity of their own laws. Their minds flow in the divided stream.

The elements of these contradictions, which I have illustrated at such length, are contained in every piece of naturalistic writing. There is always the tension between hope and despair, between rebellion and apathy, between defying nature and submitting to it, between celebrating man's impulses and trying to educate them, between embracing the universe and regarding its dark abysses with terror. The dynamics of transcendentalism demanded evolution, in order to give life to the system. Emerson frequently refers to the "aspiration" in nature: "Striving to be man, the worm Mounts through all the spires of form." Spencer used his evolutionary philosophy to justify predatory capitalism and the elimination of the "unfit" in sweatshops or mine explosions. Another version of cosmic process saw man as an accident in a movement toward eventual lifeless rest (entropy, it was called) when all cosmic energy would be absorbed and everything would be dead and uniform. This prospect justified ruthless self-expression, the brutal "superman" who smashed his way over natural and human obstacles. Yet Nietzsche's superman, Jack London's Wolf Larsen, and, a couple of generations down the scale, Mickey Spillane's Mike Hammer are all moral idealists.

These varieties of social and ethical confusion never entirely thrust from the writer's mind the orthodox Christian dualism that provides the framework within which naturalism reveals its intention and its meaning. The belief in free will and ethical responsibility, in a universe of rewards and punishments, in a world dominated by purpose and meaning, hovers like a ghost over almost every variety of naturalism in fiction. The naturalistic novelist was inspired by a zeal which he did not precisely relate to his avowed determinism and which therefore frequently turned him back toward dualism. He fell back, that is, on the tradition of Christian orthodoxy from which he had derived, unconscious of any inconsistency, the moral sanction for his belief in social justice and human rights.

From this point we can extend some of the historical perspectives of our problem: The Middle Ages saw revelation and authority solidly established over reason and nature, for reason was fallen and nature was under God's curse. But within the premises set by authority, reason was phenomenally active, and there was certainly more respect for *logical consistency* in those times than there is today. Today we are so used to assuming an absolute union of logical consistency with *exact observation* that we must be reminded that such a connection is not inevitable, that, in fact, it required five or six centuries for exact observation to overtake logical consistency. Medieval logicians could define their premises and argue from them as well as most modern scientists — perhaps better — but if there was an issue between observation and authority they automatically relied on the latter. Perhaps the cardinal fact of modern times is not that people observe more carefully, but that they rate observation first. Somewhere between the Middle Ages and the high Renaissance the premise that observation was more reliable than authority took hold. This process of taking hold extended painfully over at least a couple of centuries, for it took the idea that long to become established. But never completely established, for it is deeply seated in human psychology that one always tends to see what he expects to see — what his previous experience has conditioned him to look for. As far back as the thirteenth century a monk named Roger Bacon wrote a work on optics in which he explained the form and position of the rainbow with a perfect union of objective observation and logical consistency. As recently as the eighteenth century vaccination for smallpox was assailed with absolute horror by the medical profession; and less than a hundred years ago, clear proof that the infection of puerpural fever could be carried from one mother to another on the hands of a doctor was passionately rejected.

Nevertheless, at some point the premise was accepted and first-hand observation became as important as logical consistency. As this premise gained strength slowly and unevenly over the years, now in one area of knowledge, now in another, depending upon the religious, the social, the economic, or merely the emotional convictions that were challenged by such observation, nature — the thing that yielded truth to observation — rose in status, enjoying attention, respect, reverence, and fear in proportions that reflected the fluctuations of attraction and repulsion for instinct, which we have already considered.

During the seventeenth century astronomy made prodigious strides, and John Locke laid the foundations of mechanistic psychology. In the eighteenth century nature was sentimentalized under a myth that human nature was the pattern and model of divine reason:

> The proper study of mankind is man.

Ecstasy over this idea produced more complacent speculation about "nature" than observation of it. In the early nineteenth century, the romantic fusion of nature and reason, whether in Wordsworth's "presence Whose dwelling is the light of setting suns, And the round ocean and the living air," or in Thoreau's enraptured contemplation, achieved the emotional force of religion. Then, later in the century, the worship of reason-nature gathered momentum as an assault on convention, on moral and social values, hitherto unquestioned, that rested on the dualist religious authority of the past. It swept on into an affirmation of progress through knowledge of hard scientific fact; and then the facts grew dark, inscrutable, overpowering, and man cowered under the threat of forces he could not control.

SOME CRITERIA OF LITERARY NATURALISM

Literary naturalism moves among three patterns of ideas: the religion of reason-nature, revealed in an enraptured contemplation of Process; the attack on the dualist (therefore unscientific) values of the past; the recognition and slowly growing fear of natural forces that man might study but apparently could not control.

Out of the never-resolved tension between the ideal of perfect unity and the brutal facts of experience come the themes, motifs, forms, and styles through which naturalism found literary expression. These are all part of the picture of naturalism, although some are there more or less by chance. To list them briefly is to suggest the rather disorderly composition of this picture.

The major themes and motifs are *determinism, survival, violence,* and *taboo.* The theme of determinism, which is of course basic, carries the idea that natural law and socioeconomic influences are more powerful than the human will. The theme of survival grows out of the application of determinism to biological competition; the notion that survival is the supreme motive in animal life provides a point of view from which all emotion, motivation, and conflict may be approached; it fastens man to his physical roots. The theme of violence grows with the transfer of emphasis from tradition (ultimately supernatural tradition) to survival. Animal survival is a matter of violence, of force against force; and with this theme there emerge various motifs having to do with the expression of force and violence and with the exploration of man's capacities for such violence. "The lower nature of man," in short, is revealed, explored, emphasized. It is also defiantly and triumphantly brandished; it may indeed be worshiped! A generation later this theme will be found to have modulated into the discovery of psychic recesses — the acknowledgment of new kinds and qualities of emotional experience. The last link in this chain, dangling from survival and violence, comes as an assault on taboo: a host of topics that had been considered improper — sex, disease, bodily functions, obscenity, depravity — were found to be in the province of physical survival. In that province, where the naturalists focused their attention, they could not be ignored. Nobody wanted to ignore them.

The forms which the naturalistic novel assumes are *clinical, panoramic, slice-of-life, stream of consciousness,* and *chronicle of despair.* When the idea of the free, responsible human will, making ethical choices that control its fate, is set aside in favor of such concepts as determinism and survival, a new notion of social process has appeared. It is dramatized (or enacted) in these new kinds of novels. Biological determinism can be set forth in a clinical study of disease or deterioration, in which the course of the malady or mania is traced step by step as it destroys the individual. When these forces operate in or through the whole body of society, a panoramic novel appears. Zola's *Germinal,* which "studies" a coal mining community and shows the miners helplessly squeezed to the edge of starvation by laissez-faire capitalism, is the classic of this form and the archetype of the proletarian novel. The minute and faithful reproduction of some bit of reality, without selection, organization, or judgment, every smallest detail presented with "scientific" fidelity, is the formless form of a slice-of-life novel. The same approach, but to the content of the mind (all the data of experience) rather than to external reality, gives a stream of consciousness novel, in which every smallest detail of thought is presented without selection, organization, or judgment. And finally there is the chronicle of despair, in which a whole life is depicted as the weary protagonist trudges across the dreary wastes of the modern world and finds, usually, an early death. *Studs Lonigan* in 1930 or Motley's *Knock on Any Door* in 1950 have almost exactly the same form.

The reader who has followed through the second part of this chapter will by now be uncomfortable in his recognition that these five forms do not — any of them — allow for both parts of the divided stream or for the tensions which I have said were inseparable from naturalism. The point is that naturalism involved a continual *search* for form. These are the forms it would have attained if its materialistic premises had been wholly and consistently followed. The fact that such premises were not — and probably could not have been — consistently maintained accounts for the complexity and fascination of literary naturalism as a problem. The question will be explored in the last section of this chapter.

Naturalistic styles cannot be defined in any exclusive sense. They can be listed, perhaps, as *documentary, satiric, impressionistic,* and *sensational*; but these are not very accurate terms for describing styles, and they are certainly not exclusive. The ideal of a fact-freighted, uncolored, objective, "scientific" style can be stated, but it is not easy to find an example of it in the novel. Frequently the most superficially objective or restrained style is the most highly charged with bitterness or indignation — as in the minute and faithful reproductions of stupid conversations by, say, James T. Farrell, or the vitriolic attacks on the middle class by contemporaries of de Maupassant in France. At the other extreme, the style of Zola, the fountainhead of naturalism, is recognized as highly romantic by all the critics, as is the style of his closest follower in America, Frank Norris, who went to considerable pains in one of his essays to explain that naturalism was romantic rather than realistic.[1] In a "naturalistic" novel, where the subject matter is sensational, the style is likely to be restrained and objective; where the subject matter is commonplace, the style is likely to be turbulent or "romantic."

For these reasons, there cannot be a "naturalistic style." When applied to a literary movement, the term *naturalism* indicates the philosophical orientation outlined in the previous sections of this chapter. The term *romantic,* in this connection, indicates an attitude or quality — an exuberance or intensity of approach, a sense of vitality or richness, a feeling that the demands of the human spirit cannot be met by the commonplace or typical occasions of life. This romantic quality is frequently achieved by naturalistic subject matter presented (because it is sensational) in a style that is restrained and objective; here the effect would be called romantic, whereas the style would be called realistic. Where the subject matter is typically romantic, as for example in Melville's *Typee,* the romantic effect is rendered through a realistic style. Realism in style is, as everyone knows, relative: the "realistic" Dickens style has been turned by the passage of years into what might today be called romantic. Even in our time, what was the poignant, intense realism of Hemingway in 1927 has come to be considered romantic and even (God save the mark!) sentimental. When novels like Zola's *Germinal* and Norris's *McTeague* are considered naturalistic in philosophy, romantic in effect, and (though not consistently) realistic in style, it becomes very apparent that the three terms are not mutually exclusive; no one of them can characterize a novel to the exclusion of the other two. I use the term *naturalism* to indicate a philosophical orientation; *romanticism* to indicate extremes or intensities of effect; *realism* to indicate the apparent fidelity, through style, to details of objects, manners, or speech.

FROM SCIENTIFIC THEORY TO AESTHETIC FACT

The word *naturalistic,* then, labels a philosophy fairly adequately, but by the time we have passed through the varieties of social and ethical application that have been drawn from it and listed the forms, styles, and motifs that it has evoked, we dare speak of the "naturalistic" novel only with the reservations implied by quotation marks. The significant form of a novel cannot be deduced from the fact that its writer is a philosophical naturalist, for naturalism does not account for spirit, imagination, and personality. A work that was perfectly controlled by the theory of materialistic determinism would not be a novel but a report. It is not surprising, therefore, that critics have run aground or afoul of each other when they have tried to characterize the naturalistic novel with sweeping generalizations. Current theories about the nature of naturalism disagree in general and in detail. They disagree so fundamentally that they give diametrically contrary statements about the matter. The focus of discord seems to be the question of whether the naturalistic novel is "optimistic" or "pessimistic." Some critics insist that the essence of naturalism is "pessimistic determinism," expressing resignation or even despair at the spectacle of man's impotence in a mechanistic universe; others claim that the naturalistic novel is informed with a bright, cheerful, and vigorous affirmation of progress — of man's ability through science to control his environment and achieve Utopia.[2]

The hostility of such points of view might lead one to expect that their proponents were writing about entirely different groups of books, but they are not. It is true that one writer excludes Dreiser from the naturalistic movement, whereas another finds its epitome in his work; but on the whole these antipodal camps are dealing with the same works. The cause of the discord lies in the relation between science and literature: specifically, in the idea that scientific attitudes produce equivalent aesthetic effects. One group starts with the assumption that science is essentially optimistic and concludes that the naturalistic novel must therefore express an optimistic social purpose. Another group starts at the opposite end with the assumption that most novels of the naturalistic movement reveal a "pessimistic determinism" and concludes that the materialism of science must therefore be a philosophy of gloom and despair and that no novel written from its tenets can express any social purpose. A third set of critics, realizing that naturalistic novels embody "pessimistic determinism" and that scientists are generally idealists, innovators, and believers in progress, conclude that in the critical woodpile there is indeed a nigger, whom they cannot find.

The key to this puzzle (for it can be solved) lies in a distinction between what the socially minded man thinks and what the work of art is. The scientist who wants to improve the lot of man through knowledge and manipulation of the material world faces two obstacles: lethargy and unbelief. Some people think mankind is doing well enough. Others do not think that anything can be accomplished with "human nature" by scientific methods. The scientist-reformer therefore has to establish the validity of two assumptions: that the state of man needs to be improved, and that human conditions are determined by the operation of material causes which can be traced, recorded, understood, and, finally, controlled. The pieces of the puzzle fall into place when we understand that the best possible way to illustrate and validate these two assumptions is to write a "naturalistic" tragedy in which a human being is crushed and destroyed by the operation of forces which he has no power to resist or even understand. The more helpless the individual and the more clearly the links in an inexorable chain of causation are defined, the more effectively documented are the two assumptions which underlie the scientists' program of reform, for the destruction of an individual demonstrates the power of heredity and environment over human destinies. And if the victim's lot is sordid, the need for reform is "proved." The more helpless the character, the stronger the proof of determinism; and once such a thesis is established the scientist hopes and believes that men will set about trying to control the forces which now control men.

Thus can the scientists' "optimistic" purpose be served by a "pessimistic" novel; and thus we see how the deduction that both must be either optimistic or pessimistic is untrue. In the works of Zola we frequently see pictures of degeneration and depravity flourished with the enthusiasm of a side-show barker describing a two-headed lady. The zeal is such that one imagines the author rubbing his hands in delight over his monsters. The most casual reading of *L'Assommoir* will identify this fusion of opposites — of sordid degeneracy and soaring enthusiasm — which troubles only the logical and abstracting critic.

The optimism of the scientist is undeniable; I shall not discuss here the formidable probability that it is not justified by his philosophy of naturalism. Nor do I mean to maintain that naturalistic novelists like Zola and Frank Norris grasped the distinction between a social policy, which proposes action, and a work of art, which is essentially self-contained. There is, on the contrary, a sharp discrepancy between what Zola announced in *Le Roman Expérimentale* and what he performed in his novels; it corresponds to the discrepancy between Theodore Dreiser's socialism and the inexorable fatality that controls *An American Tragedy*. Returning for a moment to our optimism-pessimism dilemma, we should not be surprised to find the critic who proceeds from social theory to literary practice affirming that *An American Tragedy* is authentic naturalism because Dreiser suggests that "radical social reforms are imperative"; [3] whereas another might deduce, if he proceeded from the novel to the social theory, that the philosophy of naturalism is grimly pessimistic because the protagonist of the novel is utterly helpless to control his fate. But I should say that the novel is an almost ideal example of naturalism because within its framework Dreiser makes no proposals. He shows how, given certain hereditary and environmental conditions, what did happen had to happen; and he communicates this conviction because he is able to present so detailed an account of events that Clyde Griffiths is shown as powerless to choose at the very climax of the action and is never held morally responsible for his "crime."

Within its aesthetic frame the novel is completely deterministic and might be called pessimistic (though I should prefer merely to call it faithful to fact); it is for this reason that it can be considered an unusually consistent (and powerful) expression of the naturalistic philosophy. No novel, of course, can actually render the total context of an event. But it can create the *illusion* of doing so; and this is the fundamental aim, as well as the criterion, of this type of naturalistic novel. The writer's opinions about social justice cannot and will not interfere with the form of the work.

Observing the operation of determinism in *An American Tragedy,* the reader may well be led to conclude that something should be done to change the conditions that produce such tragedies. But this happens to the reader, not in the novel; and I believe it can be shown that it happens after and apart from the aesthetic experience of the novel, although of course it is an effect of the book and undoubtedly the author's intention. The force of this social conclusion depends, paradoxically, on the very inexorable fatality of the action. The ultimate social implications of the action are doubtless with the reader as he reads, too, since no man can stay constantly within the framework or be constantly and exclusively controlled by the assumptions of the work he is reading; indeed his awareness of social conditioning and of the effect of social and financial ambition on Clyde Griffiths is an important element in his awareness that the work of art which he contemplates is unique and self-contained. The conditions as given are absolute for Clyde, although for America they can be improved. Reading a naturalistic tragedy in which the hero appears to have no freedom, one can know that one is performing an act of freedom in reading the book, and can sense that the author is by no means contained by the determinism which controls his novel, for he appeals to the reader's freedom and idealism as he shows that his hero is trapped. Thus the heightening of the reader's social consciousness (and any impulse to social action which he may subsequently experience) comes precisely because the movement of *An American Tragedy* is so perfectly "fatalistic," presenting in its massive and lumbering fashion a superb integration of structure and underlying philosophy. Observing this, the reader enjoys an access of wisdom that would not come if he were being systematically exhorted to action.

But *can* anything but despair emerge from such a spectacle? And by what right do we call a naturalistic novel tragic, when its premises strip the protagonist of will and ethical responsibility? The answer lies, surely, in the fact that will is not really absent from the naturalistic novel. It is, rather, taken away from the protagonist and the other characters and transferred to the reader and to society at large. The reader acknowledges his own will and responsibility even as he pities the helpless protagonist. But the protagonist is not an automaton: his fall is a tragic spectacle because the reader participates in it and feels that only by a failure of his will and the will of society could it have taken place. What appears as an error of choice or a weakness of character in the plays of Aeschylus and Shakespeare is thus transferred to society in the naturalistic tragedy; society has destroyed the hero and thus has destroyed a part of its immortal self — and pity and guilt result. It is guilt instead of terror, because the social forces which crush a hero are finally subject to man's will and do not have the fatal power and mystery of cosmic forces. This curious wrenching of the novel's enclosing frame, which permits the "guilty" reader to enter the action, explains, in part, why so much criticism of naturalism has dealt with the problem of social intent. It also shows that the Aristotelian definition of tragedy is so fundamentally true that even a writer who believes he denies its premises nevertheless contrives to fulfill its conditions. If we can admit that *An American Tragedy* is tragic in this quasi-Aristotelian sense, we can take a further step and conclude that it is irrelevant to ask whether it is optimistic or pessimistic. The question is whether it is true. And whatever its ultimate social intent, naturalistic fiction does not exhort the reader to action. If some of Zola's best novels are still read it is because of their logical, integrated, relentless movement toward disaster — not that *L'Assommoir* will discourage drunkenness, or *Germinal* usher in the Revolution, or *Nana* apprise us of the evils of sexual license in a decadent society.

When we grant that a novelist may promote his ideas on social reform by writing a novel in which he seeks to embody a thorough-going materialistic determinism, we evoke two formidable objections. First, carried through to perfection, such a work would be a report, uncolored by ideas of human personality or recognition of the freedom of the human spirit. Such a work does not exist as a novel, and one would be fairly safe in affirming that it could not exist and be a novel. Second, the conflict between confidence in progress-through-human-effort and a belief in scientific determinism is not reconciled by my showing that "tragic" novels can document social optimism. The conflict remains. It is the chief problem that any "naturalistic" novel presents to a thoughtful reader; and we shall watch its Protean changes in the novels discussed in this volume. Like the critical controversy over optimism and pessimism, it is evidence of the divided stream — of a profound uncertainty as to whether science liberates the human spirit or destroys it. Novels, novelists, and critics consistently reflect this modern tension between science as god and science as devil, between progress and despair, between the hope of the future and the values of the past, between the two faces of human and physical nature.

A final observation on these contradictions: Naturalistic fiction which purports to receive its sanction from the scientific method and deterministic philosophy usually reveals, to the dispassionate observer, affiliations with several aspects of the aesthetic of ugliness, and these are apt to play a larger part in the novel's form than may appear to us if we keep our attention too closely on such concepts as science and reform. Art is anthropocentric. It it created by men whose dominant concern is to domesticate the physical universe to the uses of man's spirit. This aim is accomplished — or approached — by the artist's attempts to impose patterns of human thought upon the endless and eternal complexity of the physical universe. No matter how ardently he appears to be denying the worth or importance of man, the autonomy of the will, the permanence of life, the value of man's spirit, or the power of his knowledge, he is always in some fashion affirming these very things, for art is exercise and proof of them. The naturalistic novelist while he portrays with loathing and bitterness the folly and degradation of man is also affirming his hope and his faith, for his unspoken strictures imply an equally unspoken ideal which stimulates and justifies his pejorative attitude toward the world about him. The act of criticism, furthermore, is an exercise of creative intelligence which in itself denies what it may be saying about the futility of life and the folly of man.

This denial is a term in the dialectic of art; it is as much a part of the total effect of the work of art as its stated or implied scientific hypothesis. Hence all "naturalistic" novels exist in a tension between determinism and its antithesis. The reader is aware of the opposition between what the artist says about man's fate and what his saying it affirms about man's hope. Both of these polar terms are a part of the "meaning" of a naturalistic novel.

II

Zola: The Fountainhead of Naturalistic Theory and Practice

ZOLA is the fountainhead of naturalism, in a double and possibly a triple sense. He is a source of naturalistic theory, he is a model for many novelists, and he is to a lesser degree a source of critical method in the interpretation of fiction. I shall begin with the theory, proceed to consider the extent to which the theory controls the structure of his novels, and conclude with a glance at Zola's criticism of his own and other naturalists' writings. The discrepancies between the theory and the practice have a double interest in that they are an important source of the variety and complexity of American naturalism, and show how impossible it is to reduce naturalism to any single formula. We shall also find that an examination of Zola's work brings us to more elementary problems than those presented in Chapter I.

〜 〜

The ideas which led to Zola's "experimental novel," as he termed it, grew from contemporary scientific practices as well as from the philosophy of positivism which inspired and directed them. Zola was convinced that science at its best and most useful is research science. Observation and recording of facts appeared to him to be of relatively small value; in order to discover fundamental truths, the scientist must arrange and observe his data so as to conduct experiments under perfectly controlled conditions. By such procedures the researcher could discover exactly how certain phenomena occur — and this "how" was the end and the ideal of positivism. He believed that a novel could be a controlled scientific experiment in human relations or in the psychological development of an individual.

As early as 1866 Zola was deeply impressed by the scientific fidelity of the Goncourts' *Germinie Lacerteux*. Reviewing it he wrote, "The drama is terrific; it has the powerful interest of a physiological and psychological problem, of a case of physical and moral illness, of a story which has to be true." [1] In the same review he notes with interest and approval that in another milieu the heroine would not have succumbed to degradation and death — "Give her a husband and children to love, and she would be an excellent mother." Here is the germ of the experimental idea that was to drive Zola for more than twenty years.

Zola was also influenced by Taine's claim that manifestations of literary genius could best be accounted for in terms of the race, the milieu, and the moment.[2] But Taine did not at first appear to give proper emphasis to the importance of individual temperament in art, and Zola challenged him for this neglect. In fact, he insisted that art was opposed to nature, that it consisted of the artist's observation of reality plus the falsehood that he added to it. Reality had to be converted into art. He came to accept Taine when he concluded that the latter's allowance for temperament and for the artist's selection and organization of his materials permitted the ultimate mystery of genius to remain untouched. This concern for temperament (which Zola felt deeply) produces some baffling complications in his theory, as we shall see.

Zola's complete turn to the outlook that produced *Le Roman Expérimentale* came when he had absorbed the doctrines of Dr. Claude Bernard and applied them to his craft as novelist. Bernard's *Introduction a l'Etude de la Médecine Expérimentale* (1865) was an extension of the positive method of Comte to the practice of medicine, which had until then been largely empirical. Bernard insisted that it could become a true science if it would apply the experimental method to the study of physiology. He distinguished between simple observation and experimentation with controlled conditions, and he expounded the method of proceeding by hypotheses which were to be continually tested in the light of new data.

Zola appropriated this exposition bodily, claiming that the procedure of the novelist should be exactly like that of the doctor — both fiction and medicine having previously been considered "arts" — and that therefore he had only to cite Bernard in order to document his own assertions. He begins *Le Roman Expérimentale* by explaining (to paraphrase loosely) that this work of criticism involves merely a labor of adaptation, because the experimental method has been established with wonderful force and clarity by Claude Bernard in his great work. I find in this book, he says, the whole question treated, and I shall confine myself, for irrefutable arguments, to making the necessary quotations from it. I shall usually have only to substitute the word "novelist" for the word "doctor" to make my thought clear and to bring to it the rigor of scientific truth. Bernard shows that the experimental method, used in physics and chemistry, must likewise be used in the study of living bodies, through physiology and medicine. I shall try to show, in my turn, that if the experimental method gives insight into physical processes it can also lead to the understanding of the emotional and intellectual life. It is merely a question of steps in the same direction — from chemistry to physiology, then to anthropology and sociology. The experimental novel is the last step.[3] Novel writing could become a science by basing its study of character upon a sound psychology, which for anyone who had been influenced by Comte and Taine depended upon physiology.

In the preface to *Thérèse Raquin* (1867) — an experimental novel that precedes the Rougon-Macquart series in which he carried his theories through twenty volumes — Zola writes like an experimental scientist: "I have tried to study temperaments rather than characters. There is the whole book. . . . The loves of my two heroes are the satisfaction of a physical need; the murder they commit is a consequence of their adultery. Thus what I have been obliged to call their remorse ["obliged" by popular ignorance] is simply an organic disorder. . . . If one reads the novel with care

he will see that each chapter is the study of an interesting physiological case." [4] The assumption underlying these sentences is that
mental phenomena are controlled by physical phenomena or,
more precisely, that mental phenomena are physiological and can
be truly understood only as chemical reactions are. The scientific
novelist will set up an experiment involving carefully defined
characters who are subjected to certain carefully defined influences,
and from their reactions he will deduce scientific conclusions which
can in time be reduced to laws. These laws will ultimately cover
the fields of sociology and physiology in a perfected science of man.
This was the ideal that Zola later defended in the heat of controversy.

In justice to him it should be noted that he was not at first
completely sure of the scientific value of his "findings," for in 1868
he was writing himself a note of reassurance: "It is not important
that the underlying assumption [of his experimental novel] be
absolutely true; it will be a scientific hypothesis borrowed from
medical treatises. But when this fact is assumed, when I shall have
accepted it as an axiom, I can then deduce the whole volume
mathematically from it." [5] He explains that he assumes a philosophical manner not in order to explore minutely a whole system
of thought but merely to give a continuity to his work — and that
the materialistic outlook will serve his purpose best because he
will not have to explain its details to the reader.

But twelve years later, when the Rougon-Macquart series was in
full cry and controversy raged to his utter satisfaction, he could
confidently place the novelist's services to society beside those of
any "other" scientist. He affirms that when enough laws are known
it will be possible to operate upon people and their environments
so as to produce the ideal society; and he announces this sublime
achievement: "To be master of good and evil, to regulate life, to
regulate society, to resolve at length all the problems of socialism,
above all to bring solid bases to justice in resolving the problems
of criminality by experience, — is not that the most useful and
moral aim of human endeavor?" [6] Zola's heroic labors on his
novels, the mountains of documentation that he accumulated be-

fore writing a line, added to the fact that he was the focus of a tremendous literary controversy, help to explain how he could persuade himself that he was conducting scientific experiments in his novels. The notion that a novel can actually be the laboratory of an objective, controlled experiment may seem naïve and amusing today, but it was taken very seriously then.

— —

Turning from these theories to the Rougon-Macquart series, we find a surprising emphasis upon heredity. The whole work is conceived as tracing certain hereditary powers and maladies through a family that spreads into every social and professional level of the Second Empire in France. The preface to the first volume explains Zola's general design. He will show how twenty individuals who appear profoundly dissimilar are demonstrated by analysis to be intimately connected. Resolving the double problem of temperament and environment, he will trace the links which lead *mathematically* from one man to the next. The family he proposes to "study" is characterized by the profligacy of appetite of his time; it "throws itself upon sensual indulgence." Physiologically, he explains, the Rougon-Macquarts reveal the succession of maladies depending on disorders of nerve and blood which appear in a family as the result of an original organic "lesion." Historically, they give a sort of cross section of the Second Empire.[7]

Twenty years later in the final volume, the central figure, Doctor Pascal, who stands more or less for Zola, reviews the whole grand plan of the series. He begins with a catalogue of the laws of heredity revealed in the family tree, using terms which now appear as remote as the jargon of phrenology. In "direct heredity" there are *elections* (i.e., inheritance of traits) from either father or mother, of which he cites several examples. Then there are three kinds of mixture (*mélange*) of traits: by union (*soudure*), by dissemination, and by fusion. There is a fourth, "very remarkable" case of *mélange équilibre,* or balanced mixture of traits from the two parents. There are variations in which physical resemblance to the father accompanies the inheritance of the mother's nature, or vice versa.

There is collateral or indirect heredity, illustrated by the remarkable resemblance of Octave Mouret to his uncle. Zola has only one example of "heredity by influence" — the astonishing resemblance of Anna, the daughter of Gervaise and Coupeau, to Gervaise's former lover! But he is very rich in cases of "heredity by reversion" in which the traits of Aunt Dide jump one, two, and three generations. This he thinks must be exceptional, because he does not believe in atavism and would rather expect to see the elements contributed by husbands and wives who marry into the family efface the particular traits which the Rougon-Macquarts inherit from their common ancestor.[8] Here Zola writes as if he were convinced that the characters had actually lived and that he was observing and commenting on facts.

It is obvious that the unity which this grand plan brings to the twenty-volume series is entirely an invention of the author's. It is an artist's creation, not a scientist's observation. A scientist, further, would object that the terms used cover more ignorance than they reveal knowledge. Calling the resemblance of an individual to his grandfather "heredity by reversion" is not making any contribution to knowledge that Galen could not have made equally well in the second century. The critic will ask how these bogus clinical phrases can have a part in the significant form of the novels — and this question is as hard to answer as the scientist's. When Doctor Pascal in the final volume outlines the action of each novel in the series, it becomes apparent that the functioning of hereditary processes has no part in any of them. All the technical paraphernalia amounts to is the statement that certain characteristics run through the family. These are attributed to a "lesion" in the brain of Adelaïde Fouque (Aunt Dide), the mother of the line. Let us look at Zola's own summary of *L'Assommoir* as it is given here, for this book is frequently cited as the apogee of his naturalistic method. Doctor Pascal says: "Gervaise Macquart arrives with her four children, Gervaise bandylegged, pretty, and hard-working, who is thrown by her lover Lantier on the pavements of the slums, where she becomes acquainted with the roofer Coupeau, the good sober worker whom she marries, — so happy at first, having three

35

helpers in her laundry, falling then with her husband to the inevitable decay of the milieu, he conquered little-by-little by alcohol, taken by fierce madness and death, she perverted, becoming slothful, corrupted by the return of Lantier, in the easy squalor of a *ménage à trois*, then a pitiable victim of secret misery which finishes by killing her one night, her belly empty." [9]

Zola tells us that Gervaise lives under the "election" of an alcoholic father, and it is true that she degenerates through drunkenness and dies of starvation; but this hereditary force has to be taken on faith alone, for it has no part in the action of the story. There she is jolly, eager, ambitious, and strong; and she is prospering splendidly in her laundry until the accident of her husband's falling from a roof and breaking his leg. During his recovery, the husband takes to drink, Gervaise joins him by degrees, and they plunge into orgies of drink and debauchery which lead Coupeau to delirium tremens and Gervaise to starvation. Coupeau's fall is an accident; Gervaise's taking to drink is the result of Coupeau's reaction to his accident. The sequence does not appear to be inevitable or to prove anything scientifically.

If there is a theme or a meaning in the form of this novel, I should say it was that life is unpredictable and contains strange misadventures. One regards the degeneration of Gervaise and Coupeau with wonder and pity. It is fantastic and astonishing, yet credible. I do not believe that it touches the reader morally, so that he identifies himself with the plight of these people. It is a fantastic spectacle, possible rather than probable, not quite tragic yet very pitiful — and withal abounding with the author's extravagant gusto for life.

Little as heredity has to do with the action of *L'Assommoir*, it has even less to do with that of *Germinal*, which takes us with Etienne Lantier to the coal mines and reveals there the appalling struggle of the miners against tyranny and starvation. The workers are degraded to a point where they have become as promiscuous as animals and where the light of the mind is almost put out by the exhausting toil of their lives. Etienne promotes a strike, but the owners cannot afford to raise wages; and after horrible suffering the miners return to the pits and a future as hopelessly black as the coal they dig. *Germinal* is a great proletarian novel, one of the most tremendous and searching novels of the century, but it has nothing to do with the hereditary laws which it is said to exemplify and establish.[10]

Completing his recital of the novels, Doctor Pascal concludes that this family could provide evidence enough for science, "whose hope is to establish someday, mathematically, the laws of the diseases of nerve and blood which appear in a family following an original organic lesion and which determine, according to the milieus, the sentiments, the desires, the passions, all the human manifestations, natural and instinctive, of this family, of which the products are called virtues and vices." [11] A moment later he exclaims enthusiastically that here are all hereditary cases, enough to prove his entire theory that all these strange creatures are merely the logical and inevitable results of their common ancestry.[12] The words "hereditary cases" are significant. They point to the fact that most of the central characters in the novels, particularly those who derive from the Macquart side of the line, are "cases," clinical studies of some extreme form of physical or mental ailment such as hysteria, convulsions, madness, instability, acute alcoholism, nymphomania, imbecility, and ataxia. That the whole gamut of physiological monstrosities should conveniently spring from a single line is not more surprising than the bland assumption that the inevitability of such products, given the original "lesion," has been scientifically demonstrated. Zola makes that assumption, and seems to believe it, although he is powerless to explain the real causes of the various maladies. He evades the issue completely by the simple expedient of saying nothing about it. If there is any functioning of determinism in these novels, it is not to be found in the operation of hereditary forces. Despite all the theory, such "forces" simply do not exist in the novels and so cannot operate in their significant forms.

This situation is typical in naturalistic fiction. Having a theory or making an assumption does not enable an author to construct his novel so that a new form embodies the new idea. This is what makes the study of naturalism a study of the problems and tensions of the modern world. Just as science has not been able to impose its reasonable and luminous forms upon society, although social engineering and the planned society have become familiar terms, so the lucid formulations of naturalism have by no means been able to control or account for what actually happens in the "naturalistic" novel and have inaugurated rather a baffled search for form that still continues.

The naturalism in Zola's novels appears, not in the operation of hereditary forces, but in the themes and motifs described in Chapter I — violence, taboo, and the concept of determinism replacing the old moral setting in which characters were free to choose and therefore responsible for the consequences that followed. The teeming life on their stages combines with Zola's enormous gusto to create a different sort of "moral" quality. It is a belief in life, an enthusiasm for it, and a conviction that science can and must correct the conditions under which man suffers.

In a half-dozen of the Rougon-Macquart series an idea of determinism actually controls the form. In every instance this appears in the convincing power of environmental forces over the lives of the characters. Where a novelist like George Eliot is concerned with doing full justice to the limitations within which the will of man acts, Zola shows that man does not, finally, act but is acted upon. The interest of watching a character make a fateful choice is supplanted by the interest of watching evidence of external pressures pile up until there is no longer an assumption that the character is capable of choice. As I have said, this effect is accomplished in only a few of the novels, for there is a constant battle between the vitality of Zola's characters and the phalanxes of documentation that he marshals to overwhelm them. Where the documentation triumphs we have novels that seem to embody his theories about environmental forces. Where it does not we have a variety of structures and effects that might be said to constitute degrees of naturalism — or, perhaps, to embody dramatically the contradictions and tensions discussed in Chapter I.

Mechanistic psychology is another concept that would, like

these masses of documentation, overwhelm character if allowed full sway in the novel. The implications of the phrase *mechanistic psychology* are completely naturalistic. They are that cerebration is a physiological and ultimately a chemical process. Hippolyte Taine, whose famous criticism is a bridge between Comte and Zola, conveyed the same idea when he affirmed that the emotions were products of chemical reactions just as surely as sugar and vitriol were; and Zola continually refers to the mind as an aspect of physiology and thought as a physical or chemical process.

But if statements about heredity do not by themselves bring hereditary forces into the action and structure of a novel, we may wonder whether theories of mechanistic psychology are not equally difficult to dramatize. Actually, they are more difficult. It is possible to present situations in which a character's actions will recall hereditary patterns or forces which have been described earlier in a novel, and in this way the patterns or forces may appear to participate in the action. But the mechanics or chemistry of the mind is most elusive: basically, this is because nobody knows what the mind is; to say that thought is a chemical reaction is to utter pure theory. Even if the physiologists have by now discovered something about the synapses or chemicals in the brain (as they had not in 1860), these facts cannot be made to function in the action of a novel. When you get into the tissues of the brain and trace an impulse through the gray matter (if you can) you have left personality far far behind; you are no longer dealing with a person in a dramatic action. Even if you could show the "mechanism" of the brain making a choice, you would not be in the domain of personality, where the novel lives.

In the work of Zola, hereditary forces and mechanistic psychology have very much the same status. They are basic — almost axiomatic — in naturalistic theory, but neither of them has in fact been made to function centrally in the action of a novel. So both are as conspicuous for their absence in structure as for their presence in theory. If a novelist cannot pursue a thought through the tissues of the brain, how does he deal with it "mechanically"? Heir to the tradition of presenting mental events in terms of ethical

problems and choices, novelists have experienced the greatest difficulty in displaying thought under any other conditions. What does
a character think about if not a decision? He may observe, experience, or respond, yes, but if he is involved in an action, the reader
is waiting to see what he will finally *do*; and if his thoughts are
revealed along with his actions, they are most likely to be concerned
with volitions and decisions. These convey the impression of personal identity and freedom: if a character thinks at all vividly
about a decision, it has not yet been possible for a writer to show,
at the same time, the chemistry of such thought.

L'Assommoir illustrates these points. The degeneration of Gervaise and Coupeau is presented as an inevitable result of forces
over which they have no control. The reader does not judge them;
he observes — or so the author intends. The action does not depend
upon acts of will (these are carefully avoided) but upon the mechanical impulse and reaction arising from external stimuli. Gervaise and Coupeau go down and down. The reader sees, imperfectly of course, the how and the why of their degeneration. He
knows that their actions are "determined," and he perhaps infers
their thoughts from these actions; for in this novel Zola never
devotes any particular attention to what his characters are thinking
except insofar as he shows, in the interests of his deterministic
hypothesis, that they are not capable of elaborate thought. When
the will, making its ethical choices, determines the action, thoughts
are the very substance of a novel. But when will is denied,
thoughts are correspondingly neglected in favor of those external
forces which *do* cause the events.

We arrive thus at an important truth about "mechanistic psychology": to explain cerebration as a physiological or chemical
process is to remove its fundamental significance in the novel. The
naturalistic novel which assumes a mechanistic psychology is not
nearly so "psychological" — to judge from the amount of attention
devoted to thinking — as the novels of George Eliot or, for that
matter, Samuel Richardson. In practice, mechanistic psychology
tends to eliminate mental events from the novel because it has to
ignore them. If Zola had dwelt upon the thoughts of Gervaise and

Coupeau, those thoughts would inevitably have overshadowed his "mechanism" by creating the impression of free will. Indeed, this is what happened in the Rougon-Macquart novels that deal with the Rougon branch of the family. These latter move in high social, financial, and political circles. They are said by Zola to enjoy certain hereditary traits in common; but because they are complicated, sophisticated, and successful people there is never the illusion that even their actions — to say nothing of their thoughts — are rigidly controlled either by heredity or chemistry.

More recent experiments have explored other ways of eliminating the ethical will from the novel. Thoughts could be "disembodied" from action in the stream of consciousness novel which does not go outside the theater of the mind into the world of physical activity — but even there the notion of will is kept in the background only insofar as the writer, by studiously avoiding choices and actions, is able to confine himself to a representation of the *quality of experience* rather than to the interactions between the character and the world outside him. The contemporary hard-boiled detective-story writer achieves a sort of neutrality by telling what his hero does and says (often in the first person) but not what he thinks or wants. He neither affirms the will nor denies it; the hero is violently acted upon, but he is violent himself and his personality makes strong impressions on the other characters. He acts a little bit like an automaton, buffeted by violent forces; yet some semblance of a free mind is inferred from his actions. It adds up to a tricky balance between mechanism and moral values. Contemporary existentialists like Sartre and Paul Bowles have created characters whose thoughts are presented in minutest detail without any impression of free will. Sartre's Mathieu, in *The Age of Reason*, is painfully conscious of his own lack of will and seeks continually for some act by which he can become a willing and therefore a moral agent. Bowles's little people (*Let It Come Down* and *The Sheltering Sky*), who plunge into the depravities of the Arab world in North Africa in their search for meaning, are not able even to analyze their own plights, and they achieve only the vaguest sort of focus through violence or self-destruction. The existentialist is at the furthest extreme from mechanistic psychology. His assumptions are far more sophisticated and desperate than those of the early naturalists.

～ ～

Zola himself admitted that "Naturalism is only a method. The works remain apart." [13] The difficulty here is that he did not let naturalism stand as a method but went further to say that this method should determine the form (in that the novel should contain great masses of documentation) and the purpose (the discovery of laws) in a way that made it impossible for the work of art to remain outside of (*en dehors*) the method.

We may further observe that in actual practice Zola's concern with the individual or stylistic elements of art outweighs his passion for truth. He goes so far in his insistence on the personal style (motivated perhaps by the desire to justify his own) that he leaves the way clear for almost any sort of writing and makes the transforming hand of the writer more significant, from a theoretical as well as an artistic point of view, than the scientific accuracy of the materials employed. Writing of Daudet, for example, he speaks of the intimate connection between that writer and the materials stored up in his visual memory, claiming that art is produced only when the raw material of perception is transformed through the personality of the artist. In fact, he says, "In this intimate union the reality of the scene and the personality of the novelist are no longer distinct. Which details are true, which invented? It would be very difficult to say. What is certain is that reality was the point of departure, the force driving the novelist; he pursued reality; he represented the scene essentially; by giving it a life that was special and that was uniquely his . . . The essence of originality is here in such a personal expression of the real world." [14] Zola emphasizes the value of temperament so earnestly that he appears to forget his pretensions to scientific fidelity. Yet he does continually stress his belief that the writer must begin with reality, even though reality must be seized through a temperament and transformed by that temperament into a work of art. As a revolt against romantic extravagance this naturalistic manifesto is a strong plea for truth and the use of actual life in the novel. As a genuine plea for scientific objectivity, however, it is more than neutralized by Zola's insistence upon the element of temperament.

When he deals with the problem of form, the ambiguities of his theory become even more pronounced. Genius, he says, is found not only in idea and sentiment, but also in form and style: "However, method and style are independent [*distinctes*]. And naturalism, I repeat, exists solely in the experimental method, in the application of observation and experience to literature." So far he is eminently reasonable; but he proceeds: "If you want my opinion precisely, it is that the importance of form is exaggerated today. . . . Basically, I believe that method itself becomes form, that a language is only a system of logic, a natural and scientific structure. We shall not write best by galloping madly among hypotheses, but by moving straight among truths." [15] Here he appears to be saying that naturalists will not achieve greatness by galloping madly among hypotheses but by perfecting method (*qui marchera droit au milieu des vérités*) until it becomes form. The point is not clear, and Zola himself seems to be using the words *form* and *method* very loosely. These sentences tend to neutralize the conventional opinions he has uttered about the preeminence of individual style in literature. Anyone who has come to regard science as distinct from literature can see that to adopt a scientific method of gathering data does not inevitably point to an equally scientific manner of presenting them in literature. Yet Zola reflects the devout worship of science of his time by suggesting here that the scientific method of observation could indeed become a method of composition (i.e., a style) which would in turn by some mysterious alchemy become the form of the novel.

The ambiguities here are not resolved; Zola always emphasizes the importance of temperament while insisting that naturalism should supply the method of observation, never entirely facing the fact that one cannot see life scientifically and *à travers un tempérament* at the same time, that the two approaches are incompatible. The lines quoted above display considerable mystical fervor for science, a fervor that makes Zola attempt to extend what he has but a moment before been limiting as a method into that very form with which method, as he has said, should never be confused. Zola's enthusiasm is divided between the ideal of science and the knowledge of his own genius. His work, too, is divided between these two streams.

III

Adumbrations: Harold Frederic and Hamlin Garland

BECAUSE naturalism is linked with social protest and reform, the first traces of its influence in the American novel appear in the works of such writers as Joseph Kirkland, Henry Blake Fuller, Harold Frederic, and Hamlin Garland, who debunked the small town, espoused the single tax, deplored the spiritual poverty of the farm, and were bitter about the ethics of business. We should not expect to find a thoroughly formulated philosophy of naturalism in their works, or a rigorous application of scientific method. What does appear is an infusion of vigorous new blood into the pale and attenuated Victorian forms then available to the American writer. It adds tone, vigor, a new dimension — and it is a powerfully disrupting element in novels which are unable finally to accommodate it into a structure that remains coherent. Here nevertheless are early attempts at case studies of the depressing effects of impoverished or culturally narrow environments upon the lives of representative Americans. Here are the beginnings of a new approach to human and social relations.

～ ～

Harold Frederic (1856–1898) wrote two novels dealing with the narrowness of farm and small-town life. We shall look at both in some detail. *Seth's Brother's Wife: A Study of Life in the Greater New York* (1887) opens in a tone which suggests that the story is to deal primarily with the deadening effects of country life.

45

The attitude in such a passage as the following needs no comment:

"Oh, it must be such a dreary life! The very thought of it sets my teeth on edge. The dreadful people you have to know: men without an idea beyond crops and calves and the cheese-factory; women slaving their lives out doing bad cooking, mending for a houseful of men, devoting their scarce opportunities for intercourse with other women to the weakest and most wretched gossip; coarse servants who eat at the table with their employers and call them by their Christian names; boys whose only theory about education is thrashing the school teacher, if it is a man, or breaking her heart by mean insolence if it is a woman; and girls brought up to be awkward gawks without a chance in life, since the brighter and nicer they are the more they will suffer from marriage with men mentally beneath them — that is, if they don't become sour old maids." [1]

This comes from a city girl. A moment later we are warned against the romantic idealization of nature: "Perhaps there may have been a time when a man could live in what the poet calls daily communion with nature and not starve his mind and dwarf his soul, but this isn't the century." Toward the end of the book the dying grandmother utters a bitter summary of what the farm has meant to her — spiritual and physical defeat:

"P'raps it'll sound ridiculous to yeh, but yeh don't look unlike what I did when I was your age. The farm ain't had time to tell on yeh yit. But it will! It made me the skeercrow that you see; it'll do the same for you. When I was a girl, I was a Thayer, the best fam'ly in Norton, Massachusetts. We held our heads high. . . . But I married beneath me, an' I come up here into York State to live, on this very farm. With us, farmin' don't mean a livin' death. P'raps we don't hev sech fine big barns ez yeh build here, but our houses are better. We don't git such good crops, but we pay more heed to education and godly livin'. It's th' diff'rence 'twixt folks who b'lieve there's somethin' else in life b'sides eatin' and drinkin' an' makin' money, an' folks that don't. . . . Look at Lemuel Fairchild's wife Cicely — she was a relation of yours, wasn't she? — see how the farm made an ole woman o' her, an' broke her down, an' killed her! You're young, an' you're good lookin' yit, but it'll break yeh, sure's yer born. Husban's on these farms ain't what they air in the cities."

46

Not only do these and many similar passages go unanswered, so that they dominate the tone of the novel; they also reveal a plain and clear concept of determinism which is underlined when the "hero," Seth, is portrayed as ignorant, lacking in taste, and thwarted. The first hundred pages of the book call for an action that grows out of these miserable conditions.

But Frederic was unable to make such a story. The action of *Seth's Brother's Wife* swarms in and out of journalism, politics, murder, and not one but two love triangles. The writer, furthermore, is idealistic, polemical, and burning with moral indignation against the conduct of his rural people. When the murder is traced to the hired man, the district attorney explains:

"The rural murderer (I am speaking of native Americans now) plans the thing in cold blood, and goes at it systematically, with nerves like steel. He generally even mutilates the body, or does some other horrible thing, which it makes everybody's blood boil to think of. And so long as he isn't found out, he never dreams of remorse. He has no more moral perspective than a woodchuck. But when detection does come, it knocks him all in a heap. He blubbers, and tries to lay it on somebody else, and altogether acts like a cur — just as this fellow's doing now, for instance."

Frederic makes his reader hate the insolent servants who gossip in the kitchen. He forces the erring wife of Seth's brother (who through sheer boredom has engaged in epistolary flirtation with Seth to the point where he is ready to declare his love and elope with her) to confess that she is "a wicked woman!"

The crowning instance of ethical rather than naturalistic motivation appears when the corruption of the local political scene is corrected by the eleventh-hour conversion of the most vicious and powerful of political bosses into a pillar of righteousness. The change is not probable; it is not prepared for; it does not carry out the expectations of rural viciousness or backwardness that have been established in the rising action of the story. The spirit of this conversion endows a scoundrel with the "homely democratic virtues" that have been traditionally associated with the hard-working American farmer. Frederic begins the novel blaming the farm with unscientific indignation for what it has done to the poor farmer. Presently he is blaming the rural oaf for being a scoundrel. And finally he contrives the triumph of morality by what appears to be a completely unmotivated change of heart.

There were various more consistent ways of working out the possibilities of these materials. Frederic could have let his protagonist bring about his own destruction because his narrow background and lack of experience unfitted him for effective action or judgment in a crisis. It was probable that Seth should have become infatuated with his brother's wife — and probable that he should have got into inescapable difficulties with her. In another form, the material could have been developed as no story but a barren and dreary waste of futility in which nothing happened because the dreary environment paralyzed its people. A third form would have maintained a completely objective tone and presented the characters' thoughts and motives in a way that would have demonstrated their subjection to their environment without pretending to prove that the outcome of the story was inevitable. With complete objectivity and meticulous attention to the details of the background, such a story would have been massively consistent and convincing. In none of these forms does it appear that a happy solution is possible, for the conditions as given hold out no hope of any considerable improvement for anybody who is deeply involved with them.

But Frederic's idealism gets mixed into the action — early and earnestly. He is indignant with the deprivation of the rural life, and as he writes his way into the story he concentrates his outrage on what has happened to the people until — and the turn is not surprising when we see how it happens — he vents his wrath upon them. Finally, having damned them with his rage, he transfers the will-to-decency to the political boss and has him save the day with a story-book finish.

Frederic's literary technique was better fitted for exploring people than for demonstrating the large-scale operation of social forces. It is doubtless very presumptuous to undertake to read the minds of dead authors, but I am tempted to suggest that Frederic was frustrated by his inability to sustain a naturalistic technique, that this frustration turned into rage at his unmanageable materials, and that the rage expressed itself in the moral indignation which he directed at his characters. The initial vitality of *Seth's Brother's Wife* is impressive; it is a pity to see it diverted.

Frederic's more famous novel, *The Damnation of Theron Ware: or Illumination* (1896), although more mature, more interesting, and better written, falls into very much the same confusion. The opening sections of the book lead one to suppose that it will explore the blighting effects of fundamentalism and Puritanism upon the spirit of an eager young minister; it turns into a study, lacking in charity and compassion, of a mean spirit, a character who is condemned by his creator as both weak and vicious.

The town to which Theron Ware is sent is narrow and miserable, full of people whose "idea of hell is a place where everybody has to mind his own business." Those who control the church do not want any newfangled ideas, they do not want Theron's wife to dress at all gaily, nor do they want to spend a cent more than they must to keep the young minister alive and presentable:

"We are a plain sort o' folks up in these parts," said Brother Pierce, after a slight further pause. His voice was as dry and rasping as his cough, and its intonations were those of authority. "We walk here," he went on, eying the minister with a sour regard, "in a meek an' humble spirit, in the straight an' narrow way which leadeth unto life. We ain't gone traipsin' after strange gods, like some people that call themselves Methodists in other places. We stick by the Discipline an' the ways of our fathers in Israel. No newfangled notions can go down here. Your wife'd better take them flowers out of her bunnit afore next Sunday." [2]

At this stage of the story Theron is a young man full of hope and enthusiasm. He is perhaps weakly fond of the good things in life; but he is also sincerely devout, eager to perfect himself in the salvation of souls, stirred with vague yearnings after a richer spiritual and intellectual life.

We have been prepared for an action in which the blighted environment would somehow work on the characters, but just at this point it ceases to act at all. The rest of the novel is devoted

to the disintegration of Theron's character and the disappearance
of the good qualities which he had earlier displayed. The instruments of his damnation are the three people in the town who have
any cultural background. They are Father Forbes, a Catholic
priest; Dr. Ledsmar, retired, who dabbles in obscure science; and
the beautiful, wealthy, and talented Celia Madden, who draws
the men together. Theron is at first welcomed into this group;
they are attracted by his candor and his eagerness to plunge into
more spacious realms of thought than he has hitherto been able to
attain. Theron's "illumination," however, brings about his destruction. He becomes the most contemptible sort of person,
speaking slightingly of his loyal wife, losing his grip on his parishioners, feeling himself to be too good for his situation in life,
persuading himself that he is in love with Celia Madden, and, at
length, foolishly pursuing her to New York. When they meet there
she sums up the whole situation, indeed the whole novel, in a com-
prehensive utterance:

"We were disposed to like you very much when we first knew
you. . . . You impressed us as an innocent, simple, genuine young
character, full of mother's milk. It was like the smell of early
spring in the country to come in contact with you. Your honesty
of nature, your sincerity in that absurd religion of yours, your
general naïveté of mental and spiritual get-up, all pleased us a
great deal. We thought you were going to be a real acquisition. . . .
But then it became apparent, little by little, that we had misjudged
you. We liked you, as I have said, because you were unsophisticated
and delightfully fresh and natural. Somehow we took it for granted
you would stay on. But that is just what you didn't do, — just what
you hadn't the sense to try to do. Instead, we found you inflating
yourself with all sorts of egotisms and vanities. We found you
presuming upon the friendships which had been mistakenly extended to you. Do you want instances? You went to Dr. Ledsmar's
house that very day after I had been with you to get a piano at
Thurston's, and tried to inveigle him into talking scandal about
me. You came to me with tales about him. You went to Father
Forbes, and sought to get him to gossip about us both. Neither of
those men will ever ask you inside his house again. But that is
only one part of it. Your whole mind became an unpleasant thing
to contemplate. You thought it would amuse and impress us to

hear you ridiculing and reviling the people of your church, whose money supports you, and making a mock of the things they believe in, and which you for your life wouldn't dare let them know you didn't believe in. You talked to us slightingly about your wife. What were you thinking of not to comprehend that that would disgust us? You showed me once, do you remember? — a life of George Sand that you had just bought, — bought because you had just discovered that she had an unclean side to her life. You chuckled as you spoke to me about it, and you were for all the world like a little boy, giggling over something dirty that older people had learned not to notice. These are merely random incidents. They are just samples, picked hap-hazard, of the things in you which have been opening our eyes, little by little, to our mistake. I can understand that all the while you really fancied that you were expanding, growing in all directions. What you took to be improvement was degeneration. When you thought that you were impressing us most by your smart sayings and doings, you were reminding us most of the fable about the donkey trying to play lap-dog. And it wasn't even an honest, straightforward donkey at that!" [3]

As this passage shows, the novel is well written. The tone and manner, new and fresh, suggest the new era. The reader follows the adventures of Theron's decaying spirit with keen interest, and the other characters are very much alive. The spirit in which the setting is depicted — the moral and spiritual setting — suggests that the cause of Theron's disintegration must surely be that his Methodism and his limited social experience had failed to give him a cultural tradition upon which he could base his conduct. Thus when confronted with a new and attractive set of values in the outlooks of the priest, the girl, and the doctor, he had nothing to guide or restrain him. In these terms the novel could be a penetrating analysis of cultural forces. But this is not what comes out. One's judgment of Theron cannot be impersonal because his lack of background is not enough to account — to the reader's emotional satisfaction — for his contemptible weakness. This is laid to some personal failing within him, a failing which every line of the book suggests that he is ethically responsible for. The modern reader is apt to think, upon reconsideration, that Frederic is too hard on Theron — that he fails to see how helpless Theron's meager outlook is before the first sophisticated people he has known. Frederic condemns instead of explaining.

Many elements of the American Dream appear in this strong novel and participate in its vitality. There is the flouting of mere conventional morality, the belief in a scientific or rationalistic view of man and his relations, and the earnest faith in intelligence, human dignity, and freedom. There is also, initially, a firmly monistic sense of the interdependency of nature and spirit: both the rasping piety of the community and the personal inadequacy of Theron are introduced as functions of the environment. But, just as in *Seth's Brother's Wife*, the stream of moral earnestness separates from the stream of scientific analysis, and presently it appears that Frederic has slipped back into the simple formula of orthodoxy which says that a person who displays moral weakness is one of the damned. What appears to be an intellectual confusion and inconsistency that leads to a complete reversal of attitude is probably not that but a failure of technique. The novel leaves the impression that Frederic was full of his subject and that he had thought long and earnestly upon it and reached fairly subtle conclusions. But again, as in *Seth*, he was unable to dramatize them into a demonstration of environmental forces at work. Instead he penetrated Theron's character so deeply that his moral earnestness became focused upon what he found there and he lost sight of the environment completely. What appears in the novel as the indignant condemnation of Theron for his moral deterioration began as Frederic's moral indignation with the small town. Because he did not have the technique to lay out the whole spiritual landscape, he funneled his passion into the study of Theron — and there it appears, transformed but still providing the novel's vitality and interest.

A comparable shift of focus from the environment to the mind of the central character appears a generation or more later in some of the novels of James T. Farrell. Again the cause for the shift seems to lie in the fact that the naturalistic technique uses materials which are not as compelling or interesting as the inner life of a character. And again there appears in Farrell's work the excess of idealism which frustrates the artist's control of his material and transforms itself into attitudes toward the characters and the values by which they mistakenly live. These writers almost span our naturalistic movement, and they shadow forth its pattern and its problem as a tug-of-war between zeal and form.

～ ～

Hamlin Garland's biography (1860–1940) is a success story that would do credit to Horatio Alger. Reared on a middle western farm under conditions of toil and privation which he bitterly resented, he contrived to educate himself, escape to New England for further education at Harvard, and finally achieve literary fame and social position. One of his earliest passions was a zeal for reform, inspired by the bitter memories of his youth and his later observation of the Boston slums. He became a single-taxer and wrote a couple of earnestly polemic novels dealing with political corruption and land-grabbing (*Jason Edwards*, 1892, and *A Spoil of Office*, 1892). For these works he earned the reputation of being the foremost literary radical of his day. But his social ardor was short-lived. Lionized in literary and academic circles, he affected a velvet coat, drank tea, and forgot about abolishing the unearned increment.

As his interest in reform waned he turned to advocating the American scene as subject matter for American fiction, a program for which he pleaded in *Crumbling Idols* (1894). "Veritism" is his name for the kind of writing which should express the new regionalism. Again and again he assails fixed standards: "Life is always changing, and literature changes with it." Fiction must be true, mercilessly true if need be, but the novelist can be hopeful, too, seeing "life in terms of what it might be as well as in terms of what it is. . . . He aims to hasten the age of beauty and peace by delineating the ugliness and warfare of the present." [4]

Garland constantly invokes Truth as the lodestar of fiction; but as he grew older his truth became more refined. He was befriended by Richard Watson Gilder,[5] and that apostle of the genteel tradition gently persuaded him toward a literary and ethical outlook that promised more comfortable preoccupations than harsh Reform and bold Truth. Hence *Crumbling Idols* contains many an aside which assures the genteel reader that Garland holds no brief for the sexual candor of naturalism. The novelist, he says, "sighs for a lovelier life. He is tired of warfare and diseased sexualism [the reference to Zola is unmistakable], and Poverty the mother of Envy. . . . Life is to be depicted, not lovelife. Sexual attractions and perplexities do not form life, but only part of life." [6] He demands a truthful picture not of the raw impulses of life but of the grandeur and glory of its American setting. He emphasizes this belief in writing of the new literature which he hopes will spring from the West: "This literature will not deal with crime and abnormalities, nor with deceased [*sic*] persons. It will deal, I believe, with the wholesome love of honest men for honest women, with the heroism of labor, the comradeship of men, — a drama of average types of character, infinitely varied, but always characteristic." [7] To follow this formula would cause few idols to crumble.

Garland, as it appears from this evidence, was drawn in several directions at once. As a consequence his ideals were softened and his energies vitiated. But even before his turn to veritism (and long before he turned to writing placid romances of the High Sierras and, finally, tracts on spiritualism), Garland struggled with inadequate technique and irreconcilable ideas in a manner that is both interesting and painful to behold. We have seen that Frederic was able to make a convincing description of the poverty and meanness of the rural spirit but got into technical difficulties when he attempted to construct a plot. Garland had the same trouble when he moved from sketches to novels. The powerful sketches written before 1890 which appeared as *Main-Traveled Roads* (1891) and *Prairie Folks* (1893) justified the literary reputation they made for him. The change in quality from them to his early novels would be almost incredible if it were not possible to show how it happened.

Garland's early sketches deal with the influence of environment in the lives of frontier farmers. They present the effects of long hours, grim toil, and spiritual barrenness on people who live without benefit of culture. The characters in the various stories react differently to this brutal environment. Some match it with dogged bitterness. Some try pitifully to escape, without the resources or education necessary. Some develop a cynical cruelty that adds to their own woe and to the woes of those about them. A few exhibit noble qualities of endurance and fortitude. The foil against which these hard gems of determinism shine is the moral order in which Garland angrily lives. Somebody, we feel, is to blame for these wasted lives. Sympathy, tolerance, and wisdom should prevail, and these starved spirits should be able to treat each other more humanely. Something should be done by the rich East to ease the burden on those who win the West. We for whom the West has been won should feel guilt for the sufferings of these pioneers. Men should not have to suffer such privation. And so on. There is a quality of reproach and indignation in every line.

Whenever we see a powerful assertion of determinism we know that the writer is working under emotional stress. Determinism is not, in fiction, objective, although it certainly is objective in theory. These early sketches put the reader in an emotional strait-jacket. Every line asserts the need to be free. They press out against the confining determinism in which they are phrased. There is emotional appropriateness in this condition, moreover, for the confinement of the sketches, conveyed through a sense of tension and exasperation, expresses the writer's revolt against whatever order permits such conditions.

These sketches are tight and confining in the further sense that they do not move, and their aesthetic effect lies in this painful constriction; it expresses a sort of outraged, speechless indignation that such things can be. They do not move because the effect of environment has already asserted itself; the characters are trapped. The content is retrospective, looking back on what has happened, on the one chance to escape that was missed ten years ago, on the aspirations of youth now lost. The future is confined by a blank wall. The form of such a piece is perfect; it creates and it embodies its meaning.

But what happens when Garland introduces, as he occasionally does, movement? Then we have something like "A Branch Road," a story in which the hero loses his fiancée because of his own bad temper in prolonging a misunderstanding, disappears into the West for seven years, and returns to find the girl married to a brutal and tyrannical oaf. The bitterness of her life and the sense of tragic destiny which forges a dark chain of necessity from a single error are powerfully evoked. Garland has an insight here which could be left to speak for itself as a tragic fact of experience, but he cannot stop. The returning lover paints a dazzling word-picture of love, travel, luxury, Europe (he has of course made his fortune in the intervening years), and while the vicious husband is driving his old father to church the hero carries off the wife and her babe to a brave new world of bliss.

It is scarcely necessary to say that we expect some degree of wisdom, rather than daydreams, from a serious artist; we expect that he will pursue the logic of his situations to the bitter end. Garland's determinism, however, is pure protest; it is his mode of defining the injustice that has scarred his own soul; and it is not surprising that he should jump from definition to defiance by writing a story in which the iron chain is broken.

A more consistent working out of a situation appears in "Under the Lion's Paw," from *Main-Traveled Roads*. This, Garland's best known short story, deals with a tenant farmer who works like a galley slave for three years improving a run-down farm which he hopes to buy for twenty-five hundred dollars. When his heroic labors have brought him to the point of being successful, the owner of the farm tells him that the price is now fifty-five hundred dollars: "It was all run down then; now it's in good shape. You've laid out fifteen hundred dollars in improvements, according to your own story." The farmer is considerably in debt, exhausted, and because he cannot meet the new price he sees that he will have to go off absolutely penniless after his three years of sacrifices and back-breaking toil. He had a plain understanding about the price of the farm, but he did not have it in writing. This is all painfully logical, but the effect of the story is not controlled by its "naturalism" because the closing scene makes the landowner unnaturally vicious. He is not forced by economic necessity to ruin the poor farmer's life. On the contrary it is made clear that he has a great deal of money and more land than he can manage. He squeezes his victim, it appears, because he is an innately evil man, a hateful character who enjoys making others suffer. A modern psychologist would undertake to account for this landowner's personality, perhaps as a product of the same grinding and rapacious milieu which makes his victim so appallingly energetic, but Garland only gives him to us as a bad man who must be indignantly denounced. The reader is confused by the emotional and logical inconsistencies of this story; the idea of very good and very bad people is not placed in any clear relation to the notion of economic determinism, and one is uncertain how to react.

Compared with any of Garland's early novels of social protest, "Under the Lion's Paw" is a miracle of unity and coherence. The problem of plotting is more formidable in a novel, and the difficulties of integrating inconsistent elements are tremendously greater. At the risk of appearing to beat a dead horse, I should like to examine one of the early novels in some detail because Garland's problems are instructive.

Jason Edwards: An Average Man is a caricature of orthodox dualism locked in mortal combat with the forces of scientific materialism. It is a novel of protest against the crushing forces of economic determinism as they operate in Boston industry and in western prairie farming. In Boston, Jason is squeezed to the edge of starvation between rising rents and falling wages. He and those like him are doomed to horrible squalor and misery. Conditions are described in passages of surprising power:

. . . as Edwards looked in at the foundry door on his way back, about five o'clock, men were "pouring." It was a grew-some sight. With grimy, sooty shirts, open at the throat, in a temperature of deadly heat, they toiled like demons. There was little humanity in their faces, as the dazzling metal threw a dull-red glow on them.

Here and there, with warning shouts, they ran, bent like gnomes, with pots of shining, flame-colored liquid lighting their grimy faces. Here toiled two stalwart fellows, with a huge pot between them; with hoarse shouts they drew up beside a huge "flask" or moulding-box. The skimmer pushed away the slag, the radiant metal leaped out and down into the sand, sending spurts of yellow-blue flame out of a half-hundred crevices. . . . Jason Edwards remained a long time looking at this scene. Its terror came in upon him as never before. That men should toil like that for ten dollars per week . . . was horrible.[8]

So Jason takes his family west — to fall into the clutches of heartless capitalists who control all the land near the railroad and hold mortgages on seventy per cent of the farms, farms which, drought-cursed and sun-baked, fail to support the poor souls who toil upon them. Here, after intolerable privations, Edwards's daughter pleads with the mortgage holder:

"Then take the land!" cried Alice, despairingly, "Don't delude us with the idea of ownership where we're only tenants."
"But we don't want the land," explained the judge. "All we want is the interest. We've got more land than we know what to do with."
He had made it too plain. The girl's face lifted, lit by a bitter indignant smile —
"I see! It's cheaper to let us think we own the land than it is to pay us wages. You're right — your system is perfect — and heartless. It means death to us all and all like us!" she said, as the whole truth came upon her.

Such lines show the mixture of moral indignation and economic determinism so characteristic of Garland's early work.

These passages suggest a novel in the Zola tradition, with the bitter consequences inevitably following. But this matter of mortgages and foreclosures is not the plot of *Jason Edwards*. The plot is concerned with the activities of Jason's daughter, Alice, who is confronted by various difficult choices between love and duty. In Boston, where she has trained her voice and her manners so well that she has risen quite above her economic class, she inspires the love of a rising Bostonian who offers her culture and security if she will stay behind and marry him instead of going west with the family. Duty wins, but the undaunted hero follows Alice and proposes again. His arrival at the town nearest Edwards's farm is the occasion for a chapter or two of expository dialogue from which the reader again learns how bad are conditions and how cruel the men who prey upon their fellows. But the deterministic forces are not shown in operation — they are merely discussed — and they have only the most rudimentary relation to the plot. The action continues to turn upon questions of love against duty. When the hero proposes a second time, duty again triumphs in Alice's refusal. But as the hero is driving away, nature saves the day with a hailstorm and cloudburst which destroy the wheat and prostrate the old man with a stroke. These catastrophes satisfy the frontiersman's sense of honor and make it reputable for Jason to abandon the unequal struggle and return to the green East to live with his daughter and son-in-law.

Genteel elegance and romantic compromise prevent Garland from carrying the grim expectations of his situation through to their tragic consequences. It would be attractive to explain this structural collapse by invoking the eager spirit of American democracy — to say that the West was bold and confident and that the writer was carried along by this spirit to renounce the "pessimistic determinism" of European naturalism. But this patriotic explanation will not do. Returning to the comfortable East to live with genteel culture is not a victory for the pioneer spirit but an abandonment of it. A happy ending of this sort does not express frontier optimism. Paradoxically, a grimly tragic "naturalistic" ending would have revealed the author's belief in the ultimate triumph of democracy over natural and institutional obstacles. It would have demonstrated his eagerness to present the hard facts in all their hardness, so that democracy would know exactly what had to be done. Such a pessimistic conclusion would have been an affirmation because it was intellectually bold and consistent. The happy ending of *Jason Edwards* shows that Garland was already yearning to abandon the hard life of a radical for the comfortable prestige of literary circles. His failure to manage the implications of determinism, in his plots, must not, therefore, be laid merely to the fact that he was not a master of naturalistic techniques or not entirely sure of the philosophy. The same uncertainties appear in criticism of the American novel of 1920 to 1940. Those who wrote most honestly, most courageously, and most notably in the tradition of American idealism were accused of pessimism and of undermining America's faith in her destiny. The accusation was genteel.

Garland made another and more ambitious attempt to write a problem novel. Published in 1895, before he went to the High Country for romantic subjects, *Rose of Dutcher's Coolly* has been considered his best novel. The work contains a freshness and reality of scene that take it far beyond conventional romance or local color. It begins on a middle western farm, showing an unusual girl who seeks more from life than can be found in the backward community near which she lives. Garland's charming description of Rose as a little girl — the sturdy, sunburned, bramble-scratched waif who trudges independently about the farm, tasting all kinds of leaves and berries, inquiring into everything she sees, fearing nothing, and loving only her widowed father — is an appealing child portrait. When she grows up she attends the University of Wisconsin and later goes to Chicago in an effort to discover some occupation worthy of her force and talent. These materials are real; they bring the reader into close touch with the American scene; they are a far cry from the historical romances that were being devoured by the hundreds of thousands during the nineties.

Two thirds of *Rose*, however, is given up to a romantic love story that hinges on the imperfectly realized problem of whether Rose, who has risen from farm life to a degree of social prestige, should marry the rich man she loves or remain free to develop her intellectual powers in a career. The problem is further complicated by the hero's uncertainty as to whether he, an older man, has the moral right to marry a beautiful young girl. These issues are not very compelling. Rose's vacillation between passion and career is unconvincing because Garland fails to give her any particular talent or interest to draw her away from the man she loves. Without such a particular interest, with only a vague longing for creative activity, Rose faces a thoroughly romantic problem; and most of the action consists of her movement through time-filling incidents and sentimental conversations. The most specific talent she demonstrates is a melodious whistle which helps her through the crisis of her first social encounter. Her love is consummated in fittingly idyllic beatitude when she and her betrothed meet at the farm under the loving eyes of her old father. The narrowness of farm life, which had originally driven Rose forth, is forgotten in the need for a mellow atmosphere that will give the proper setting to lovers' vows.

So much for the general tenor of *Rose of Dutcher's Coolly*. There are, however, a few vestigial remains of Garland's veritism and his leanings toward naturalistic values. They have nothing to do with the plot or structure of the novel, and yet they account for its being mentioned in literary histories and for the modest survival of Garland's name. There is, first, something of Zola's feeling for the way a passion can sway a group of people in the incident of the pretty teacher who comes to the unsullied country community and soon has all the boys competing for her favors. The whole school is corrupted into ominous (though unnamed) misconduct: "At school the most dangerous practices were winked at. The older boys did not scruple to put their arms about the teacher's waist as they stood by her side. All the reserve and purity which is organic in the intercourse of most country girls and boys seemed lost, and parties and sleigh-rides left remorse and guilt behind." [9] Rose, child though she is, participates in this obscure misbehavior, but after the teacher has been dismissed and Carl, Rose's friend, has been rebuked, "they popped corn and played dominoes all the evening, and the innocency of their former childish companionship seemed restored." Coy as this presentation may be, something might nevertheless have been done with the material. Its presence shows that Garland was aware of the new thought that was beginning to overstep the boundaries of conventional literary inhibition. If the impulse was not strong enough to supersede the standard sentimental attitudes and motivations in the structure of the novel, the impropriety of the lines quoted above was shocking enough to cause the novel to be banned from the shelves of public libraries.

Other wraiths of the new thought hover near the fringes of the action. When Rose goes to Chicago the stage is set for a naturalistic treatment of the effect of the sordid elements of city life on an unspoiled country girl. Will it poison her morals, corrupt her ideals, destroy her faith in life? These dangers, along with the presence of male vultures lying in wait for innocent girls, are suggested but they never materialize in the action. There is propaganda for veritism, too. Rose's college essays are said to be lifeless because they are tied to the dead past: "They represented study and toil, but they did not represent her real self, her real emotions, any more than her reading represented her real liking. Her emotions, big, vital, contemporaneous, had no part in this formal and colorless pedantry." When she returns from Chicago to the Coolly, she writes fluent, natural poetry about farm life and country memories — poetry which the author tells us is very beautiful, even though nothing in Rose's character or development makes this seem probable. Actually, it is the literary tradition of country simplicity and beauty — straight from the eighteenth century — that controls Garland at this point, although he thinks he is proposing a veritistic treatment of the contemporary American scene. Another conscious effort to celebrate the American scene and the American hero occurs in the description of a storm on Lake Michigan, watched by Rose and the man she later marries.

The exposure of Garland's inconsistencies will not appear uncharitable if the reader sees in them the impassable abyss that yawned between the genteel tradition and the first stirrings of naturalistic theory in our literature. Because writers like Garland were unsophisticated and therefore completely at the mercy of the literary techniques which they absorbed from their Victorian world, it is understandable that they could not integrate the new ideas into a fictional structure. If a novel, like a play, is, as Aristotle said, an action, then these ideas cannot live if the writer does not know how to put them into an action where they can breathe. And if the action that is used comes from the literary forms and attitudes of a sentimental tradition, it will inevitably, as it has with Garland, determine the quality of its subject matter. Garland's rather pathetic failures are painful first tries to break away from the genteel tradition, attempts to cross the abyss that had to be made by someone. Garland had the idea, if not the style and technique to make them live.

— —

Some of the problems of naturalism are boldly illustrated in the contemporary drama, where contrasts of moral and naturalistic values are especially clear because they are sharp and simple. To comfort the outraged ghost of Hamlin Garland it might be appropriate at this point to show how the very same problems, in a more sophisticated guise, have tripped a recent playwright.

An example so striking that it might have been written to illustrate the present study is *Craig's Wife* (1925) by George Kelly. On the scientific axis it is a study of a neurotic woman. Mrs. Craig lived with a stepmother for twelve years and developed a feeling of rejection and insecurity. She marries in order to have a home absolutely her own — perfect, impeccable, envied. To this end she must gain such complete control over her husband that he will not share in or threaten her ownership; she must distrust every overture of neighborliness or friendship because they represent to her the sinister efforts of the outside world to break into her haven; and she must keep her house so fantastically neat that servants, made to feel like criminals, will not stay. From the opening curtain the neurotic compulsiveness of Mrs. Craig's conduct is apparent; indeed it is the key to most of her actions. She will not let her husband smoke in the living room; she makes the maids use the back stairway; she will not have flowers because the petals fall; she cannot have a hat, a bag, or a slip of paper lying on a table, and she dismisses a maid for leaving a ticket behind an ornament on the mantle; she treats a friendly neighbor with cold suspicion. The upshot is that she drives away neighbors, friends, relatives, and finally husband and comes into icy and abandoned possession of her big cold house. Thus her neurosis has severed her bonds with humanity, and her plight at the end of the play is a terrible one.

But on the moral axis there is a different play. Mrs. Craig is lying, suspicious, mean, scheming, cold, and *hateful.* Every act makes her more hateful. She insults the friendly neighbor. She lies to her husband and spies on him. She tries to convince him that he may be implicated in a murder, and indeed in order to preserve her fancied propriety she risks involving him with the police. Her hateful egocentricity is brought out by every act and speech, until the audience (and even the reader) is ready to see her boiled in oil. And then the wish is granted, as her husband finds her out for a dishonest, unloving prig, denounces her roundly, and makes a dramatic exit with his hands full of suitcases. On this axis the play seethes with moral indignation, and the audience expands with gratified resentment when Mrs. Craig is abandoned by everyone.

The experience of the play is unquestionably an emotional one, in which the reader or, more strongly, the audience identifies with the abused and patient husband. But the character of Mrs. Craig is presented through psychological concepts, for it is only by knowing the symptoms of the neurotic-compulsive that George Kelly is able to dramatize Mrs. Craig in such immediately and effectively unpleasant terms. He uses these psychological insights to represent a character as hateful, and here there is something basically uncomfortable and wrong, for one knows that these concepts from the world of objective clinical analysis should not be used to present a character as morally hateful. One does dislike Mrs. Craig, but one is not at peace in doing so, because one knows that as presented she is a sick woman who needs therapy rather than chastisement. The aesthetic experience of the play cannot be satisfactory because the two frames of reference do not coincide. And here is the dilemma of naturalism in a well-made three-act nutshell.

As writers became more sensitive to the pitfalls of the clinical approach, they subordinated their psychological concepts to their moral insights. Playwrights a generation later make fun of the psychiatrist or show, in play after play, that the neurotic character must be brought back into the stream of human love or, if he is evil, judged for the harm he does to others. A novelist like Faulkner is always deeply aware of the psychological intricacies of his characters, but he never for a moment lets us forget that he is taking a moral attitude toward moral agents. In such novels as *Absalom, Absalom!, Light in August,* and *The Sound and the Fury* he may look with an almost clinical awareness at the sources of his characters' appalling neuroses, but he also knows that these are the universal problems of men and that for all their ghastly psychic distortions they are still people like himself and have to work out their destinies as best they can. He neither condemns nor justifies. He shows that life includes all terrible aberrations in its pattern, and for him there is no line where the moral agent ceases and the sick mind takes over. They are always co-existent and co-operative. That is man's tragedy. When this view has been sufficiently explored and realized by a Faulkner, the naturalistic movement has ceased to be in the vanguard of literary experiment.

IV

Stephen Crane: Naturalist and Impressionist

THE inchoate naturalism of Frederic, Garland, and even lesser figures like Joseph Kirkland, Henry Blake Fuller, and H. H. Boyesen, is never strong enough to take control of the action of their novels.[1] They believe, with at least part of their minds, in determinism; they talk about scientific materialism and the influence of environment on the lives of their characters; they show the influence of the new candor that was being practiced by Zola and his followers in France; but they have not developed techniques that enable them to construct their novels according to strictly naturalistic principles. They usually begin with self-conscious emphasis on the molding power of environment and then veer off into ethical choices when they have established the setting and turn to the plot. These writers can describe the theory and the operation of determinism, but they cannot make it control a plotted action because they cannot eliminate personal choice and they cannot resolve the logical discord between action-by-choice and action caused by evironmental pressure.

The works of Stephen Crane (1871–1900) are an early and unique flowering of pure naturalism. It is naturalism in a restricted and special sense, and it contains many non-naturalistic elements, but it is nevertheless entirely consistent and coherent. It marks the first entry, in America, of a deterministic philosophy not confused with ethical motivation into the structure of the novel. Ethical judgment there is, in plenty. To define Crane's naturalism is to understand one of the few perfect and successful embodiments of the theory in the American novel. It illustrates the old truth that literary trends often achieve their finest expressions very early in their histories. *Mutatis mutandis*, Crane is the Christopher Marlowe of American naturalism — and we have had no Shakespeare.

Crane's naturalism is to be found, first, in his attitude toward received values, which he continually assails through his naturalistic method of showing that the traditional concepts of our social morality are shams and the motivations presumably controlled by them are pretenses; second, in his impressionism, which fractures experiences into disordered sensation in a way that shatters the old moral "order" along with the old orderly processes of reward and punishment; third, in his obvious interest in a scientific or deterministic accounting for events, although he does not pretend or attempt to be scientific in either the tone or the management of his fables. Crane's naturalism does not suffer from the problem of the divided stream because each of his works in so concretely developed that it does not have a meaning apart from what happens in it. The meaning is always the action; there is no wandering into theory that runs counter to what happens in the action; and nowhere does a character operate as a genuinely free ethical agent in defiance of the author's intentions. Crane's success is a triumph of style: manner and meaning are one.

～ ～

In *Maggie: A Girl of the Streets,* published pseudonymously in 1892, Crane opened fire with a loud bang. A story of the New York slums, it sounds in synopsis like a perfect bit of sordid determinism: a girl raised in violence and squalor, charmed, seduced, and abandoned by her flashy lover, rejected by her family, descends rapidly through streetwalking to suicide.

In telling this story, Crane fuses elements of poverty, ignorance, and intolerance in a context of violence and cruelty to create a nightmarish world wavering between hallucination and hysteria. The language establishes this tone through violent verbs, distorted scenes, and sensory transfer. A sampling of the first three pages discovers such terms as "howling," "circling madly about," "pelting," "writhing," "livid with the fury of battle," "furious assault," "convulsed," "cursed in shrill chorus," "tiny insane demon," "hurling," "barbaric," "smashed," "triumphant savagery," "leer gloatingly," "raving," "shrieking," "chronic sneer," "seethed," and "kicked, scratched and tore," which immediately suggest that the people are hurled through a nightmare. The device of sensory transfer appears in "lurid altercations," "red years," "dreaming blood-red dreams," and "various shades of yellow discontent." When Maggie's brother comes in bloody from fighting, "The mother's massive shoulders heaved with anger. Grasping the urchin by the neck and shoulder she shook him until he rattled. . . . The babe sat on the floor watching the scene, his face in contortions like that of a woman at a tragedy. The father . . . bellowed at his wife. 'Let the kid alone for a minute, will yeh, Mary? Yer allus poundin' 'im. When I come nights I can't get no rest 'cause yer allus poundin' a kid. Let up, d'yeh hear? Don't be allus poundin' a kid.' " [2]

In the same vein, Maggie's parents are depicted in insanely drunken battles during which they break up whole roomfuls of furniture and crockery several times during the brief story. After one such battle, "A glow from the fire threw red hues over the bare floor, the cracked and soiled plastering, and the overturned and broken furniture. In the middle of the floor lay his mother asleep. In one corner of the room his father's limp body hung across the seat of a chair." And a bit later, Maggie's "mother drank whiskey all Friday morning. With lurid face and tossing hair she cursed and destroyed furniture all Friday afternoon. When Maggie came home at half-past six her mother lay asleep amid the wreck of chairs and a table." Now, such people would not have more than one set of furniture, and it is improbable that they would in an ordinary drunken quarrel reduce it to matchwood, although of course one grants the likelihood of a table overturned or a chair smashed. The rather fantastic but obviously intentional exaggeration of these passages renders Crane's sense that this world is so warped as to be mad. His tone unites despair and moral outrage with the self-protection of a sort of wild humor.

A dominant idea that grows from this landscape of hysteria is that these people are victimized by their ideas of moral propriety which are so utterly inapplicable to their lives that they constitute a social insanity. Maggie is pounced upon by the first wolf in this jungle and seduced. When she is abandoned and returns home, her mother's outraged virtue is boundless:

"Ha ha, ha!" bellowed the mother. "Dere she stands! Ain't she purty? Look ut her! Ain't she sweet, deh beast? Look ut her! Ha, ha! Look ut her!" She lurched forward and put her red and seamed hands upon her daughter's face. She bent down and peered keenly up into the eyes of the girl. "Oh, she's jes' dessame as she ever was, ain't she? She's her mudder's putty darlin' yit, ain' she? Look ut her, Jimmie. Come here and look ut her."

Maggie is driven forth with jeers and blows and presently commits suicide. Crane tells how her mother responds to the lugubrious consolations of her neighbors in this classic paragraph:

The mourner essayed to speak, but her voice gave way. She shook her great shoulders frantically, in an agony of grief. The tears seemed to scald her face. Finally her voice came and arose in a scream of pain. "Oh, yes, I'll fergive her! I'll fergive her!"

The impressions that these people are not free agents, and that their freedom is limited as much by their conventional beliefs as by their poverty, are naturalistic concepts completely absorbed into the form of the story. One might object upon sociological grounds that Crane's ideas of the family are unsound, but his literary technique here is a triumph. It creates a coherent if terrible world, and there are no serious loose ends — no effect of tension or contradiction between abstract theory and human event. Crane's hallucinatory inferno is a gift of his style. What he says and what he renders are one. Indeed, he does not comment because the whole work is one grand roar of mockery and outrage. The hysterical distortions symbolize, image, and even dramatize the confusion of values which puts these social waifs in a moral madhouse.

The discrepancy between the Victorian pieties and the jungle reality of the slums is conscientiously explored. At a play to which Maggie is taken by her seducer, "Shady persons in the audience

69

revolted from the pictured villainy of the drama. With untiring zeal they hissed vice and applauded virtue. Unmistakably bad men evinced an apparently sincere admiration for virtue. The loud gallery was overwhelmingly with the unfortunate and the oppressed. They encouraged the struggling hero with cries and jeered the villain, hooting and calling attention to his whiskers." "Maggie always departed with raised spirits from these melodramas. She rejoiced at the way in which the poor and virtuous eventually overcame the wealthy and wicked."

Another interesting passage begins when Maggie's mother is evicted, drunk, from a bar; the brother, Jimmie, tries to take her home, and a great battle ensues:

She raised her arm and whirled her great fist at her son's face. Jimmie dodged his head, and the blow struck him in the back of the neck . . .
"Keep yer hands off me!" roared his mother again.
"Say, yeh ol' bat! Quit dat!" yelled Jimmie . . .

And presently he defeats her. Whereupon the conquered mother, in high moral dudgeon, evicts his erring sister: "Yeh've gone t' d' devil, Mag Johnson. . . . Yer a disgrace t' yer people. . . . Git out. I won't have sech as youse in me house!" The next time she is drunk, the pity of it overcomes her:

"She's d' devil's own chil', Jimmie. . . . Ah, who would t'ink such a bad girl could grow up in our fambly, Jimmie, me son. Many d'hour I've spent in talk wid dat girl an' tol' her if she ever went on d' streets I'd see her damned. An' after all her bringin'-up, an' what I tol' her and talked wid her, she goes teh d' bad, like a duck teh water."

Confused by the fact that it was he who brought the seducer to the house, Jimmie curses manfully but does nothing until he finds that the fall of Maggie is causing rude comment from the neighbors; then he proposes to salvage the family's reputation by bringing Maggie back home. But the mother screams with indignation, "What! Let 'er come an' sleep under deh same roof wid her mudder again? . . . Shame on yehs . . . dat ye'd grow up teh say sech a t'ing teh yer mudder — yer own mudder." Sobs choke her and interrupt her reproaches.

Jimmie does not renew his suggestion, "But, arguing with himself . . . he, once, almost came to a conclusion that his sister would have been more firmly good had she better known how. However, he felt that he could not hold such a view. He threw it hastily aside." Here Crane's technique flags for a moment and betrays his tone, even though he does not fall into inconsistency. Elsewhere the tone is complicated, beyond the needs of his thesis, into further impressionisms which demonstrate virtuosity of auctorial impression (and style) rather than exploration of the subject. In the dirty street, for example, Maggie — as a little girl — is dragging her infant brother Jimmie along: "He fell on his face, roaring . . . He made *heroic* endeavors to keep on his legs, *denounced* his sister, and consumed a bit of orange peeling which he chewed between the times of his *infantile orations*." The italicized words come from a world of reference beyond this grisly slum. They convey a stylistic exuberance; they introduce humor and psychic distance, or what Joyce terms aesthetic *stasis*. But to call a grubby child's screams infantile orations is to deflect the impact of the scene and make us aware of the writer. The deflection is studiously grotesque: there is just enough truth in the pictorial comparison between a child waving its arms and opening its mouth to scream and an orator with hand raised and mouth wide in campaign eloquence to elicit a flash of recognition. But the comparison makes a comment on the orator, not on the child. One thinks of the current fad of infant portraits with subtitles pointing to adult conduct. With this abrupt wrenching of the attention the effect of hysteria and wild confusion spreads out from the scene itself into the world that includes the writer and the reader, suggesting that if our world includes Maggie's world then it is insane too. Thus the impressionism renders the scene as it strikes the observing author, giving his involvement with this impression and uttering the comment that this scene outrages the sense of order and decency to the point where — like Hamlet jumping into the grave and outboasting Laertes — one responds in self-defense with an outburst of wild mockery.

But we have not done. A still further effect is attained because Crane's detachment motivates the reader to an involvement which he might otherwise resist, and we come finally to sense the horror of this life when, after a climactic drunken brawl between the horrible parents, "The father had not moved, but lay in the same death-like sleep. The mother writhed in a uneasy slumber, her chest wheezing as if she were in the agonies of strangulation. Out at the window a florid moon was peering over dark roofs, and in the distance the waters of a river glimmered pallidly."

A perennial controversy about naturalism concerns whether it is optimistic or pessimistic — whether it dwells in the horrors it portrays or believes it can correct them. The problem achieves an epitome in *Maggie*: however stark the horror, no reader can feel that Crane is scientifically disinterested or unconcerned. Where his method does, through its fascinated concern with detail, achieve a ghastly fixation, it is the quality of Goya rather than the cold form of Velasquez. The story shows that nothing can be done for Maggie and her family, for they are lost; but it presents the exact reality with an intensity that defies indifference. I say the exact reality. It seems exact, but it would be more accurate to say that Crane objectifies and renders exactly his spirited and intentional distortion of the grotesque world that he has exactly seen.

— —

The frantic impressionism we have seen in *Maggie* is the signature of Crane's fiction, yet it varies in each work enough to give it particularity. "The Blue Hotel" is a satire on causation in which the action is the argument, as it was in *Maggie*. An easterner, a cowboy, and a furtive tenderfoot Swede alight in a blizzard at a hotel on the Nebraska prairie. The Swede is sneaky, vehement, or jocose in unpredictable spasms because he is afraid of the wild West. During a lull in the card game that follows, he says, "I suppose there have been a good many men killed in this room." [3] His statement evokes angry denials from the proprietor's son, Johnnie, and the cowboy, and these in turn frighten the Swede into further immoderate statements. His fear grows to terror, and he cries, "Gentlemen, I suppose I am going to be killed before I can leave this house!" Finding the Swede yelling in fright, the proprietor accuses Johnnie of troubling him — and as a result three people are now tense.

Motivated largely by pride, the proprietor gives the Swede a great drink of whiskey to calm him and prove that the establishment is not a death trap. But the Swede goes into a manic phase from the drink and becomes as brash and aggressive as he was before timid and insecure. At a second card game, after dinner, he accuses Johnnie of cheating. Naturally there is a fight, and the Swede defeats Johnnie. He than insults the proprietor, the easterner, and the cowboy, who have to eschew reprisals because they have been accused of "ganging up," and roars out to a saloon. There he gets drunk and insults, threatens, and assaults a professional gambler who is, incidentally, the most scrupulous gentleman in the story. "In all affairs outside his business . . . this thieving card-player was so generous, so just, so moral, that, in a contest, he could have put to flight the consciences of nine tenths of the citizens of Romper." The gambler, a small frail man, kills the burly Swede with one thrust of his knife and is subsequently convicted and sentenced to three years in prison.

Some months later the easterner and the cowboy attempt to fix responsibility. It transpires that Johnnie did cheat at the card game, and the easterner saw him but refused to stand up for the Swede. "And I refused to stand up and be a man. I let the Swede fight it out alone. And you — you were simply puffing around the place and wanting to fight. And then old Scully himself! We are all in it! This poor gambler isn't even a noun. He is a kind of an adverb. Every sin is the result of a collaboration. . . . Usually there are from a dozen to forty women really involved in every murder . . ."

The Swede was branded by the gods for the slaughter, made mad by the death he carried in his craven and ignorant heart. The pattern of blind fate-ridden folly suggests an authentic tragic effect, but Crane has distorted it by giving the details of the Swede's undoing so precisely that every bit of what has happened is accounted for quite plainly and clearly. Instead of a dark mystery, we see finally a clear outrage caused by human folly and ignorance.

The characters have volition and ethical judgment — they are not driven by overwhelming forces — and they use these powers everywhere in the story. Their reactions are controlled by what they are as people, but the point of the story is that they are typical people, with humor, passion, and weakness in reasonable proportions. Yet their "choices" entangle them in nets of circumstance from which they cannot be extricated. The conventional notion of a moral order presided over by the forms of public morality is made indefensibly ludicrous by the action. Everybody in this story is conscious, has ideas about fairness and decency which are with him constantly, and tries to act in a way that he can justify. But the outcome is beyond anyone's control, and the social verdict of the gambler's conviction is a gross fraud.

The final effect of this story hovers somewhere between indignation with conventional morality and an approach to the pity and terror of tragedy. It is obviously not on the grand scale of Sophocles, but it is authentic. The tragic pretensions are modified by Crane's sardonic tone, so that he seems not to be defining man's place in the universe so much as commenting on the naïve foolishness of his conventional morality. The tragic overtone comes out in the fact that the characters involved, foolish and erratic as they may be, are not specifically guilty of the Swede's murder. They act about as well as their sort of people could be expected to act in such a situation. It is the whole cosmic scheme that is out of key with man's notions of what properly should happen. The Swede is a fool, indeed, but he is understandably terrified by his first meeting, on a distant and snowswept prairie, with cowboys and gamblers.

Crane's naturalism is descriptive: he does not pretend to set forth a proof, like a chemical demonstration, that what happened must have happened, inevitably. This is what Zola was forever saying he did, and it is for these pretensions of scientific demonstration and proof that he has been chided by later critics. Crane simply shows how a sequence of events takes place quite independently of the wills and judgments of the people involved. The reader is convinced that it happened that way, and he sees that the ordinary moral sentiments do not adequately judge or account for these happenings. The writer does not have to argue that he has proved anything about causation or determinism: he has absolutely shown that men's wills do not control their destinies.

~ ~

The Red Badge of Courage (1895),[4] Crane's Civil War story, is the most controversial piece in his canon. It has been much discussed and most variously interpreted, and the interpretations range about as widely as they could. Is it a Christian story of redemption? Is it a demonstration that man is a beast with illusions? Or is it, between these extremes, the story of a man who goes through the fire, discovers himself, and with the self-knowledge that he is able to attain comes to terms with the problem of life insofar as an imperfect man can come to terms with an imperfect world? It is tempting to take the middle road between the intemperate extremes; but let us see what happens before we come to the paragraphs at the end that are invoked to prove each of the explanations:

He felt a quiet manhood, non-assertive but of sturdy and strong blood. He knew that he would no more quail before his guides wherever they should point. He had been to touch the great death, and found that, after all, it was but the great death. He was a man.

So it came to pass that as he trudged from the place of blood and wrath his soul changed. He came from hot plowshares to prospects of clover tranquilly, and it was as if hot plowshares were not. Scars faded as flowers.

. . . He had rid himself of the red sickness of battle. The sultry nightmare was in the past. He had been an animal blistered and sweating in the heat and pain of war. He turned now with a lover's thirst to images of tranquil skies, fresh meadows, cool brooks.

It is not obvious whether the young man who thinks these thoughts is deluding himself or not. To judge the quality of his self-analysis we must look in some detail at what he has been through. The book opens with a scene at a Union encampment in which the uninformed arguments of the soldiers are described in a manner that recalls the mockery of "infantile orations" in *Maggie*. The phrase pictures a squalling child colorfully, while it conveys the

75

author's private amusement at the image of a shouting politician. In *The Red Badge* there is continually a tone of mockery and sardonic imitation of men who are boisterous, crafty, arrogant, resentful, or suspicious always in an excess that makes them comical, and the author seems to delight in rendering the flavor of their extravagances. An element of the fantastic is always present, the quality apparently representing the author's feeling for the war, the situations in it, the continual and enormous incongruities between intention and execution, between a man's estimate of himself and the way he appears to others, between the motivations acknowledged to the world and those which prevail in the heart. It is with these last that the book is centrally concerned — with the problem of courage — and it is here that the meaning is most confusingly entangled with the tone.

In the opening scene the men are excited over a rumor that the troop is about to move, for the first time in months, and immediately the tone of mockery appears. A certain tall soldier "developed virtues and went resolutely to wash a shirt. He came flying back. . . . He was swelled with a tale he had heard from a reliable friend, who had heard it from a truthful cavalryman, who had heard it from his trustworthy brother. . . . He adopted the important air of a herald in red and gold." Another soldier takes the report "as an affront," and the tall soldier "felt called upon to defend the truth of a rumor he had himself introduced. He and the loud one came near to fighting over it." A corporal swears furiously because he has just put a floor under his tent; the men argue about strategies, clamoring at each other, "numbers making futile bids for the popular attention."

From this outer excitement we turn to the excitement in the heart of the youth who is to be the hero of the tale. He has crept off to his tent to commune with himself and particularly to wonder how he will act when he confronts the enemy. He has "dreamed of battles all his life — of vague and bloody conflicts that had thrilled him with their sweep and fire. . . . He had imagined peoples secure in the shadow of his eagle-eyed prowess." He had burned to enlist, but had been deterred by his mother's arguments that he was more important on the farm until — the point is sardonically emphasized — the newspapers carried accounts of great battles in which the North was victor. "Almost every day the newspapers printed accounts of a decisive victory." When he enlists, his mother makes a long speech to him — which is presented by Crane with no trace of mockery — but he is impatient and irritated. As he departs, there is a tableau described, for almost the only time in the book, with unqualified feeling:

Still, when he had looked back from the gate, he had seen his mother kneeling among the potato parings. Her brown face, upraised, was stained with tears, and her spare form was quivering. He bowed his head and went on, feeling suddenly ashamed of his purposes.

Vanity amid dreams of Homeric glory occupy him thenceforth — until battle is imminent. Then he wonders whether he will run or stand; and he does not dare confide his fears to the other men because they all seem so sure of themselves and because both they and he are constantly diverted from the question by inferior concerns. When the first rumor proves false, its carrier, the tall soldier, in defense of his honor, "fought with a man from Chatfield Corners and beat him severely." (This tall soldier, whose name is Jim Conklin, has been identified symbolically with Jesus Christ by some critics.) In a similar instance, "A man fell down, and as he reached for his rifle a comrade, unseeing, trod upon his hand. He of the injured fingers swore bitterly and aloud. A low tittering laugh went among his fellows." This petty reaction alienates the boy. The tall soldier offers more theories, is challenged, and there are endless debates: "The blatant soldier often convulsed whole files by his biting sarcasms aimed at the tall one." Another soldier tries to steal a horse, is defied by the girl who owns it, and precipitates wild cheers from the men, who "entered whole-souled upon the side of the maiden. . . . They jeered the piratical private, and called attention to various defects in his personal appearance; and they were wildly enthusiastic in support of the young girl."

Approaching the first engagement, the youth perceives with

terror that he is "in a moving box" of soldiers from which it would be impossible to escape, and "it occurred to him that he had never wished to come to the war . . . He had been dragged by the merciless government." He is further startled when the loud soldier, a braggart, announces with a sob that he is going to be killed, and gives the youth a packet of letters for his family. The engagement is described with terms of confusion: the youth feels "a red rage," and then "acute exasperation"; he "fought frantically" for air; the other men are cursing, babbling, and querulous; their equipment bobs "idiotically" on their backs, and they move like puppets. The assault is turned back, and the men leer at each other with dirty smiles; but just as the youth is responding in "an ecstasy of self-satisfaction" at having passed "the supreme trial," there comes a second charge from which he flees in blind panic: "He ran like a blind man. Two or three times he fell down. Once he knocked his shoulder so heavily against a tree that he went headlong." As he runs, his fear increases, and he rages at the suicidal folly of those who have stayed behind to be killed.

Just as he reaches the zone of safety, he learns that the line has held and the enemy's charge been repulsed. Instantly he "felt that he had been wronged," and begins to find reasons for the wisdom of his flight. "It was all plain that he had proceeded according to very correct and commendable rules. His actions had been sagacious things. They had been full of strategy. . . . He, the enlightened man who looks afar in the dark, had fled because of his superior perceptions and knowledge. He felt a great anger against his comrades. He knew it could be proved that they had been fools." He pities himself; he feels rebellious, agonized, and despairing. It is here that he sees a squirrel and throws a pine cone at it; when it runs he finds a triumphant exhibition in nature of the law of self-preservation. "Nature had given him a sign." The irony of this sequence is abundantly apparent. It increases when, a moment later, the youth enters a place where the "arching boughs made a chapel" and finds a horrible corpse, upright against a tree, crawling with ants and staring straight at him.

From this he flees in renewed panic, and then there is a strange turn. A din of battle breaks out, such a "tremendous clangor of sounds" as to make the engagement from which he ran seem trivial, and he runs back to watch because for such a spectacle curiosity becomes stronger than fear. He joins a ghastly procession of wounded from this battle, among whom he finds Jim Conklin, his friend, gray with the mark of death, and watches him die in throes that "caused him to dance a sort of hideous hornpipe." The guilt he feels among these frightfully wounded men, in this chapter which comes precisely in the middle of the book, should be enough to make him realize his brotherhood, his indebtedness, his duty; but his reaction as he watches the retreat swell is to justify his early flight — until a column of soldiers going *toward* the battle makes him almost weep with his longing to be one of their brave file. Increasingly, in short, Crane makes us see Henry Fleming as an emotional puppet controlled by whatever sight he sees at the moment. He becomes like Conrad's Lord Jim, romancing dreams of glory while he flinches at every danger. As his spirits flag under physical exhaustion, he hopes his army will be defeated so that his flight will be vindicated.

The climax of irony comes now, when, after a stasis of remorse in which he does indeed despise himself (albeit for the wrong reason of fearing the reproaches of those who did not flee), he sees the whole army come running past him in an utter panic of terror. He tries to stop one of them for information, and is bashed over the head by the frantic and bewildered man. And now, wounded thus, almost delirious with pain and exhaustion, he staggers back to his company — and is greeted as a hero! Henry is tended by the loud soldier, who has become stronger and steadier. Henry's reaction to his friend's care and solicitude is to feel superior because he still has the packet of letters the loud one gave him a day before, in his fear: "The friend had, in a weak hour, spoken with sobs of his own death. . . . But he had not died, and thus he had delivered himself into the hands of the youth." He condescends to his loud friend, and "His self-pride was now [so] entirely restored" that he began to see something fine in his conduct of the day before. He is now vainglorious; he thinks himself "a man of experience . . .

chosen of the gods and doomed to greatness." Remembering the terror-stricken faces of the men he saw fleeing from the great battle, he now feels a scorn for them! He thinks of the tales of prowess he will tell back home to circles of adoring women.

The youth's reaction to his spurious "red badge of courage" is thus set down with close and ironical detail. Crane does not comment, but the picture of self-delusion and vainglory is meticulously drawn. In the following chapter Henry does fight furiously, but here he is in a blind rage that turns him into an animal, so that he goes on firing long after the enemy have retreated. The other soldiers regard his ferocity with wonder, and Henry has become a marvel, basking in the wondering stares of his comrades.

The order comes for a desperate charge, and the regiment responds magnificently, hurling itself into the enemy's fire regardless of the odds against it; and here Crane devotes a paragraph to a careful and specific analysis of their heroism:

But there was a frenzy made from this furious rush. The men, pitching forward insanely, had burst into cheerings, moblike and barbaric, but tuned in strange keys that can arouse the dullard and the stoic. It made a mad enthusiasm that, it seemed, would be incapable of checking itself before granite and brass. There was the delirium that encounters despair and death, and is heedless and blind to the odds. It is a temporary but sublime absence of selfishness. And because it was of this order was the reason, perhaps, why the youth wondered, afterward, what reasons he could have had for being there.

Heroism is "temporary but sublime," succeeded by dejection, anger, panic, indignation, despair, and renewed rage. This can hardly be called, for Henry, gaining spiritual salvation by losing his soul in the flux of things, for he is acting in harried exasperation, exhaustion, and rage. What has seemed to him an incredible charge turns out, presently, to have been a very short one — in time and distance covered — for which the regiment is bitterly criticized by the General. The facts are supplemented by the tone, which conveys through its outrageous and whimsical language that the whole business is made of pretense and delusion: A "magnificent brigade" goes into a wood, causing there "a most awe-inspiring racket. . . . Having stirred this prodigious uproar, and, apparently, finding it too prodigious, the brigade, after a little time, came marching airily out again with its fine formation in nowise disturbed. . . . The brigade was jaunty and seemed to point a proud thumb at the yelling wood." In the midst of the next engagement, which is indeed a furious battle, the youth is sustained by a "strange and unspeakable hatred" of the officer who had dubbed his regiment "mud diggers." Carrying the colors, he leads a charge of men "in a state of frenzy, perhaps because of forgotten vanities, and it made an exhibition of sublime reckless-ness." In this hysterical battlefield the youth is indeed selfless and utterly fearless in "his wild battle madness," yet by reading closely we see that the opposing soldiers are a thin, feeble line who turn and run from the charge or are slaughtered.

What it all seems to come to is that the heroism is in action undeniable, but it is preceded and followed by the ignoble senti-ments we have traced — and the constant tone of humor and hysteria seems to be Crane's comment on these juxtapositions of courage, ignorance, vainglory, pettiness, pompous triumph, and craven fear. The moment the men can stop and comment upon what they have been through they are presented as more or less absurd.

With all these facts in mind we can examine the Henry Fleming who emerges from the battle and sets about marshaling all his acts. He is gleeful over his courage. Remembering his desertion of the wounded Jim Conklin, he is ashamed because of the possible dis-grace, but, as Crane tells with supreme irony, "gradually he mus-tered force to put the sin at a distance," and to dwell upon his "quiet manhood." Coming after all these events and rationaliza-tions, the paragraphs quoted at the beginning of this discussion are a climax of self-delusion. If there is any one point that has been made it is that Henry has never been able to evaluate his conduct. He may have been fearless for moments, but his motives were vain, selfish, ignorant, and childish. Mercifully, Crane does not follow him down through the more despicable levels of self-delusion that are sure to follow as he rewrites (as we have seen him planning to do) the story of his conduct to fit his childish specifications. He has been through some moments of hell, during which he has for moments risen above his limitations, but Crane seems plainly to be showing that he has not achieved a lasting wisdom or self-knowledge.

If *The Red Badge of Courage* were only an exposure of an ignorant farm boy's delusions, it would be a contemptible book. Crane shows that Henry's delusions image only dimly the insanely grotesque and incongruous world of battle into which he is plunged. There the movement is blind or frantic, the leaders are selfish, the goals are inhuman. One farm boy is made into a mad animal to kill another farm boy, while the great guns carry on a "grim pow-wow" or a "stupendous wrangle" described in terms that suggest a solemn farce or a cosmic and irresponsible game.

If we were to seek a geometrical shape to picture the significant form of *The Red Badge,* it would not be the circle, the L, or the straight line of oscillation between selfishness and salvation, but the equilateral triangle. Its three points are instinct, ideals, and circumstance. Henry Fleming runs along the sides like a squirrel in a track. Ideals take him along one side until circumstance confronts him with danger. Then instinct takes over and he dashes down the third side in a panic. The panic abates somewhat as he approaches the angle of ideals, and as he turns the corner (continuing his flight) he busily rationalizes to accommodate those ideals of duty and trust that recur, again and again, to harass him. Then he runs on to the line of circumstance, and he moves again toward instinct. He is always controlled on one line, along which he is both drawn and impelled by the other two forces. If this triangle is thought of as a piece of bright glass whirling in a cosmic kaleidoscope, we have an image of Crane's naturalistic and vividly impressioned Reality.

～ ～

The same grim joke of a world is more quietly portrayed in a story that has received little critical attention, perhaps because it is so unpleasant to think about — "The Monster" (1899).[5] This tale explores the consequences of an act of brotherhood which is forced by the nature of things to become involved with pride. Dr. Trescott's little son is saved from a fire by Henry, a Negro coachman, whose face is horribly burned for his heroism. The doctor is urged to let the poor Negro die, but he exerts all his skill to save him — and thereby produces a faceless and witless monster. It is a small town, where the effects of this conscientious "blunder of virtue" multiply. Disgust, revulsion, fear, guilt, and hostility poison the town. The doctor has to pay to have the monster cared for by some very unwilling relatives. The head of this household, complaining that "he looks like er devil, an' done skears all ma frien's away, an' ma chillens cain't eat, an' ma ole 'ooman jes' raisin' Cain all the time . . . and him not right in his haid," and so on, demands a regular salary of six dollars a week. When Henry "escapes" one evening and rambles through the town, he causes a panic of fright which straightway turns into hostility toward Dr. Trescott. The good doctor finds his child taunted, his wife ostracized, and himself solemnly waited upon by a delegation of businessmen who demand that Henry be institutionalized. The doctor has to take Henry back to his own home, and the town's hostility mounts to hysteria; he loses his practice and his standing; his son's little friends are forbidden to play with him; his wife is heartbroken.

And there the story ends, without a solution. The Negro's heroism, followed by the doctor's gratitude and humanity, have evoked as unlovely a series of human responses as one could imagine. There is a suspicion that the doctor is guilty of stubborn pride in standing by his decision and refusing to commit Henry to an institution. But Henry is not really insane, as the doctor knows, and the doctor would not have been the town's leading citizen if he had not been a man of strength and integrity; so it is hardly a culpable pride that leads him to defy the irrational hostility which has sprung up around him like the fire that started the trouble. For such cosmic jokes there does not seem to be a human or decent solution, and this is what the story finally means. It may not be typical, but it is too certainly possible. All the characters are bound by their virtues and limitations (it does not matter which) in the circumstances given, and apparently no will can extricate those involved from the social deterioration that ensues. As usual, Crane's style expresses the grotesque and hallucinatory quality of his subject and in so doing embodies a grim comment on the moral insanity of a world that produces such maniacal fantasies.

The same values appear in Crane's famous story, "The Open Boat," [6] where four survivors of a shipwreck battle exhaustion and the open sea, and three of them survive. The bravest of the group is drowned in the waves as they finally beach, but the irony of his death is offset by the quiet heroism which all four have displayed through their ordeal. As in "The Monster," Crane sees no cosmic order or purpose, but here the human values of courage and brotherhood are able to live for a time. Are these men better — or are their circumstances merely luckier? Crane does not say.

～ ～

There is an interesting connection, which scholarship has not yet traced, between what we speak of as Crane's impressionism and the "expressionism" of the modern theater. Expressionism is the theatrical mode that uses distortion, violent and intense motion, and the "yell" to convey a sense of the world as it appears to one of the characters or to the author. Usually it is the protagonist whose distorted view conveys something the author wants us to see. In Kaufman's *Beggar on Horseback* (1924), the girl's aggressive brother wears a yellow bow tie with red polka dots. With each new scene this tie grows until in the dream sequence where the hero sees the consequences of marrying into her family it is about two feet long. Her father carries a telephone which grows until it is five feet tall. The scene on Fifth Avenue in O'Neill's *The Hairy Ape* (1922) has Yank, the stoker, bouncing off the well-dressed strollers as if they were granite and he rubber. Hallucination, distortion, violent and frenetic change in expressionistiq drama purport to represent the vision of the world distorted by the lens of a personality.

Yet while it thus undertakes to display the world through the private vision of a character — an enterprise that one might expect to produce a very subjective art — expressionism simultaneously makes a bold social comment. *Beggar on Horseback* deals with the commercial mind and the impingement of business values on private lives. Its distortions make the business world seem grotesque and inhuman. *The Hairy Ape* develops two themes — the alienation of the worker and the gross differences in our social scale. The play begins with a deck scene on a liner, where a frigid, hospital-like whiteness prevails; it then descends to the bowels of the ship, where Yank and the other stokers, casting huge shadows against the dark boilers, look like monsters of the infernal depths. When the immaculately white girl walks into this inferno, the dramatic contrast is startling. The expressionism here, it may be noted, represents the author's sense of a distorted social order, rather than that of any character. Georg Kaiser's *From Morn to Midnight* (1919) depicts the grotesque, ridiculous, and terrible aspects of the life of a bank cashier. He steals money to pursue a woman who is unaware that she has aroused him and proceeds through a series of distorted experiences of which the most lurid is a scene in a velodrome, with the crowd frenzied by betting on the cycle race and the total effect a phantasmagoria of the bewildered cashier's reality.

Each of these expressionistic plays has as a major part of its effect the revelation of social evil. In each the distortion reflects the author's sense of the dislocations in a society where human values are subordinated to business and machinery. It projects a sense of outrage, of hysterical folly, of a reality so wrenched that it appears hallucinatory. These comments apply in almost precisely the same way to Crane's writings. What appears hysterical and twisted through the mind of the protagonist is also seen thus in the longer perspective of the author's purpose. He is showing his characters baffled and harried in a crazy world, where they do not function well enough to control their own destinies, or even to understand them very well; it is a world which the author's larger view does not make any more reasonable, for what his view particularly adds is a fuller sense of the protagonist's limitations.

Crane's writings anticipate dramatic expressionism in America by twenty years, as they do also the work of Kaiser, Toller, and Wedekind on the Continent. Only the earliest expressionistic work of Strindberg is as early as Crane's impressionism. For its sources we might better look to the painting of the great modern impressionists — Cezanne, Matisse, van Gogh.

V

Jack London: Blond Beasts and Supermen

To turn from Stephen Crane to Jack London is like turning from a Jaguar roadster to a Stanley Steamer. The former is extreme, unique, and also just about perfect in its particular way. The latter was supposed to have more power than any man dared use, but it was also known to run out of steam halfway up a long hill; and everybody knows that it was a trial to start and a constant threat to explode. It may also profitably be contrasted with the slick and fragile 1956 models, for there was glamour and courage and excitement with the old Steamer. Looked at coolly and seriously, however, it was an unpractical dream, and it had its ludicrous aspects, too, along with its flair.

One thinks of London (1876–1916) as an arresting storyteller and a writer of tremendous vigor. These qualities are there in his work, but what accounts for his immense and continued popularity is his ideas. Ideas distinguish his novels and stories from the thousands of action stories that so regularly appear and disappear. His ideas have the same appeal today that they had to London's contemporaries, although today they interest somewhat less sophisticated readers than those who devoured his books in the early decades of this century. In Europe and Russia, however, he is still widely read and seriously considered by the intellectuals. He is interesting today for a further reason. He occupies a dramatic position in the flow of naturalistic writing, for he stands like a colossus, rugged but precarious, with one foot in each branch of the divided stream. He fought with his background, his environ-ment, and finally he fought his way through self-education to become famous and successful. But he never stopped fighting, and the struggle with life is no more important to his success than his struggle with ideas. One led to the other, and the battle of ideas dramatizes with extraordinary clarity the confusions and tensions which I have attributed to the divided stream. In the melee, blond beasts, ideas, and supermen drip with blood like White Fang himself.

London's experiences in the years before he began to write were brutal. Before he was twenty-one he had worked in a cannery where, if we are to accept as authentic the fictionalized use he made of the incidents in later years,[1] he frequently saw his companions lose their fingers when their attention flagged toward the end of a twelve-hour day at the machines; he had, at the age of sixteen, a mistress — the Queen of the Oyster Pirates — and became an oyster pirate himself, a man who broke the law daily and lived in the shadow of the penitentiary; he had sailed with the fish patrol of San Francisco Bay; he had shipped at the age of seventeen as an able seaman and had gone on a long sealing cruise; he had set forth for Washington, D.C., with Kelly's Army (an organization which hoped to join forces with Coxey's Army) and, when that body dis-banded in the Middle West, had hoboed his way on to the east coast and back to California; he had become a formidable drunk-ard, a tough of the most desperate order;[2] he had become an ardent socialist; he had studied for and passed the entrance ex-aminations of the University of California in three months — this with only a half-year of high school behind him; and, finally, having abandoned college as useless, he had followed the Gold Rush to the Yukon, where he saw life as a struggle for existence in which quarter was always denied and only the strong could survive.

These were the experiences that determined London's reactions to his readings in philosophy and science, insofar as experience does work in such areas; for aside from early hardship there was something inherent in London that impelled him to do things the hardest way, set himself the most impossible tasks, and thrust himself into the most perilous situations. He was able to flourish within and finally to rise above the hard conditions of his early life; and the fact that he gloried in the memory of his early adventures shows to some extent how he saw himself as embodying the bone-crushing vitality which he continually celebrated in his stories. He saw everything from farming through fighting to reading in heroic terms, and this side of his character is not without its ludicrous aspects: he could not help being self-conscious about his manliness; and the most determined admirer of Jack London must smile at such a passage as the following, quoted from his wife's biography:

George Serling [Sterling] had affectionately dubbed him "The Wolf," or "The Fierce Wolf," or "The Shaggy Wolf." In the last month of Jack London's life, he gave me an exquisite tiny wristwatch. "And what shall I have engraved on it?" I asked. "Oh, 'Mate from Wolf,' I guess," he replied. And I: "The same as when we exchanged engagement watches?" "Why, yes, if you don't mind," he admitted. "I have sometimes wished you would call me 'Wolf' more often." [3]

This ridiculous bit of dialogue illustrates what appears everywhere in the biography: that London was drawing a real or fancied portrait of himself in Sea-Wolf Larsen and in most of his other "primitive" and strong-minded heroes.

A glimpse of some of the main aspects of London's thought, before we turn to the novels, will reveal the astonishing mixture of cross-purposes and contradictions that came out of his fierce studies.

From the day when he first read Herbert Spencer, London was drunk with the new science. In a letter written in 1899, when he was twenty-three years old, he speaks straight from Spencer's *First Principles*: "If people could come to realize the utter absurdity, logically, of the finite contemplating the infinite!" [4] Eternity, said Spencer, is beyond man's powers of conception; nor can man imagine a time before time, or the creation of something out of nothing. All such ultimate problems are unanswerable because man's mind cannot grasp the elements involved in them. With this neat disposition of the Unknowable, Spencer strode on to the knowable — the physical universe. Here, London echoes him, is "LAW, inexorable, blind, unreasoning law, which has no knowledge of good or ill, right or wrong; which has no preference, grants no favors." [5] Such law frees man from worship, if not from fear. Some fifteen years later London wrote a statement of belief that reveals the same stanch materialism: "I am a hopeless materialist. I see the soul as nothing else than the sum of the activities of the organism plus personal habits, memories, and experiences of the organism. *I believe that when I am dead, I am dead. I believe that with my death I am just as much obliterated as the last mosquito you or I smashed."* [6] Elaborating upon this materialism, he denies the existence of free will. It is, he says, absurd "to think that man is the object of his own volition, inasmuch that a few of him may oppose the many in a movement which does not spring from the individual but from the race, and which received its inception before even they had differentiated from the parent branch!" [7]

Spencer was closely linked to Darwin in London's thought. The idea of life as a struggle for survival appealed to him tremendously, and it accounts for a number of loosely related ideas that occur repeatedly in his work. In the first place he argues for the pure breed: "God abhors a mongrel. In nature there is no place for a mixed breed. . . . Consult the entire history of the human world in all past ages, and you will find that the world has ever belonged to the pure breed and has never belonged to the mongrel." [8] Strength is pure. Strength is good. Weakness is therefore evil. These are moral values, of course, and they are repeatedly urged with a moral fervor that belies what London has elsewhere said about free will and sin. The tone of passage after passage asserts that the mixing of breeds is a sin against nature and assumes a moral order which London asserts (unconsciously) as the basis of good conduct, social justice, and physical survival. Concepts of strength and the purity of an unmixed breed evoke images of savage men who have survived through pure physical strength and who, being freshly minted, would not have suffered racial pollution. This notion takes us by easy steps to the concept of atavism. Atavism is a condition in which one's primitive self, with its assumed strength and ferocity, is close to the civilized surface. Its presence argues greater adaptability in its possessor, for it means that he has not been frozen into a rigid pattern; he can rise to the challenge of new conditions. London's heroes are likely to evince this atavism when they are thrust into the struggle for survival under brutal frontier conditions. When such atavistic power surges up, nothing can safely oppose them, and they exult in the glory of it. From atavism he moves by natural steps to the superman, whom he considers at one time to be superior because he is non-moral and, at another, an antisocial irritant who cannot survive in the complex modern world. He attaches virtue now to will and self-assertion, now to social adaptability.

In his theorizing about society, Herbert Spencer was extremely conservative. Since evolution would inevitably bring the Golden Day — it being a part of his theory that evolution was a law of development toward higher and higher orders of integrated complexity — it behooved man not to hamper evolution with any sort of misguided social legislation. Such efforts, he said, were generally directed to preserving the unfit, who could not protect themselves from the rigors of free competition. Hence "social" legislation was really unsocial. It interfered with the long-range working of evolution toward perfection. It interfered, that is, insofar as it had any effect, but for the most part it was as futile and ineffectual as any puny efforts of man against cosmic processes. But London, the avowed Spencerian, was a socialist. Revolutinary socialism, he wrote in 1905, "is based upon economic necessity and is in line with social evolution." [9] The words "necessity" and "revolution," which continue to associate socialism with natural law, do not hide the fact that socialism offers a program directly contrary to Spencer's most earnest convictions.

A final item of London's intellectual furniture is moral idealism. This need not be specifically documented because almost every line he wrote bristles with anger against social injustice or carries the force of uncritical belief in truth, justice, and the right of every man to a good life. These values are continually opposed by bad and selfish men, who use their superior power and cunning to impose upon the weak. Beyond this, moreover, we shall see that such qualities as courage and cowardice are used to distinguish a hero from a villain in a London novel, and are further used to make the reader adopt a highly "moral" attitude toward these characters.

This medley of conflicting and contradictory ideas represents an "advanced" mind of about 1900. Being more articulate than the average person, London expressed himself with more energy and more abundance; but the content is representative, and the ideas account for London's tremendous appeal to the reading public. The characters who come most vividly to life do so because of their ideas, and the conflicts are either dramatized in terms of ideas or draw their vitality from the clash of theories in the mind of a leading character.

— —

London's heroes are said to be supermen, and the superman must be cornered and identified before we can understand his place in London's naturalism, for his "naturalism," his determinism, and his use of so-called supermen are all involved with the same complex of ideas.

From the point of view of one critic the brute superman is a product of despair. He is invoked by the writer who abandons ethical control and substitutes impulse for intellection in his portrayal of nature's brutal creed. "The Naturalist," he says, defining the outlook of the writer who is afflicted with this despair,

lets Nature take its course, accepts the universe of science, and cares only for things "as they are," rather than for things "as they have been," or "should be." . . . Nature is a vast contrivance of wheels within wheels; man is a "piece of fate" caught in the machinery of Nature; and love is ultimately a product of the same forces that control gravitation. The world is a jungle, where men grapple with one another for life and its accessories, murder (and are in turn murdered), fly after pleasure, and resign themselves with stoic calm to whatever pain they cannot elude. Man's only duty is to discharge his energies and die, at the same time expressing his individuality as best he can.[10]

The writer burdened with this attitude, says our critic, creates a "superman" and, according to his creed of *laissez faire* (i.e., rampant individualism), allows him to fight out his own brutal destiny. Now this analysis rests upon several different concepts of what a superman is, and we may perhaps arrive most easily at a full understanding of the connotations of the word superman by distinguishing these several concepts of which it is composed.

The Nietzschean superman, to begin at the source, is the apotheosis of individualism. Materialistic monism denies the possibility of absolute values that have been ordained by a higher power. It follows from this that man must rely more upon his instincts than upon revealed doctrine, for the "will to live" — which Nietzsche read of in Schopenhauer's essays and translated into the "will to power" for his own purposes — is the one positive fact that man can recognize and by which he can be guided.[11] The superman is selfish, individual, cunning, amoral, achieving happiness through the fullest indulgence of his will to power.[12] Since pleasure comes from the fullest and most satisfying use of one's faculties, it follows that the main concern of the superman is to perfect his instincts, to develop himself into the highest conceivable type of human kind. Those ethical ideas which teach man to deny himself, to sacrifice himself for the weak, to restrain his impulses as fundamentally evil are the doctrines preached by weaklings in their efforts to protect themselves from the strong. These are the tenets of "slave-morality." Nietzsche exhorted the strong to be guided by "master-morality," for it will effect the elimination of the unfit and the consequent purification of the human race. In this latter notion we see the element in Nietzsche's thought, related to science and Darwinism, which seeks not just anarchical egoism but the constant improvement and progress which would result from evolution if its operation were not impeded by the folly of slave-morality and of preserving the unfit. It is this latter notion, furthermore, which lifts the ideal superman far above a ruthless brute who triumphs over his competitors by sheer force. The highest superman, indeed, was to surpass present man as completely as man surpasses the ape. As Mencken explains,

Nietzsche, it will be observed, was unable to give any very definite picture of this proud, heaven-kissing superman. It is only in Zarathustra's preachments to "the higher man," a sort of bridge between man and superman, that we may discern the philosophy of the latter. On one occasion Nietzsche penned a passage which seemed to compare the superman to "the great blond beasts" which ranged Europe in the days of the mammoth, and from this fact many commentators have drawn the conclusion that he had in mind a mere two-legged brute, with none of the higher traits that we now speak of as distinctly human. But, as a matter of fact, he harbored no such idea. In another place, wherein he speaks of three metamorphoses of the race, under the allegorical names of the camel, the lion, and the child, he makes this plain. The camel, a hopeless beast of burden, is man. But when the camel goes into the solitary desert, it throws off its burden and becomes a lion. That is to say, the heavy and hampering load of artificial dead-weight called morality is cast aside and the instinct to live — or, as Nietzsche insists upon regarding it, the will to power, — is given free rein. The lion is the "higher man" — the intermediate stage between man and superman. The latter appears neither as camel nor lion, but as a little child. He knows a little child's peace. He has a little child's calm. Like a babe *in utero*, he is ideally adapted to his environment.[13]

The efficient operation of the highest intellect would require adequate physique, but physical efficiency is no more than a means to the end of intellectual progress. Although Nietzsche despised Christianity, he was far from approving of degrading indulgence. His superman, acting upon the principle of expediency, would always be able to restrain his brutish impulses in order to attain to some higher goal.

Nietzsche's conception of the superman was not widely familiar in America until after 1905.[14] Until that time there were in our literature a number of manifestations which have mistakenly been called supermen by critics of a later date. There is, first, the "blond beast" or physical giant who emerges when a writer portrays the struggle for existence on the frontier or the sea — under conditions where social restraints are removed and the victory of physical "survival values" may be most effectively displayed. This combination of pseudo-science and the romantic quest for new materials does not produce a Nietzschean superman. But many people thought it did: so late as 1917 the notion prevails in an article on "Jack London as Titan," whose author deplores the Russians' adoration of London, deeming tragic "that strange twist in their 'idealism' which makes them identify life with visible action and outer victory, with the superman, — brief master of all but himself," and concludes that the finest deeds "will need a balance and sanity, an inner health and nobility for which the hurried superman of action has not time to wait." [15] The writer in these last words more or less defines the Nietzschean superman, when apparently he means to describe a higher being than "the hurried superman of action."

Science leads to the creation of supermen in another, quite different way: The naturalist has had new fields opened to him by the right which science assumes to explore all areas of thought and being. These new fields contain many horrible and disgusting subjects which the naturalist can exploit and render doubly affecting by his ostensibly scientific approach to them. Partly through his concern with such striking material, and partly through his desire to employ the deterministic outlook in his work, the naturalist is led to write about sociological extremes, for it is in the sordid side of life that the operation of external force upon man is most satisfactorily displayed. When the higher ethical nature of man is either denied or ignored, the emphasis must perforce be placed upon the physical, racial, instinctive, brutal side. There is no alternative. People who have no spiritual values are moved by physical compulsions. They can of course be purely the objects of force; but if they move themselves their characters must contain strong emotional urges.

The sociological cases of, say, Zola's *L'Assommoir* are represented as mostly animal, in order that Zola may study their reactions to their environment in the simplest terms — unhampered, that is, by any exalted spiritual yearnings in them, which would be most difficult to analyze as products of heredity or milieu. In Zola's novels such creatures are part of a larger whole, they are more or less explained by their environments, and their actions frequently take place within a broad cycle of movement that depends upon the external deterministic forces whose operation Zola attempts to study. Remove the large sociological framework and you have the atavistic, red-blooded brute who makes such wonderful material for stirring romance. To call such a creature a superman is a mistake. Rather he is instinctive, physical man set free to roam at large in wild conflicts on the frontier or the sea. He is ill-fitted to triumph in the struggle for existence of civilized society. He has little in common with the superman described by Nietzsche. But he is physically strong; the naïve transition from a creature who is only physical to one who is strong physically is quite understandable, though not therefore reasonable; and in a world where strength counts he will flourish until cunning or accident destroys him. A version of this super-brute dates back to Norse saga, or indeed to any of the heroic literatures that come from periods when physical prowess was essential to survival.

Still another kind of "superman" arises from a preoccupation with what has been called primordialism. This is the exploitation of the idea that civilization is a thin veneer and that the primitive brute is close to the surface in every human being. Combine this primordialism with the sort of exultation over physical strength that London manifests and there results the "Call-of-the-Wild" school of fiction upon which Frederic Taber Cooper has commented as follows:

There is a vast difference between thinking of man as a healthy human animal and thinking of him as an unhealthy human beast, — and the Call-of-the-Wild school of fiction is tending toward precisely this exaggerated and mistaken point of view. The chief trouble with all the so-called Back-to-Nature books is that they suggest an abnormal self-consciousness, a constant preoccupation regarding the measure of our animalism. Now, it is a sort of axiom that so long as we are healthy and normal, we do not give much thought to our physical machinery. . . . But this, in a certain way, is precisely what the characters in the average Call-of-the-Wild novel seem to be doing, or at least what the authors are constantly doing for them. They seem, so to speak, to keep their fingers insistently upon the pulse of their baser animal emotions, — and this is precisely what the primitive, healthy savage is furthest removed from doing.[16]

In this labyrinth of paths to the rugged brutes developed by Norris and exalted by London, the conception of the superman presented by Nietzsche is lost. That is, Nietzsche's writings cannot be said to account for all such creatures who appear in the American novel around the turn of the century. Yet these brutes spring from a single complex of ideas that formed about materialism, Darwinism, and science; and although many of them, because they are looking at the struggle *from within*, exhibit states of mind which do not illustrate or prove the concept of determinism, their ultimate relation to the materialism which begets that determinism is clear to anyone who has followed the analysis this far. It should also be clear that what prevents the various "brutes" described here from being Nietzschean supermen is, primarily, that they embody no ideal of perfection or progress toward it. What distinguishes London's work from mere violence and adventure is an underlying attitude — the attitude that was concerned not with the brutal details of the conflict so much as with its hoped-for outcome in a higher type of individual and a greatly improved state of society.

Thus the supermen of adventure novels do not necessarily owe much to Nietzsche, but they do have affiliations with the naturalistic philosophy. Our next problem is to see how completely London was able to pattern his novels upon his avowed materialism — to see, in short, whether the ethics of Christianity ever became confused with the survival ethics of an absolute materialist.

It has been said that a writer puts most of himself into his early work, a statement that is strikingly true of London's first novel, *A Daughter of the Snows* (1902). He subsequently lamented that he had squandered in it material for a dozen novels,[17] and he is lav-

97

ishly prodigal of ideas. Beginning, then, with the ideas, we find a wealth of exposition that sets forth most of the beliefs which have been discussed earlier in this chapter.

The operation of determinism is presented in the clearest terms, with rather pompous pedantry:

These be the ways of men, each as the sun shines upon him and the wind blows against him, according to his kind, and the seed of his father, and the milk of his mother. Each is the resultant of many forces which should go to make a pressure mightier than he, and which moulds him in the predestined shape. But, with sound legs under him, he may run away, and meet with a new pressure. He may continue running, each new pressure prodding him as he goes, until he dies, and his final form will be that predestined of the many pressures.[18]

But hard on the heels of this exposition comes a belief in primordialism. "Thus, in the young Northland," he writes, "frosty and grim and menacing, men stripped off the sloth of the south and gave battle greatly. And they stripped likewise much of the veneer of civilization — all of its follies, most of its foibles, and perhaps a few of its virtues. Maybe so; but they reserved the great traditions and at least lived frankly, laughed honestly, and looked one another in the eyes." Elsewhere this creed is expanded in a defense of atavism, of the notion that one's adaptability (and therefore one's likelihood of survival) depends upon one's nearness to a primitive state. The hero's greatest virtue lay in his not having become hardened in the mold formed by his several forbears:

Some atavism had been at work in the making of him, and he had reverted to that ancestor who sturdily uplifted. But so far this portion of his heritage had lain dormant. He had simply remained adjusted to a stable environment. There had been no call upon the adaptability which was his. But whensoever the call came, being so constituted, it was manifest that he should adapt, should adjust himself to the unwonted pressure of new conditions. The maxim of the rolling stone may be all true; but notwithstanding, in the scheme of life, the inability to become fixed is an excellence par excellence.

With such an outlook it is not surprising that London sets forth as "survival values" the cruder kinds of physical might and brute courage; but he presents them with the self-consciousness and muscle-flexing self-idolatry of one who attaches spiritual values to brute force. The emphasis in the following passage upon body, body, body, upon those muscles of which your true primitive man is wholly unconscious, is typical of this attitude toward the struggle for existence and toward the kind of beings he would like to see prevail.

Thus Frona, the heroine and superwoman, liked the man because he was a man. In her wildest flights she could never imagine linking herself with any man, no matter how exalted spiritually, who was not a man physically. It was a delight to her and a joy to look upon the strong males of her kind, with bodies comely in the sight of God and muscles swelling with the promise of deeds and work. Man, to her, was pre-eminently a fighter. She believed in natural selection and in sexual selection, and was certain that if man had thereby become possessed of faculties and functions, they were for him to use and could but tend to his good. And likewise with instincts. If she felt drawn to any person or thing, it was good for her to be so drawn, good for herself. If she felt impelled to joy in a well-built frame and well-shaped muscle, why should she restrain? Why should she not love the body, and without shame? The history of the race, and of all races, sealed her choice with approval. Down all time, the weak and effeminate males had vanished from the world-stage. Only the strong could inherit the earth. She had been born of the strong, and she chose to cast her lot with the strong.

The reader must not think for an instant that this passage authorizes any sort of sexual freedom. The heroine is unwaveringly chaste because, the tone of the book would seem to say, so fine a creature could be nothing else but chaste. A woman of questionable virtue in the story is scarcely allowed to speak to the heroine. In other words, the atavism is safely mixed with the sexual ethics of civilization — a concession partly, perhaps, to be traced to London's concern for the prejudices of his readers.

This affection for atavism merges, elsewhere, into a definition of "the will to power" that is strikingly close to the Nietzschean conception. Frona's love of bodily strength — a strength which is accompanied by a higher moral nature that shines through its splendid physical container — is presented as an ethical choice, a choice involving distinction between good and evil, rather than a choice which represents only the force of animal impulse. Her father, mighty trader of the North, expresses a higher, Nietzschean concept of will in describing the code of the strong:

Conventions are worthless for such as we. They are for the swine who without them would wallow deeper. The weak must obey or be crushed; not so with the strong. The mass is nothing; the individual everything; and it is the individual, always, that rules the mass and gives the law. A fig for what the world says! If the Welse should procreate a bastard line this day, it would be the way of the Welse, and you would be a daughter of the Welse, and in the face of hell and heaven, of God himself, we would stand together, we of the one blood, Frona, you and I.

These lines almost define the master-morality of self-assertion that Nietzsche opposed to the miserable slave-morality by which the weak sought to protect themselves from the strong. Frona Welse, likewise, combines beautiful physique and hardihood with intellectual subtlety. Bred in the North, educated in the United States, she is an ideal example, London seems to say, of the higher woman, with perfect body and piercing intellect. In the treatment of the hero the notion of the superman draws markedly away from the Nietzschean concept, the difference being measured by the hero's atavism: as he works into the spirit of the Northland his manhood waxes. "Gambling without stakes is an insipid amusement, and Corliss discovered, likewise, that the warm blood which rises from hygienic gymnasium work is something quite different from that which pounds hotly along when thew matches thew and flesh impacts on flesh and the stake is life and limb." And in a later conflict, "The din of twenty centuries of battle was roaring in his ear, and the clamor for return to type strong upon him." [19]

It would be impossible to show a logical connection between these ideas which are brought forth throughout *A Daughter of the Snows*. A satisfactory classification of them is to consider the determinism to be the conclusion of the calm philosopher who contemplates the flow of life from without; whereas the atavism, the "will to power" creed, and the glorying in physical prowess and valiant struggle represent the attitude toward the same set of facts that the intelligent and unscrupulous strong man would take when he found himself embroiled in the conflict. Caught up in the struggle for existence and hence unable to view it philosophically, he devises a plan of action that will enable him to thrive and to develop those instincts by which he is guided. It is the philosophy of a fighter, celebrating will (as vital force, which is thus subjectively identified with ethical rightness) diametrically opposed to the "experimental" calm of a Zola, and yet depending upon the same basic assumptions.

Mixed with this glowing individualism is a good deal of conventional and high-flown moral idealism; this latter element is woven into the structural pattern of the novel even more closely than the idea of ruthless self-assertion. The central complication of the story consists of a triangle: Frona Welse, superwoman, is strongly attracted to Vance Corliss, the newcomer to the North who is responding so atavistically to its challenge; but Frona's heart is ensnared by Gregory St. Vincent. Since Corliss is the hero, St. Vincent must be the villain. His villainy consists primarily in cowardice and secondarily in his lying to conceal it. The main action of the story is a series of events in which St. Vincent's cowardice is exposed to Frona while Corliss's rugged virtues are given ideal opportunities to display themselves.

The reader will doubtless recognize the fictional device by which a fine woman's heart is won by an oily-tongued rascal, while the hero, suffering but inarticulate, is recognized only after he has helped expose the baseness of his rival. In so important a situation, odd though it may seem to the realistic reader, this convention permits the superwoman to err in judgment without any shadow being cast upon her perfection. This convention, it would seem, rests upon the assumption that wrong will be punished and that a just Providence will always reward patient virtue, the assumption of a moral order, a universe properly controlled by justice and right. It is diametrically opposed to the materialism which admits no possibility of moral control of the universe. Now, although atavism and self-assertion are constantly invoked in *A Daughter of the Snows*, the reader knows that he is reading steadily toward the final triumph of the moral order through the exposure of St. Vincent and the rewarding of Corliss's love, and he is not disappointed. Thus we see that the structural pattern of the novel is woven upon a framework of ethical thought, the Moral Principle displayed in operation. Frona's purity is providentially saved from too intimate contact with the baseness of St. Vincent; and just as her goodness is manifested in a truly heroic devotion — in the face of terrible doubts — to the man to whom she has pledged her heart, so Providence rises to the occasion with a magnificent exposure that resolves all her doubts.

Even though the belief in this moral order may have come to London as a bit of story-writing technique, as a pattern, that is, which had been employed in countless earlier novels, it is used in a way that makes the writer's acceptance of it unquestionable. It is the mainspring of the action; its presence indicates London's inability to make his determinism carry the burden of his plot.

Further evidence of the idealism which is mixed with London's materialism lies in the fact that Frona and Corliss are sexually chaste, whereas St. Vincent is not. The thoroughgoing materialist would not blame a man for acting upon his natural impulses; rather he would applaud him. London was writing books to sell, and he always worked to please his readers; but it is nevertheless significant that he should slide so easily into conventional thinking. The story makes the most of the moral ardor which is kindled by its situations; the final scene is devoted to the heroine's icy denunciation of the coward:

"Shall I tell you why, Gregory St. Vincent?" she said again. "Tell you why your kisses have cheapened me? Because you broke the faith of food and blanket. Because you broke salt with a man, and then watched that man fight unequally for life without lifting your hand. Why, I had rather you had died in defending him; the memory of you would have been good. Yes, I had rather you had killed him yourself. At least it would have shown there was blood in your body."

The novel is built around acts of free will and based upon an implicit faith in a moral order. In these respects London's determinism has not penetrated to its structure. In two other respects, however, it has done so. In the first place, the action as described above takes up only a small part of the novel. In the rest of it, accompanying the digressive exposition of philosophical material- ism, is scene after scene in which the conditions of Alaskan life are depicted. Gold-hunting, starvation, the rigors of the trail, the spectacle of an ice-pack breaking up — these are some of the many sequences which make up the background of the story. In this picturesque presentation of the frozen North one sees the conditions under which the struggle for existence, as naïvely con- ceived by London, is carried on, conditions which challenge man's strength and courage. Although they are not part of the plot proper of *A Daughter of the Snows*, they nevertheless account for a large part of its content.

The other point at which London's "naturalism" enters is in his choice of cowardice as the hallmark of villainy. Cowardice argues unfitness in the struggle for existence more directly than dishonesty, deceit, or any of the "moral" failings which would impair a man's status in a more civilized community. But London brings what can only be called "moral" ardor to his championship of the clean, rugged, he-man virtues he prizes so highly. Cowardice in this story is regarded as the most loathsome of sins, so loathsome that the reader is indignant at the thought of a coward's marrying Frona Welse. In this way the moral and the amoral are inter- twined.

The materialism which went into the making of *A Daughter of the Snows* was seen through the eyes of struggling men and hence was employed as the rationale for a program of conduct which, selfish and amoral, was calculated to ensure the maximum efficiency in the fight for survival. The same general point of view dominates *The Call of the Wild* (1903), but in dealing with the adventures of an animal London is able more quickly to slough off such moral considerations as appeared in *A Daughter of the Snows* and to devote his attention to the exposition and development of that primordialism which produced, as he thought, the highest animal development and hence best fitted its possessor to succeed under savage conditions.

Like *A Daughter of the Snows, The Call of the Wild* is episodic. Buck, a splendid California ranch dog, is stolen and sold into Alaska, to become a sled-dog in the gold rush. Going thus "into the primitive" he quickly learns "the law of club and fang." "Jerked from the heart of civilization and flung into the heart of things primordial," [20] his first experience on the Alaskan coast brings home the nature of the eternal struggle. A friendly dog is knocked down in a fight, and instantly "she was buried screaming with agony beneath the bristling mass" of huskies who had been watching the unequal fight. "So that was the way," Buck learned. "No fairplay. Once down, that was the end of you."

Buck's fitness is measured by his primordialism, by the way "he was harking back through his own life to the lives of his forbears." He learns fast and is soon clever enough to steal some bacon to supplement his meager rations of dried fish. The author's comment upon this action is illuminating:

This first theft marked Buck as fit to survive in the hostile Northland environment. It marked his adaptability, his capacity to adjust himself to changing conditions, the lack of which would have meant swift and terrible death. It marked, further, the decay or going to pieces of his moral nature, a vain thing and a handicap in the ruthless struggle for existence. It was all well enough in the Southland, under the law of love and fellowship, to respect private property and personal feelings; but in the Northland, under the law of club and fang, whoso took such things into account was a fool, and in so far as he observed them he would fail to prosper.

The reader will recall that this exposition is nearly identical to one quoted from *A Daughter of the Snows*.[21] But here the "moral nature" can be thrust aside without the reader's losing respect for Buck, because Buck is a dog. Corliss in the earlier novel, for example, was a hero, regardless of his primordialism, by virtue of his higher moral nature, his honor, loyalty, chastity, and generous patience. Buck's forgotten ancestors "quickened the old life within him, and the old tricks which they had stamped into the heredity of the breed were his tricks. They came to him without effort or discovery, as though they had been his always"; and the reader seeks no higher ethical virtues in Buck.

By Chapter III, Buck is "The Dominant Primordial Beast"; and the story proceeds as the conflict for mastery between Buck and Spitz, the treacherous and hated lead-dog of the team. "It was inevitable that the clash for leadership should come. Buck wanted it. He wanted it because it was his nature, because he had been gripped tight by that nameless, incomprehensible pride of the trail and trace — that pride which holds dogs in the toil to the last gasp, which lures them to die joyfully in the harness, and breaks their hearts if they are cut out of the harness." Spitz is experienced. Buck is intelligent and big; he has imagination, and his prowess increases. Always it is the life-impulse in him expressing itself. London pauses in a muscle-flexing digression to explain the nature of this impulse:

There is an ecstasy that marks the summit of life, and beyond which life cannot rise. And such is the paradox of living, this ecstasy comes when one is most alive, and it comes as a complete forgetfulness that one is alive. This ecstasy, this forgetfulness of living, comes to the artist, caught up and out of himself in a sheet of flame; it comes to the soldier, war-mad on a stricken field and refusing quarter; and it came to Buck, leading the pack, sounding the old wolf-cry, straining after the food that was alive and that fled swiftly before him through the moonlight. He was sounding the deeps of his nature, and of the parts of his nature that were deeper than he, going back to the womb of Time. He was mastered by the sheer surging joy of life, the tidal wave of being, the perfect joy of each separate muscle, joint, and sinew in that it was everything that was not death, that it was aglow and rampant, expressing itself in movement, flying exultantly under the stars and over the face of dead matter that did not move.

This is the materialistic philosophy transformed by the celebration of the single vital and inescapable fact which even materialism recognizes as valuable — life. Seen from within, the struggle represents the surge of life, and the struggle is dominated by will. It is will in the sense of impulse, life-urge, ecstasy of power, rather than ethical choice. It is presented as an animal trait, inherited and consequently not really "free." If Buck were a man there would have to be some kind of ethical responsibility. With Buck there need be only this animal expression of the life-instinct that is derived from his "racial memory" of his ancestors.

Although the story is seen substantially from Buck's point of view, there is always inevitably present (and carefully controlled by London) the reader's moral judgment of men and their actions. Thus one admires the dogs' noble courage, hates the tenderfeet, and loves the kind John Thornton who saves Buck. Much of the aesthetic effect of the novel attaches to these feelings. Chapter VI is devoted to the love of dog and man, and here the reader's feelings are entirely human and civilized as he responds to the presentation of Buck's devotion to Thornton while in all other respects he is becoming increasingly wild. He twice saves Thornton's life and wins a $1600 wager for him by pulling a tremendous load.

Finally, on a trip into the wilderness, Buck's atavism surges up within him. He has racial dreams of remote times, when fear dominated his primitive master:

When he watched the hairy man sleeping by the fire, head between his knees and hands clasped above, Buck saw that he slept restlessly, with many starts and awakenings, at which times he would peer fearfully into the darkness and fling more wood upon the fire. . . . Through the forest they crept noiselessly, Buck at the hairy man's heels; and they were alert and vigilant, the pair of them, ears twitching and moving nostrils quivering, for the man heard and smelled as keenly as Buck . . . and Buck had memories of nights of vigil spent beneath trees wherein the hairy man roosted, holding on tightly as he slept.[22]

The same primordialism that makes him "remember" the hairy man draws him toward the wolves whom he hears howling at night. He makes friends with the pack and, when John Thornton is killed, he joins the pack and lives thereafter as a magnificent wolf — more cunning and fierce than all the others and the relentless foe of the Indians who had killed his master. In this story the conflict of animal impulse and ethical nature is successfully evaded because the hero is a dog of whom ethical action is not expected — though the most moving passages in the book are those that deal with

Buck's love for Thornton and which, consequently, appeal strongly to the reader's sense of moral rightness and goodness.

The Call of the Wild is a masterpiece of thrilling and colorful narrative, but it does not — indeed it cannot — tell anything about the nature of "atavism" or the operation of determinism.

The discrepancy between London's philosophical ideas and the "naturalistic" use he is able to make of them in his novels appears in his explanation of *White Fang,* companion volume to *The Call of the Wild.* Published in 1906, *White Fang* deals with a wolf who is domesticated through circumstances and, particularly, the love of a man. London wrote of it:

Life is full of disgusting realism. I know men and women as they are — millions of them yet in the slime state. But I am an evolutionist, therefore a broad optimist, hence my love for the human (in the slime though he be) comes from my knowing him as he is and seeing the divine possibilities ahead of him. That's the whole motive of my "White Fang." Every atom of organic life is plastic. The finest specimens now in existence were once all pulpy infants capable of being molded this way or that. Let the pressure be one way and we have atavism — the reversion to the wild; the other the domestication, civilization.[23]

As a theory this is all very well, but in the novels there is no explanation of the atavism and the domestication; their only justification is that they *happen.* No "pressures" are depicted which tell why Buck goes wild and White Fang becomes tame. The facts speak for themselves; as facts they are convincing; but the science or philosophy behind them receives no serious attention. It is less real even than Zola's famous "experimental" program.

～ ～

The Sea-Wolf (1904) contains an intensification of the divergent tendencies toward moral idealism and egotistical self-assertion which we have seen in *A Daughter of the Snows.* In the latter novel these contradictory impulses were drawing gently apart; in *The Sea-Wolf* they have rushed to opposite poles, and it is matter for astonishment that they have remained within the bounds of a single novel.

The story opens with Humphrey Van Weyden, the narrator, crossing San Francisco Bay in a fog. Humphrey is thirty-five, independent, gentlemanly, something of a literary critic and lover of poetry; and he has never confronted the harsh realities of life. When the ferry on which he is traveling is rammed, Humphrey is swept out to sea on an ebb tide; he is rescued by Wolf Larsen, captain of the sealing schooner *Ghost*, who forces him to become cabin boy.

The first third of the book is expository, presenting the slowly growing manliness of the narrator, but most of all it is devoted to the personality of Wolf Larsen. Wolf is London's idea of a superman, although he is never described by that word. He is a man of tremendous physical strength — "a strength savage, ferocious, alive in itself, the essence of life in that it is the potency of motion, the elemental stuff itself out of which the many forms of life have been moulded. . . . In fact, though this strength pervaded every action of his, it seemed but the advertisement of a greater strength that lurked within." [24] The inner strength of Wolf consists of a ruthless and powerful mind. He has educated himself, read Spencer and Darwin, and become a complete materialist. Life, to him, "is like yeast, a ferment, a thing that moves and may move for a minute, an hour, a year, or a hundred years, but that in the end will cease to move. The big eat the little that they may continue to move, the strong eat the weak that they may retain their strength." [25] Life is cheap; nature spills it out lavishly — "of course life is valueless, except to itself. And I can tell you that my life is pretty valuable just now — to myself. It is beyond price, which you will acknowledge is a terrific overrating, but which I cannot help, for it is the life that is in me that makes the rating." As a true materialist he says that the joy of living, the exultation in his powers, "is what comes when there is nothing wrong with one's digestion, when his stomach is in trim and his appetite has an edge, and all goes well. It is the bribe for living, the champagne of the blood, the effervescence of the ferment — that makes some men think holy thoughts, and other men to see God or to create him when they cannot see him."

With his piercing and cold-blooded analysis and his tigerish strength, Wolf is a brutal master whom his men fear and hate. The reason for his cruelty is not made perfectly clear. At one time he is described as an atavism. Van Weyden thinks "he is the perfect type of the primitive man, born a thousand years or generations too late and an anachronism in this culminating century of civilization. He is certainly an individualist of the most pronounced type. . . . His tremendous virility and mental strength wall him apart" from the simple sailors. In this light it is the primitive in him that is cruel. Elsewhere London lays his cruelty to a sense of frustration: having no good use for his great powers has made him bitter. Later we are told that Wolf represents the high point of self-assertion untrammeled by moral restraints:

I remarked the total lack of viciousness, or wickedness or sinfulness, in his face. It was the face, I am convinced, of a man who did no wrong. And by this I do not wish to be misunderstood. What I mean is that it was the face of a man who either did nothing contrary to the dictates of his conscience, or who had no conscience. I am inclined to the latter way of accounting for it. He was a magnificent atavism, a man so purely primitive that he was of the type that came into the world before the development of the moral nature. He was not immoral, but merely unmoral.

The product of all this exposition is an absorbing character. Reciting a bit of poetry one moment, kicking a sailor in the stomach the next — exulting in the struggle of life yet condemning ideals as trash and religion as folly, Wolf holds the reader's attention during the long opening section in which there is no particular action except passages of brutality that cause the entire crew to hate him and plot his destruction. Wolf captures the reader's interest and sympathy, even though one is not led either to understand or to condone his brutality.[26] As a superman he has all the necessary qualifications except the ability to make others serve him without endangering himself. Of course, he does not embody the Nietzschean ideal of human perfection. For this failure of personality there is no explanation except the demands of plot — where it does create an effective tension of expectancy.

The real plot complication begins when the *Ghost* rescues a handful of survivors from a wreck. Among them is a beautiful poetess, the ideal of culture and refinement. Humphrey falls in love with her; but Wolf too is attracted by her, and her danger resolves the story into a conflict between heartless egotism and ethical idealism. Humphrey can no longer be a spectator to Wolf's callousness. He must act, for, as he tells Miss Brewster, "moral courage is a worthless asset on this little floating world." And act he does. With Miss Brewster he escapes in a small boat through a stormy sea. Landing on a seal rookery they prepare in true Robinson Crusoe fashion to build and hunt against the winter. Then one night the *Ghost,* dismantled and weather-beaten, floats into their cove. Upon it is Wolf, abandoned by his crew, alone, and helpless. Humphrey could kill him, but the force of convention and the power of Wolf's personality prevent him. Throughout the story Wolf has been subject to terrible headaches that render him helpless for days at a time. Such an attack comes upon him soon, leaving him blind. Yet when Humphrey tries to restore the *Ghost* to sailing trim, Wolf, still indomitable, destroys his work in the night. The strength of Wolf's resolution and the uncertainty of living under the danger of his unpredictable action, combined with Humphrey's inability to kill him, make a situation that is rich in suspense. The knot is untied, however, not by action but by the rapid physical disintegration of Wolf. Following his blindness comes paralysis, and as the unknown ailment "destroys his nerve centers" the former superman is reduced to absolute helplessness.[27] When he dies, Humphrey and Miss Brewster sail off with their love to civilization. Thus the closing incidents of the novel do not consist of a struggle so much as a *spectacle,* with Wolf Larsen the center of interest. The force of his personality prevails even when he is unable to move, and in his living death "There was the awfulness of retribution."

The Sea-Wolf divides into two more or less independent parts. First there is the outward trip to the sealing grounds, during which Humphrey grows in stature and Larsen's character is portrayed. After Miss Brewster is added to the ship's company there are a number of acts of sheer cruelty by Larsen that emphasize her danger and urge the need of immediate action if she and Humphrey are to escape. This section of the story contains no crisis or climax, for Wolf is always in command of the situation. There are fights and deaths, but they are always incidental to the main point. Wolf is, perhaps, foiled by the escape of the two, but that escape is not something in which he can play a part. The point is that moral idealism and ruthless individualism do not *conflict* — rather the former flees from the latter. Furthermore, nothing happens to the individualism: it merely expresses itself through the destruction of several men; its *status quo* has not changed appreciably except possibly in Wolf's having cast lustful eyes upon Miss Brewster — and he does not appear to have been changed by his interest in her. No natural forces have been shown in action. No struggle for existence has gone on, because there has been no change of state in the principal character. Thus the first half of the novel sets the stage for a conflict which is suddenly avoided by the escape of the lovers.

The story of Wolf Larsen might, if carried to a natural and consistent end, take him through a number of fierce encounters into a climax in which he could be killed, could find a satisfactory outlet for his superior powers, or could triumph over, say, the rival sealers and become a Titan of the seas. Certainly the story of a hard-fisted superman should be told from a consistent point of view. This is especially true since Wolf is the unquestioned hero of the first third of the book. It is worse than inept to direct the reader's sympathies toward a particular character and then abandon him in favor of another character, with another story, seen from another point of view. Both Wolf and Humphrey cannot be the heroes of a single novel. In trying to develop them both into heroes London has been forced to abandon one story just when the scene was set for action and turn to another.[28]

The second part of the story, or rather the second story, takes place upon the seal island. Again there is no conflict between the representatives of ethical control and of "primitive" ruthlessness. Humphrey does not meet and destroy Larsen; he barely evades him until he is stricken by his mysterious ailment. Most of our attention is devoted to Humphrey's Robinson Crusoe activity in building the hut, killing seals, and, later, refitting the *Ghost,* and there is always of course his growing love for Maud Brewster. Wolf Larsen is an ominous shadow that hangs over them, spectacular rather than structural. He is the center of attention rather than of action. His being destroyed by some secret malady necessarily prevents his destruction by the working out of a plot complication. Seen in this light *The Sea-Wolf* tells the love story of Humphrey and Maud; and in that story Wolf Larsen in an elaborate *decoration.* He is the volcano in the shadow of which the lovers meet, struggle, and finally achieve happiness as the volcano gradually becomes extinct. Like the volcano's, Wolf's failure is inward and — to outward seeming — uncaused. The only overt act against him is the desertion of his ship by his crew; and no better proof of the essentially decorative function of Wolf could be adduced than the fact that this desertion is not directly represented in the novel: only the result of it is shown, the result in the form of a stranded Wolf who enters the story of the two lovers.

In the face of this evidence we come upon the statement made by London in 1905 of the meaning of *The Sea-Wolf*:

I want to make a tale so plain that he who runs may read, and then there is the underlying psychological motif. In "The Sea Wolf" there was, of course, the superficial descriptive story, while the underlying tendency was to prove that the superman cannot be successful in modern life. The superman is anti-social in his tendencies, and in these days of our complex society and sociology he cannot be successful in his hostile aloofness. Hence the unpopularity of the financial superman like Rockefeller; he acts like an irritant in the social body.[29]

In the novel itself there is no use of the word superman and, although there is reference to Darwin, Spencer, Huxley, Tyndall, and others, there is no mention of Nietzsche. It would appear that London was expatiating *ex post facto* in the statement of intention quoted above.[30] Our preliminary discussion of the superman, real and fancied, shows that London's Wolf Larsen, a mixture of egotism, cruelty, "atavism," and disillusionment, is not a genuine Nietzschean superman. Furthermore, the contention that "the superman cannot be successful in modern life" — assuming for the moment that Wolf is a true superman — cannot be said to have been demonstrated through the movement of the novel, for instead of being destroyed by social forces shown at work in the plot, he is destroyed by an unknown and adventitious something within him that could hardly be shown to represent society's hostility to his kind. It was equally inept to imply that Rockefeller could not be successful in modern life, and a novel in which Rockefeller died from a tumor of the brain after accumulating his billions would hardly demonstrate how he was unfitted to survive in society.

The structure of *The Sea-Wolf* is conventional, though its content and setting are unusual. The movement of its plot depends upon acts of will and in no sense embodies the operation of external determining forces. Wolf Larsen utters, and in his actions stands for, the point of view of the person who sees nature's determinism as acting upon himself, and hence, recognizing no values or laws but those of his own life-impulse or "will," acts upon a program of complete selfishness. If this be naturalism, it is an entirely different sort from that which Zola attempted to bring into his novels. It is a kind that celebrates rather than denies will; it has no particular effect upon the structural pattern of the novel; it does not bring the operation of determinism into the novel's movement; in short, it brings decoration in the shape of a curious philosophy, and a striking character in the person of Wolf, into a novel whose spokesman and hero stands for the conservative ethical point of view.

If we can rely upon London's reiterated statements, we must conclude that the figure of Humphrey represents his concession to popular tastes. Humphrey is too "ethical" to represent London. Wolf Larsen's position, on the other hand, is too cruel and unsocial to stand for the author (though he undoubtedly stands for London's ideal of his own physical self). London's position must be thought of as midway between the two. His beliefs drew him toward Wolf; his sociability toward Humphrey. The novel breaks apart upon the rock of this inconsistency.

VI

Frank Norris and the Search for Form

FRANK NORRIS is generally spoken of as America's out-standing naturalistic novelist. His debt to Zola is mentioned in virtually every consideration of his work, and the comparison be-tween Zola's command of mass and movement, and the epic sweep and conception of Norris's *Octopus* is inevitable. But the exact nature of Norris's naturalism has not been studied, its influence upon the structure and technique of his novels has not been ex-pounded, and the nature and importance of its influence at various times during his short literary career have not been traced. Least attention of all, perhaps, has been devoted to the exact nature of the ideology which finds expression in his work.[1]

～ ～

Frank Norris (1870–1902) was born in Chicago of wealthy parents. The family moved to San Francisco when Frank was fifteen years old. In 1888, at the age of eighteen, he went to Paris for two years. He went to study painting, and his father called him home when he found that Frank was writing romances instead of making pictures. He entered the University of California in 1890. It was at this time that he became acquainted with the works of Zola and was frequently seen carrying a yellow paper-covered edition under his arm.[2] His personality and intellectual interests at this time have been described by his biographer, Franklin Walker:

"The natural bent of his genius is observation, imagination, in-tensity, not thought, not intellect." . . . If Norris had been primarily of the intellectual type, he would have become a rebel; he would have left the university, or, realizing the puerility of his attitude (passionate protest against the sterility of university life and thought), would have sought out from books and sympathetic companions speculative bones to gnaw upon. Instead of looking for bones, he satisfied himself with cakes and ale; he joined a fraternity and supported student activities.[3]

It is not known when he first read Zola. Walker, however, says that his influence was not noticeable until Norris was in his senior year. But he reveled in Anglo-Saxon strength and fierceness and brutality from at least as early as his freshman year. "His admiration for the 'red-blooded he-man' became a form of hero worship." [4] "Likewise he saw that the 'primordial instincts' held sway in the warfare between freshmen and sophomores." [5] His thirst for blood-chilling incidents may be traced back at least as early as his twenty-first year. "The Jongleur of Taillebois," one of his earliest tales, begins with the death agony of a man struck down in medieval combat — which the victor watches curiously, reserving the final poniard thrust until the man has ceased to move.[6] This blood-thirsty turn of mind may be traced in part to Norris's admiration for Kipling, who preceded Zola as his literary ideal. "Lauth," written in his junior year and possibly suggested by Kipling's "The Mark of the Beast," reeks with blood and bestiality. It is an exercise, with special emphasis upon horror, in the degeneration theme to be carried out more fully in *Vandover and the Brute*.[7] These facts prove nothing, but they urge the conclusion that Norris did not arrive at naturalistic fiction through a rigorous intellectual discipline in the philosophy of materialism. His main concern was not with ideas.

In 1894–1895 he attended Harvard University and devoted himself to writing under the inspiring teaching of Professor Lewis E. Gates. There he wrote all of *Vandover and the Brute* and a large part of *McTeague*. The spectacle of a well-to-do young man writing naturalistic novels in the genteel atmosphere of Harvard University is an interesting one. It emphasizes the literary quality of his inspiration, and it should prepare the reader of his novels not to expect them to rest upon too substantial a philosophical foundation, for we shall see how easily the superficial, stylistic elements of naturalism may exist apart from the philosophical basis. Further proof that his aesthetic was not deeply rooted in abstract thought is not far to seek. In *Blix,* for example, we learn that Condy Rivers, the author-hero who represents Norris himself,[8] " 'went in' for accuracy of detail" no matter how trivial his story. Two or three years later, writing to a friend for technical information to be used in *The Octopus,* he concludes, "I am going back *definitely* now to the style of *McTeague* and stay with it right along. I've been sort of feeling my way ever since the *Moran* days and getting a twist of myself. Now I think I know where I am and what game I play the best. The Wheat series will be straight naturalism with all the guts I can get into it." [9] This is not the language of a man primarily — or even very largely — concerned with ideas, but a man who is first of all an author, who is more interested in people than forces, who feels within himself a creative exuberance that must find expression through the most attractive literary form he can find.

Thus although he defended "The Novel with a Purpose," [10] he did not mean it to be primarily polemic. The novelist, he thought, should above all else avoid propaganda; he should rather present the evidence from which the reader might draw conclusions. The underlying idea should be like the key of a sonata. The novelist should present life realistically, but his concern must be with people rather than theories. Norris despised the spineless productions of his contemporaries, "the amusing novels, the novels that entertain . . . a flippant paper-covered thing of swords and cloaks, to be carried on a railway journey and to be thrown out of the window when read, together with the sucked oranges and peanut shells." [11] True stories, derived from the real issues of life, he insists, would be fuller, richer, more compelling, more gripping than this trash. But always it is the literary man who speaks. Norris would no more have written novels even ostensibly to advance the cause of science, or to perfect man's control of his environment, than he would have gone over to the budding school of muckrakers. As his biographer writes,

He was interested in stories, not reforms. He was comparatively untouched by suffering and misery, and his sense of the dramatic outweighed his sympathies whether he was concerned with a murder, a fight between farmers and railroad employees, or the torturing of a cat. By nature he was almost as detached from his subjects as was Flaubert. He was much more a storyteller than a social philosopher, and there is every reason to believe that he would have remained so.[12]

By examining his novels we may determine the exact nature of his naturalism, the changes in method which mark the various stages of his short career, and possibly something about the relation between the quality of his writing and the amount of intellectual discipline that he received through his association with the naturalistic philosophy and its literary techniques.

~ ~

Vandover and the Brute was Norris's first long work and an attempt to imitate the method of the French naturalists with a particularly naturalistic subject — the destruction of an individual by a degenerative disease. *Vandover* has not the scope of *The Octopus* or the primordial violence of *McTeague*, but it contains some of Norris's most effective writing; it has, indeed, been considered his most memorable work. It stands at the opposite end of the scale of naturalistic motifs from novels dealing with the broad external workings of social and economic forces. Here the forces are internal and physiological; the book purports to be a "clinical" study of a disease.

The novelist's reason for dealing with a mental disease would seem to be his enthusiasm for science. He would, perhaps, be inspired by the experimental zeal which Zola described, the desire to show in detail how certain psychoneurotic manifestations could be clinically diagnosed and systematically presented — subjected to the clear light of knowledge so that man would know for at least one malady whether he had germs or "lesions" to cope with. This would, then, be a factual scientific report, rich with information vital to human welfare. Its interest would depend upon the new subject matter and the reader's aroused zeal for human betterment.

This hypothetical description, with its implication that the facts of the case will be scientifically related and established, leaves no place for an unpredictable element like the free human will. A disease is strictly physical; it is a problem in material cause and effect. Spiritual values, morality, or personal struggle would not seem to be relevant to an understanding of it.

Vandover is the son of a prosperous San Francisco businessman. He is a painter, but he neglects his art. "Vandover was self-indulgent — he loved these sensuous pleasures, he loved to eat good things, he loved to be warm, he loved to sleep. He hated to be bored and worried — he liked to have a good time." His disintegration begins when a girl he has seduced commits suicide in terror at the prospect of having an illegitimate child. Next his father, weakened by the shock of Vandover's deed, dies. When the reason for the girl's suicide becomes known, Vandover is socially ostracized and loses the love of Turner Mavis, a fine girl who had been a powerful influence for good in his life. After his father's death, his income is greatly curtailed. At this point Vandover resolves to reform and throws himself into his painting with furious energy. But too late. The disease, lycanthropy, first appears in a terrifying scene when he finds that he can no longer paint, that his hand will not reproduce the image in his mind; and thereafter his descent is rapid and inexorable. The dead girl's father sues him for a large sum. One of his friends, on the pretext of "handling" the case out of court, cheats him of money and property. What is left from the sale of his father's house Vandover squanders in reckless gambling and debauchery, his unnatural life punctuated by attacks of lycanthropy, during which he creeps about naked on all fours, snarling and yapping like a wolf. Finally he is living from hand to mouth, dirty, unkempt, estranged from friends, sometimes near starvation — a hopeless wreck. The story ends with a pitiful scene in which Vandover is cleaning a filthy kitchen for the friend who had defrauded him.

An appearance of factual reality is created by the method Norris employs. The style and tone of *Vandover* suit the commonplace unromantic people and setting of the story admirably. Details of

Vandover's life and activity are accumulated with meticulous and dispassionate thoroughness. This was a new note in American letters. The quantity and "meanness" of the detail, with the objective tone, give the effect of authentic "documentation" in the best naturalistic tradition. We are shown, step by step, how "In his idleness he grew to have small petty ways. . . . It became a fad with him to do without matches, using as a substitute 'lights,' tapers of twisted paper to be ignited at the famous stove. He found amusement for two days in twisting and rolling these 'lights,' cutting frills in the larger ends with a pair of scissors, and stacking them afterward in a Chinese flower jar he had bought for the purpose and stood on top of the bookcases. The lights were admirably made and looked very pretty. When he had done he counted them. He had made two hundred exactly. What a coincidence!"

Structurally, the novel is not "well made" or dramatic, in the sense of being organized around a conflict between free moral agents. Instead Norris has conformed his structure to the steady and "inevitable" disintegration of Vandover under a succession of blows from forces over which he has no control. In one passage Norris announces a deterministic philosophy very explicitly. It is when Vandover, after his first attack of the disease, prays for help:

There was no answer, nothing but the deaf silence, the blind darkness . . . there was nothing for him. Even that vast mysterious power to which he had cried *could* not help him now, could not help him, could not stay the inexorable law of nature, could not reverse that terrible engine with its myriad spinning wheels that was riding him down relentless, grinding him into the dust.[18]

There is no climactic choice in the story; it moves evenly on a chain of circumstances.

These elements of style, tone, documentation, structure, and explicit determinism constitute the naturalism of *Vandover and the Brute*. But they do not really account for the novel. In spite of its explicit determinism, the conflict in this novel is a thoroughly moral one. It is a conflict between Vandover's free and responsible spirit and a series of circumstantial influences (the disease is merely one of several) which win out over him largely because of his culpable moral weakness. Examination reveals that Vandover is morally responsible for his downfall, that the forces which thrust him down are circumstantial rather than inevitable, and that the novel has the form and effect of a tragedy. It appears, also, that the tragic effect would have been stronger if Norris had not allowed so much moral condemnation to intrude; if, that is, he had held to a more rigorous determinism!

The tone of moral judgment appears in passages like the following, where Vandover broods on his decline:

And with the eyes of this better self he saw again . . . the eternal struggle between good and evil that had been going on within him since his very earliest years. He was sure that at the first the good had been the strongest. Little by little the brute had grown, and he . . . luxurious, self-indulgent . . . had shut his ears to the voices that shouted warnings of the danger, and had allowed the brute to thrive and to grow, its abominable famine gorged from the store of that in him which he felt to be the purest, the cleanest . . .

Again:

It was gone — his art was gone, the one thing that could save him. That, too, like all the other good things of life, he had destroyed.

And:

It was the punishment that he had brought upon himself, some fearful nervous disease, the result of his long indulgence in vice, his vile submission to the brute that was to destroy his reason . . . till he should have reached the last stages of idiocy.

Although these passages are presented as Vandover's thought, they come as auctorial comment also, for it is clear that Norris's attitude is represented in these and many other passages like them. One is reminded of Milton's

> But, when lust
> By unchaste looks, loose gestures, and foul talk,
> But most by lewd and lavish act of sin,
> Lets in defilement to the inward parts,
> The soul grows clotted by contagion,
> Imbodies, and imbrutes, till she quite lose
> The divine property of her first being.

Far from illustrating the operation of determinism, Vandover's degradation is presented as the result of some internal failure which allows the brutish side to grow and thrust out the good. Vandover's moral responsibility depends on his being a person of intelligence and social position; regardless of the author's intention, the naturalistic approach is disrupted because the human being is more important, more intimately known, and therefore more credible than the forces which supposedly dominate him.

There is no established set of forces, either hereditary or environmental, which can bring about his degeneration in such a way that it appears to be inevitable. Vandover is not shown to inherit qualities from his parents that would make him subject to lycanthropy. He does not move in a society that is notable for the pressure it exerts upon its members. He is free from the sort of influences that obtain in industrial areas, or among the poorer classes anywhere. In all these respects he is free from the forces which can be shown, even in the contrived simplicity of the novel, to have shaped a character or bent it toward an unalterable end. Thus the bars which prevent the invasion of his beast must be withdrawn by chance, that is, by pressures which are not presented as an inescapable part of the milieu; and half of the book is devoted to the impact of various kinds of chance upon him. There is nothing typical, nothing that might contribute to the science of sociology in the events by which he is destroyed. At any time Vandover might take a turn for the better. The events which thrust him down are more coincidental than the acts of fate that destroy some of Hardy's characters. But nevertheless they are presented with such a wealth of convincing detail that the average reader accepts them as probable.

It appears, then, that the beast — the disease — is an external and adventitious factor like the suicide of the girl or the swindle by the friend. The disease is not studied for its own sake. Vandover does not become a mere organism subjected to clinical examination. The shred of manhood, of free will, that he retains is always at the focal point of attention. The question is not what new form will the disease take, or what does one learn from the data about its growth and operation, but what is the last tiny bit of conscious individuality thinking and feeling and suffering as it approaches the moment of final extinction. The reader's attention is not fixed by the progress of the disease but by wonder and pity at the fact that the human spark continues so long to survive and so to suffer. The conflict, then, is between a free but fallible individual and a fatal but indefinable enemy. We never see the operation of "That vast terrible engine with is myriad spinning wheels." What we see is a real young man with a well-developed personality and a whole set of convincing mannerisms, who succumbs because of the impact of circumstances upon him — and not the least of these circumstances is the disease lycanthropy, for it is not "scientifically" traced to a source or accounted for. Chance, of course, does not exist in the theory of naturalism. When it appears we know that another frame of reference has been introduced, whether intentionally or not.

There are two extreme points of view which produce inferior art. One extreme is the belief in pure mechanistic determinism. When this attitude is "pure," it is expressed in scientific reports dealing perhaps with pathological or physiological disturbances of the human organism. The "person" being described or examined does not, for the purposes of the report, exist. He is merely a certain amount of tissue, part of which is isolated as a breeding ground for germs or tumors. In pure science, this attitude may be essential for the study of disease per se, although even scientists are not so sure as they were fifty years ago that a disease is anything per se, apart, that is, from the nature of the organism in which it lives. The same impersonal attitude is pure in statistical studies of social trends, and it is perhaps approximated in sociological reports. It is doubtful whether it can be anywhere near pure in a work of fiction. Employed by a very cynical writer who despised the human race and delighted to portray the helpless wrigglings of men impaled on the pins of Fate, it would in effect be an assertion of the writer's superiority and spiritual independence. If it were free of such ironic overtones, it would produce a dismal and boring novel with little or no feeling for the dignity of man. At the other extreme, there is plenty of fiction which fatuously assumes that nature is benign and man is perfectly in tune with it and with himself. From this view come novels which present an easy universe where justice is always done, evil punished (but merely for the delight and beatitude of the Good), and ambitions fulfilled. It is the world of easy pleasure, happy people, and barren complacency. It is a moral world, constructed entirely for the protection of little men. Its perfect "artistic" expression is Hollywood's doctrine of the unique temptation, according to which one has to resist evil only once in order to be forever blessed.

Between these extremes moves the tragic view, which underestimates neither man nor the forces against which he contends. The greatest men face the greatest oppositions and suffer most greatly; therein lies the grandeur of the Greek and Shakesperian tragedy — and the foremost tragic artists show man rising to greatness as he pits himself against forces over which he can never triumph. To acknowledge the might of these forces while not losing faith in the men who challenge them is to possess the tragic view of life.

Vandover and the Brute is in this tragic area. The hero, an ordinary attractive young man, is caught and crushed, not in the "vast terrible engine" that Norris describes, but by social and personal forces which twentieth-century man knows all too well. Insofar as he blames Vandover for moral weakness, Norris moves toward the pole of fatuity, for by doing so he assumes that a moral man would avoid conflict with the moral order. Insofar as he talks about the vast terrible engine, Norris moves toward the pole of inhuman mechanism. But in reality the effect of his novel is between these extremes, if only because the reader is pulled in both directions. Vandover is accepted for what he is — not judged — and the reader, I believe, identifies himself with the struggling spirit of the protagonist *as well as* with the social and personal evil which destroys him. The tragic conflict is within the individual and also between him and the society which is composed of the fallible wills of all individuals.

The modern hero is ruined in the milieu which modern man has made, and the reader participates in the tragic *agon,* aware of the social forces he represents, yet in a manner somewhat different from that of the spectator of a Shakespearian tragedy, for the terrible forces against which Shakespeare's heroes contend are viewed with awe and wonder and fear; not only are they unconquerable, they are indeed beyond man's power of comprehension. The catharsis of pity and terror is to be reached only through art. The modern tragedy locates the opposing forces in society and the nature of man, where they are not quite so terrible and where they produce guilt rather than terror. Hence the conflict cannot be as grand as Shakespeare's. The idea of progress, the necessity for social action, creep into these modern tragedies and offer an alternative or added release for the emotions which Shakespeare purges through pity and terror alone. The modern tragedy thus unconsciously presents two orders of symbolic action: one shows man struggling with Fate and his own nature. The other "attacks" the social order as the embodiment of injustice and heedlessness.

Vandover and the Brute is a modern tragedy in a minor and imperfect key. If the book had been more exhaustively "naturalistic," it would have shown more fully the nature of the social (i.e., human) forces that destroy the hero, and there would have been correspondingly less need to impose a Sunday-school moral censure upon him. Thus the weakness of *Vandover* shows very clearly the potential strength of naturalism as a foundation for tragedy — so long as it is not carried to a point of diminishing returns in lifeless mechanism. In short, so long as it is essentially transcendental, naturalism will give full recognition to the power and immensity of the physical world but will also assume a meaning in it that is akin to and ideally accessible to the mind of man; so that man achieves tragic dignity as he strives to penetrate and master his own nature and the physical universe which repeats the tension of actual and potential, real and ideal, fate and will, evil and good, and matter and spirit, that is in the nature of man. Seen in this light, naturalism is no revolutionary departure from the world-view of Shakespearian tragedy. It is rather a mode of presenting in realistic "modern" terms the forces, microcosmic and macrocosmic, against which man has always tragically contended. Naturalism is the modern approach to Fate. It is more hopeful in

that it suggests rational means of coping with Fate; if it is "pessimistic" it is so only because it has to accord less dignity to man.
As the twentieth century passes, the stature of man has, in fact,
diminished, and the tragic effects of early naturalism have been
achieved less frequently.

Writing for the San Francisco *Wave* in 1896, when he was still
at work on *McTeague,* Norris averred that

> The naturalist takes no note of common peole, common in so far
> as their interests, their lives, and the things that occur in them are
> common, are ordinary. Terrible things must happen to the charac-
> ters of the naturalistic tale. They must be twisted from the ordi-
> nary, wrenched from the quiet, uneventful round of everyday life
> and flung into the throes of a vast and terrible drama that works
> itself out in unleashed passions, in blood, and in sudden death.[14]

This pronouncement identifies at once the literary quality of Zola
and the attraction which Norris found in his work. It was the
surging vitality of Zola's style, the power of his conceptions, the
superabundance of life in his work that Norris emulated. He did
not care for theories except insofar as they released forces within
him. The scientific outlook, the patient documentation, the use of
physical and sociological monstrosities become with Norris, as
they were in the work of Zola, the instruments of a new vigor as
much as they are the causes of it. As in *Vandover,* these naturalistic
qualities free *McTeague* from the lifeless vapidness of contemporary romance and create the effect of newness — of new people seen
with new closeness doing new and real things.

McTeague is the story of a semi-moronic dentist, a great dumb
brute of a man who has learned his trade in a short apprenticeship
with a traveling practitioner and who consequently has no college
diploma. His thoughts are few and his pleasures come with the
satisfaction of physical needs:

> It was Sunday, and, according to his custom on that day,
> McTeague took his dinner at two in the afternoon at the car
> conductors' coffee-joint on Polk Street. He had a thick gray soup;
> heavy, underdone meat, very hot, on a cold plate; two kinds of

vegetables; and a sort of suet pudding, full of strong butter and sugar. On his way back to his office, one block above, he stopped at Joe Frenna's saloon and bought a pitcher of steam beer. It was his habit to leave the pitcher there on his way to dinner.

Once in his office, or, as he called it on his sign-board, "Dental Parlors," he took off his coat and shoes, unbuttoned his vest, and, having crammed his little stove full of coke, lay back in his operating chair at the bay window, reading the paper, drinking his beer, and smoking his huge porcelain pipe while his food digested; crop-full, stupid, and warm. By and by, gorged with steam beer, and overcome by the heat of the room, the cheap tobacco, and the effects of his heavy meal, he dropped off to sleep. Late in the afternoon his canary bird, in its gilt cage just over his head, began to sing. He woke slowly, finished the rest of his beer — very flat and stale by this time — and taking down his concertina from the book-case, where in week days it kept the company of seven volumes of "Allen's Practical Dentist," played upon it some half-dozen very mournful airs.

The six lugubrious airs that he knew, always carried him back to the time when he was a car-boy at the Big Dipper Mine in Placer County, ten years before.[15]

He is a man of tremendous physical strength:

For McTeague was a young giant, carrying his huge shock of blond hair six feet three inches from the ground; moving his immense limbs, heavy with ropes of muscle, slowly, ponderously. His hands . . . were hard as wooden mallets, strong as vices . . . Often he dispensed with forceps and extracted a refractory tooth with his thumb and finger.

And his main ambition is to possess a huge gilded tooth to hang in front of his office.

Into his life comes Trina Sieppe, who is sent by his friend Marcus Schouler to have a tooth repaired. Trina is the daintiest and most beautiful thing he has ever seen, and as he works on the difficult problem of repairing her tooth, McTeague falls in love with her. Marcus, who has been friendly with Trina, steps aside for McTeague; and Trina accepts her "big bear." Just before their marriage she wins five thousand dollars in gold in a lottery, an event which determines the further course of the story. Trina becomes a miser, a spirit concentrated in greed, her whole soul devoted to keeping her money intact. She cheats McTeague, insists on living in the cheapest possible quarters, and devotes her spare time to earning further pennies by whittling wooden animals for a toy store.

Marcus Schouler, his jealousy aggravated by his friend's good fortune, discloses to a rival dentist that McTeague has no college degree. Forced to abandon his profession, fretted by idleness and a fractious, miserly wife, McTeague turns surly. He fishes, loafs in saloons, and drinks more than his dull brain can master. When Trina becomes insufferably stingy, he takes to biting her fingers till the bood comes in order to force her to give him money. Yet while their lives deteriorate, Trina nurses her hoard of gold. When she has amassed an additional four hundred dollars, which she converts into gold and adds to her hoard, McTeague steals it and deserts her. She degenerates into a slattern, contracts blood-poisoning in her bitten fingers from the "nonpoisonous" paint used on her wooden animals, and when McTeague next sees her she has a claw instead of her right hand.

He returns, drunk, to collect from her the money for which she has sold his beloved concertina. She pleads and fights until he kills her; then he flees with her five thousand dollars in gold (she had kept it by her to play with) back to the Big Dipper Mine where he had worked as a boy. The end of the story tells of his flight from the pursuers whom he instinctively detects on his trail. Striking across Death Valley with a mule, he meets Marcus Schouler, who has joined the pursuing posse. Marcus has a gun, but when Mc-Teague's mule runs away he empties it into the beast — which in falling crushes the canteen. The men, crazed by heat and thirst, fight:

McTeague thrust Marcus backward until he tripped and fell over the body of the dead mule . . . McTeague tore the revolver from Marcus's grip and struck out with it blindly. Clouds of alkali dust, fine and pungent, enveloped the two fighting men, all but strangling them.

McTeague did not know how he killed his enemy, but all at once Marcus grew still beneath his blows. Then there was a sudden last return of energy. McTeague's right wrist was caught, something clicked upon it, then the struggling body fell limp and motionless with a long breath.

As McTeague rose to his feet, he felt a pull at his right wrist; something held it fast. Looking down, he saw that Marcus in that last struggle had found strength to handcuff their wrists together. Marcus was dead now. McTeague was locked to the body. All about him, vast, interminable, stretched the measureless leagues of Death Valley.

When Norris is dealing with his physical setting, he sets forth the details plainly, carefully, and objectively. The material appears to speak for itself, and the style approaches the studied reserve of the case study. As in *Vandover,* he chooses details which carry a smell and feel of reality. The technical language of dentistry — rubber dams, sponge-gold, gutta-percha fillings, hard-bits, hoe-excavators, half-cone burrs, glycerite of tannin — is included as if it contained the only terms in which one could write about the profession. It neither apologizes for nor yet exalts the lowly material; its existence is its justification for being included in the novel. Merely because of the nature of the subject, there is more place in *McTeague* than there was in *Vandover* for this sort of documentation. In the latter novel the disease was the outstandingly naturalistic material, and the descriptions of it were closer to the aesthetic of horror than to the simple reality which attaches to hard-bits and hoe-excavators.

It will be obvious by this time that *McTeague* deals with the sordid side of life. McTeague is a brute, a primitive man unnaturally placed in a civilized environment. His life with Trina is degraded and ugly, and his lack of mentality makes his connection with his environment more intimate than it could be if he had those qualities of will or "soul" which, in different kinds of stories, cause characters to stand out as self-sufficient and autonomous in spite of whatever physical conditions may oppress them. Since it is in this respect that most American naturalistic novels fail to achieve inner consistency, the preponderance of sordid milieu over individual will may profitably be emphasized. McTeague probably thinks and chooses, but the novel concerns itself with the objects and actions that exist outside of his mind; in the crises, the actions of the leading characters are fully treated, while the accompanying cerebration is assumed to be a part or function of the action rather than its cause. The causes are physical, instinctive, and dependent upon external circumstance. In this respect the resemblance between *McTeague* and Zola's *L'Assommoir* is striking.

The lower spiritual plane upon which *McTeague* moves accounts for a difference in ethical tone from that which obtains in *Vandover* and suggests that it comes considerably closer to fulfilling the theoretical criteria of naturalism. The hero of *Vandover* starts from a social and moral plane as high as that of the average gentle reader, who consequently identifies himself with Vandover and in some degree judges and condemns him for the kind of moral lapses that he would condemn in himself. But where McTeague's rudimentary moral gropings appear beside his gigantic and instinctive activities, the reader feels no impulse to identify himself with their possessor; and if McTeague does make a reasoned choice (which he scarcely does in the whole book) the reader hardly thinks of judging it. Rather he observes — with curiosity, fascination, wonder, and pity. The terror proper to tragedy is absent. There is interest but no purgation.

Furthermore, the tone of *McTeague* is frequently facetious. Norris treats his characters as if they were exhibits in a side show, ridiculous monsters, or conversation pieces. He seems to delight in exhibiting their follies, to be grimacing at the reader over their shoulders, to be saying that these freaks from the grubby levels of society are at least as funny as they are pathetic. McTeague is absurd except when powerful emotion makes him terrifying. Trina is repulsive. Marcus Schouler, who is symbolically represented by yapping dogs, is vain, combative, petty. And as if this were not enough, Norris has introduced minor freaks. There is a crazy servant, Marie, who says, "I had a flying squirrel but I let him go," and who tells a burlesque miser about chests full of gold plate till she has him wild with avarice. And there is a pathetic old couple, Miss Baker and Old Grannis, who commune through the wall of the rooming house where they live, never daring to speak to each other. The assemblage of big and little monsters creates a sense of sociological extremes — of people or creatures who have to be seen in the new dimension of Darwinian thought rather than in the established frames of social conformity and orientation. For all the humor, there is a grotesque and nightmarish quality here that recalls similar effects in the work of Stephen Crane. This is the jungle at our back door, full of creatures who do not answer to the social norms.

That the philosophy is broadly deterministic is obvious from the character of the story. How explicitly so is another matter, for the forms of naturalism may be assumed without the writer's caring much about its theoretical basis. Let us see how Norris goes about working either internal or external determining forces into his action. With reference to the former, he gives careful attention to McTeague's heredity. His father died of acute alcoholism, and the evil is said to have been transmitted to the son: "Below the fine fabric of all that was good in him ran the foul stream of hereditary evil, like a sewer. The vices and sins of his father and of his father's father, to the third and fourth and fifth hundredth generation, tainted him." His physique and his intellectual slowness are also obviously products of his heredity which show why he does not act like the "ideal" social creature who thinks and chooses with perfect moral freedom. We are told of the forces which produce McTeague's "will," though his individuality is not impaired thereby. Trina's greed, further, is derived from her Swiss ancestry. Equal care is devoted to the external forces which operate upon the hereditary endowment of McTeague to bring about a change of state. But these external forces — Trina's greed, and Marcus's jealousy, especially — do not represent broad social or economic pressures and so do not in their operation demonstrate any sociological truths. In other words, the story of *McTeague* is put in motion by circumstance, by external forces which do not join perfectly together to form a chain of cause and effect. Norris points to the unalterable destiny that was created when McTeague and Trina met: "Their undoing had already begun. Yet neither of them was to blame. From the first they had not sought each other. Chance had brought them face to face and mysterious instincts as ungovernable as the winds of heaven were at work knitting their lives together."[16]

In this story, however, we are not to witness the interaction of heredity and environment according to scientific rules, but to observe the web of circumstances which brings about the destruction of the leading characters. The structure of the novel, therefore, depends neither upon a "cycle of degeneration" in which internal forces direct the movement, nor upon a cycle of change induced by external pressures operating in their regular courses. The structure consists, rather, of very much the sort of plot that might be found in any novel of adventure or intrigue — except that it is not conceived in terms of free will. Its interlocking of cause and effect in such incidents as the winning of the lottery, the loss of McTeague's practice through Marcus's jealousy, and the finding by McTeague of his concertina which Trina had sold, is as statistically improbable as the melodrama of the conclusion. Yet the fact that the action is slow, so that there is ample time for detailed presentation of what appears to be a *complete* picture of the lives of McTeague and Trina, makes the incidents seem inevitable as they occur. In this sense of inevitability lies much of the aesthetic effect of the story. In spite of the comic overtones the reader is touched by the pathos of McTeague's situation, by his dumb and helpless struggling against a sequence of events for which he is not personally responsible, and by the pathetic sense of isolation which attaches to a character who moves in a course which he cannot change.

The plot is one extra-naturalistic element in *McTeague* that accounts for its interest. Instead of illustrating natural laws, the structure of the novel draws the reader's attention to the people who move through it. The result is that one knows McTeague and Trina as individuals who do think and desire and struggle: instead of robbing them of their personalities, the deterministic forces direct us to feel the pathos of their inability to cope with the pressures which overcome them. It is a feeling for the desperation of human, or subhuman, impotence that the book communicates. The humanity of the characters is minimized somewhat by Norris's facetious tone, but nevertheless it comes through, sometimes forcefully, almost in spite of the author.

Because the writer's concern is always with his characters, we get only an inkling of his attitude toward nature. It is malignant toward McTeague, but he is not a representative American. Norris expresses no teleology; yet he does not deny one. He exhibits religious feeling which seems not to be related to his inchoate materialism. So shadowy are the philosophical assumptions, indeed, that he can endow McTeague with a sharp power of intuition through which, in the long final section devoted to his flight into the mountains and across the desert, he is constantly aware of his pursuers and knows when he must thrust on further into the hinterland. The suggestion is that this power of instinctive perception belongs to the atavistic animal nature which is strong in him. It is also a preview of the natural dynamism which derives from the romantic roots of naturalism and of which we shall see much more in *The Octopus* and *The Pit*.

McTeague is an advance toward pure naturalism beyond *Vandover* in that its characters are more convincingly dominated by a sordid milieu. The difficulty in *Vandover* was that Norris could produce no effective milieu in San Francisco. In *McTeague* he found one but lightened its burden by leaning heavily upon heredity and circumstance to control his action. The carefully wrought plot represents a literary advance; it does not draw away from "pure" naturalism so much as it distinctly and consciously subordinates it to the literary intention which was always uppermost with Norris. If it ends in outlandish melodrama rather than a controlled demonstration of inevitable consequences, it is merely because Norris shifted from the theory to the romantic extremes of naturalism.

Following *McTeague* Norris wrote three novels which carry out the expectations set up in the first two books so well that one would like to think he could have predicted them. These three books exploit the sentiment, the primordialism, the violence, and the energy that make the first two as good as they are. But they have no serious intellectual core, and so they can be regarded only as potboilers tossed off to answer popular demand for excitement and sensation. *Blix* (1899) is a pleasant love story of *Ladies' Home Journal* quality. *Moran of the Lady Letty* (1898) is somewhat tougher. Ross Wilbur of San Francisco's elite is shanghaied aboard a dirty Chinese schooner bound south to collect sharks' liver oil. They sight a derelict whose lone survivor is a Norse blonde titan of a girl, Moran. Violence piles on violence as they engage in mortal conflict with a group of murderous Chinese. Moran calmly files down the teeth of a miserable captive until he tells where his fellows are hiding. Ross kills a man in hand-to-hand combat. "Never had he conceived of such savage exultation as that which mastered him at that instant." [17] Shortly thereafter he vanquishes Moran in a primordial wrestling match — and she turns feminine and adores him. The problem of how to bring a savage like Moran back as a wife to sophisticated San Francisco society is solved in a manner which reveals the structural bankruptcy of the novel. At the eleventh hour she is murdered by the Chinese whose teeth she filed, who thereupon hoists sail and abandons ship as it boils out through the Golden Gate before a spanking breeze, carrying Moran to a Viking's funeral.

A Man's Woman (1900) is the most extreme of Norris's novels. In it his interest in horrible "scientific" detail and his celebration of brute strength are carried to fantastic lengths. Only the quality of the writing saves the story from being ridiculous, for it is made of the stuff of the most extravagant thrillers. The extremes to which the dominant motifs are carried can be adequately rendered only by quotation. The hero is an epitome of forthright strength: "The rugged unhandsome face; the massive jaw, huge almost to deformity; the great, brutal indomitable lips; the square-cut chin with its forward, aggressive thrust; the narrow forehead, seamed and contracted, and the twinkling, keen eyes so marred by the cast, so heavily shadowed by the shaggy eyebrows." [18] His courage and power win the love of the man's woman, Lloyd Searight, who, rich, cultivated, and able, is nevertheless described in phrases reminiscent of those applied to Moran: "She was tall and of a very vigorous build, full-throated, deep-chested, with large, strong hands and solid, round wrists. Her face was rather serious; one did not expect her to smile easily; the eyes dull blue, with no trace of sparkle and set deep under heavy, level eyebrows. Her mouth was the mouth of the obstinate, of the strong-willed, and her chin was not small." In order to be of use in the world, she has adopted the profession of nursing. The crisis of the story is a titanic struggle between the wills of these two. Bennett refuses to permit her to take the risk of nursing his best friend and unsuccessful rival for her hand, who is dying with virulent typhoid fever. Her career, her ideals, her loyalty, her stubbornness are helpless before the power of his will. At the end of the tale, a man's woman to the core, she sends him back to the arctic that he may continue to be a man worthy of her love.

These red-blooded people move in the vivid setting that Norris is always able to create. Everything is authentic, from the details of arctic exploration to the profusion of exact scientific terminology that is applied to descriptions of Lloyd's activities as a nurse. Scenes which carry naturalistic horror to extremes are made even more striking through the "scientific" treatment of detail. The following picture of disease and starvation in a stricken polar expedition is outstanding:

In the strange and gloomy half light that filled the tent these survivors of the *Freja* looked less like men than beasts. Their hair and beards were long, and seemed one with the fur covering of their bodies. Their faces were absolutely black with dirt, and their limbs were monstrously distended and fat — fat as things bloated and swollen are fat. It was the abnormal fatness of starvation, the irony of misery, the huge joke that arctic famine plays upon those whom it afterward destroys. The men moved about at times on their hands and knees; their tongues were distended, round, and slate-colored, like the tongues of parrots, and when they spoke they bit them helplessly. Near the flap of the tent lay the swollen dead body of Dennison. Two of the party dozed inert and stupified in their sleeping bags. Muck Tu was in the corner of the tent boiling his sealskin footnips over the sheet-iron cooker. Ferriss and Bennett sat on opposite sides of the tent, Bennett using his knee as a desk, Ferriss trying to free himself upon the sleeping bag with the stumps of his arms. Upon one of these stumps, the right one, a tin spoon had been lashed.

The tent was full of foul smells, the smell of drugs and of mouldy gunpowder, the smell of dirty rags, of unwashed bodies, the smell of stale smoke, of scorching sealskin, or soaked and rotting canvas that exhaled from the tent cover — every smell but that of food.

In the first edition there was a description of the excision of a little girl's hip joint — so unpleasant that the publishers were constrained to remove it from later printings.

The naturalist has had new fields opened to him by the right which science assumes to explore all areas of thought and action. These new fields contain many hideous and revolting subjects which the naturalist can exploit and render doubly effective by this ostensibly scientific approach to them. Partly through his concern with such striking material, and partly through his desire to employ the deterministic outlook in his work, the naturalist is led to write about "sociological extremes," for it is in the sordid and unpleasant side of life that the operation of external force upon man is most satisfactorily displayed. When the higher ethical nature of man is either denied or ignored, the emphasis must perforce be placed upon the physical, racial, instinctive, brutal side. There is no alternative. People who have no spiritual values are by the same token sure to be moved by physical, instinctive compulsions, for there is nothing else to make them move. They can, it is true, be purely the objects of force; but if they move themselves their characters must contain strong emotional urges.

From the sociological cases of Zola's *L'Assommoir*, who are shown to be mostly animal in order that Zola may study their reactions to their environment in the simplest terms — unhampered, that is, by any exalted spiritual yearnings which would be most difficult to analyze as products of heredity or milieu — from these people it is but a short step to the "abnormal" brute who vents his "primordial" passions upon the outskirts of civilization. Such characters abound, as I have said, in the novels of Zola, where they are to a large degree explained by their environments. Remove the large sociological framework and you have the atavistic, red-blooded brute whom we have already encountered in the pages of Jack London. To call such a creature a superman, as both Norris and London do, is an error. He is instinctive, physical man set free to roam at large in conflicts outside the conditioning influences of society. He is not capable of endless conquest under any conditions. He has little in common with such a bona fide superman as Dreiser's Frank Cowperwood. His strength alone identifies him with the superman of Nietzsche's philosophy, and he will flourish only where it is the prime survival value. The McTeagues and Sea Wolfs and Bennetts are not supermen but sociological monstrosities taken out of the conditions that might have produced them; they are creatures-once-removed from the mythical "pure" naturalistic novel, given a partially new set of characteristics, and set in motion under entirely new conditions.

Instead of representing a world stripped of ethics and ideals, these brutes of Norris's seem rather to embody his search for meaning in life. For if science and philosophy had poured the chilling waters of doubt over the ideals and activities of civilized men, still with strong-willed Titans in violent struggles there was never an instant's doubt as to the final value of their activity. Such figures would provide an escape from the civilized world that had come to question its old absolutes.

A Man's Woman celebrates force and ferocity — naturalistic method brought as literary device to a tale which glorifies the human will as far as it could be glorified in fiction. Of determinism there is none. *A Man's Woman* illustrates the protean nature of Norris's naturalism. It was a literary garment that, like the chameleon, could assume any color; and like the chameleon it lived, so far as its philosophical basis was concerned, upon air.

～ ～

The sweep of Norris's *Octopus* (1901) is so big that no adequate account of the book can be given in small compass, but some description of it must be attempted if one is to analyze its structure and discuss its place in the naturalistic movement.

The story, built around an incident in California history (the Mussel Slough affair) which Norris altered to suit his literary purposes, is concerned with the wheat ranchers of the San Joaquin Valley who have taken up land every alternate section of which belongs by federal grant to the Pacific and Southwestern Railroad. When the ranchers first settled, the Railroad promised to sell them its half of their land at two dollars and a half an acre. After some eight years, when the ranchers have dug irrigation ditches, improved the land, built houses, and, after two dry years, are about to gather a bonanza harvest, the Railroad announces that the lands are now for sale — to anyone who will buy — at prices ranging from twenty-two to thirty dollars an acre. Such prices mean ruin; they mean that the Railroad will take over the land with all its improvements and its rich crop of growing wheat because the ranchers cannot possibly meet the price. The men are desperate. To protect themselves they form a league to fight the case in the courts and to promote the election of a friendly majority on the Board of Commissioners in order to bring about a favorable revision of the freight rates on wheat. To the latter end the leaders of the league resort, unknown to its members, to bribery — only to be sold out by the man whose election they buy. This man, Lyman Derrick, son of the president of the League, betrays his trust for Railroad money. Pledged to secure a reduction, the commission reduces rates drastically between points where no wheat is ever shipped.

Hard upon this disaster, the Railroad, which has meanwhile sold the ranch lands to its own dummy buyers, wins its suits to evict the ranchers. The evictions are effected when the ranchers are away at a barbecue, and only eleven of the six hundred return to prevent the dispossession. In an unexpected clash between these farmers and the United States marshal and his deputies, eight men are killed — eight who include the central figures of the story, the leaders of the League. After this catastrophe the rest of the ranchers are ruined, and Magnus Derrick, grand old leader of the League, is disgraced for his part in the election and broken into abject misery. The Railroad maintains absolute control of the situation:

Instantly Bonneville had been isolated. Not a single local train was running, not one of the through trains made any halt at the station. The mails were not moved. Further than this, by some arrangement difficult to understand, the telegraph operators at Bonneville . . . refused to receive any telegrams except those emanating from railway officials. The story of the fight . . . was to be told to San Francisco and the outside world by . . . the local P. and S.W. agents.[19]

Around the central complication are grouped enough related events to give the novel impressive breadth and fullness. The story is largely told through Presley, a poet who is staying at the Derrick ranch for his health. He thinks a great deal about the nature of the epic of America which he hopes to write. When he becomes tremendously concerned with the struggle of the ranchers against the Railroad, he arrives at what seems to be Norris's conclusion — that the epic of America will be the real story of the People. After the massacre he writes one successful poem, *The Toilers,* which is read everywhere; and at a mass meeting he bursts into an impassioned plea for liberty and justice:

"They own us, these task-masters of ours; they own our homes, they own our legislatures. We cannot escape from them. There is no redress. We are told we can defeat them by the ballot-box. They own the ballot-box. We are told we must look to the courts for redress; they own the courts. . . . No outrage too great to daunt them, no petty larceny too small to shame them; despoiling a government treasury of a million dollars, yet picking the pockets of a farm hand of the price of a loaf of bread."

Shortly after delivering this tirade he dynamites the home of the railroad agent, but S. Behrman is miraculously unharmed.

Supporting the main action like the subplot in *Lear* runs the story of Dyke. A former railroad engineer, he risks his savings in hop growing. When the crop is flourishing he borrows money from the railroad agent on a mortgage. He began his enterprise with an unofficial "promise" of a freight rate of two cents a pound on his hops. As soon as he has sold his crop for what seems a handsome profit he is told that the rate has been advanced to five cents. He is ruined, as irrevocably as the ranchers. In the fury of despair he demands that the railroad agent explain his basis of applying freight rates.

"Yes, what's your rule? What's your basis?" demanded Dyke, turning swiftly to him.

S. Behrman emphasized each word of his reply with a tap of one forefinger on the counter before him:

"All — the traffic — will — bear."

In desperation Dyke robs a train and flees into the mountains, where he is finally captured after a long chase, the outcome of which presages the larger tragedy that is to follow.

Showing the villainy of the Trust through another of its effects upon society is the death by starvation in the streets of San Francisco of Mrs. Hooven. She is the wife of one of the ranch workers, a German immigrant. Penniless, she and her little daughter are put out of their room:

> Sometimes leading and sometimes carrying Hilda, Mrs. Hooven set off upon her objectless journey. Block after block she walked, street after street. She was afraid to stop, because of the policemen. As often as she so much as slackened her pace she was sure to see one of these terrible figures in the distance, watching her, so it seemed to her, waiting for her to halt for a fraction of a second, in order that he might have an excuse to arrest her.

So they walk, and at night sleep on park benches. Begging prolongs her agony, but she cannot live on what she is given. The combination of ignorance and stupidity which prevents her from getting proper assistance is unforgettably portrayed. While Mrs. Hooven is struggling through her last evening, Presley is dining with a wealthy San Francisco family, thinking, "Because the farmers had been killed at the irrigating ditch, these others, Gerard and his family, fed full. They fattened on the blood of the People, on the blood of the men who had been killed at the ditch. It was a half-ludicrous, half-horrible 'dog eat dog' of unspeakable cannibalism."

It is clear from this outline of the plot that *The Octopus* is in the naturalistic tradition in its delineation of the broad sweep of economic forces. It is naturalistic in the Zola tradition, and its qualities may be further elucidated by comparison with those of Zola's novel which it most closely resembles, *Germinal*.

The most striking quality that the two works have in common is the epic sweep. Zola is famous for his ability to handle great movements, for the tremendous canvas which he is able to paint before his readers' eyes. In this, Norris's first attempt to deal comprehensively with a social and economic movement, he reproduced much of Zola's magnitude. *The Octopus* seems to picture the heart of the California social body: the reader senses that his eye is directed toward that point where the maximum number of social forces converge; he is constantly made to feel that all the activity of city and ranch is going forward while his attention is confined to a particular sequence of events. The richness of Norris's conception is illustrated by this magnificent description of the spring plowing:

The ploughing, now in full swing, enveloped him in a vague, slow-moving whirl of things. Underneath him was the jarring, jolting, trembling machine; not a clod was turned, not an obstacle encountered, that he did not receive the swift impression of it through all his body, the very friction of the damp soil, sliding incessantly from the shiny surface of the shears, seemed to reproduce itself in his finger-tips and along the back of his head. He heard the horsehoofs by the myriads crushing down easily, deeply, into the loam, the prolonged clinking of trace-chains, the working of the smooth brown flanks in the harness, the clatter of wooden hames, the champing of bits . . . the sonorous, steady breaths wrenched from the deep, laboring chests, strap-bound, shining with sweat, and all along the line the voices of the men talking to the horses . . .

Such a passage is reminiscent of the celebration of the earth's fecundity in *La Terre,* and it is comparable to many of the descriptions in *Germinal.* Its tone and quality are probably not conscious and specific imitations of Zola, for it is characteristic of Norris whether he is writing romance or "naturalism" to reach out for the epic sweep. But this tendency to create pictures of gigantic movement and force is more and more frequently to be observed in his last two novels. It satisfies, perhaps, the epic conception of his trilogy and the symbol underlying it;[20] it reflects an increasing indebtedness to the style and method — the literary qualities — of Zola; it has little relation to the intellectual conception upon which the work rests.

Another Zolaesque element in *The Octopus* is the use of symbols to give emotional weight to the forces which play so large a part in its movement. In *Germinal* the black buildings and tower of the Voreux, the coal mine, are pictured again and again as symbols of the alien force which crushes the miners. Early in *The Octopus* a flying locomotive cuts through a herd of sheep:

The pathos of it was beyond expression. It was a slaughter, a massacre of innocents. The iron monster had charged full into the midst, merciless, inexorable. To the right and left, all the width of the right of way, the little bodies had been flung; backs were snapped against fence posts; brains knocked out. Caught in the barbs of the wire, wedged in, the bodies hung suspended. Under foot it was terrible. The black blood, winking in the star-light, seeped down into the clinkers between the ties with a pro-longed sucking murmur . . .

Again and again, at rapid intervals in its flying course, it whistled for road crossings, for sharp curves, for trestles; ominous notes, hoarse, bellowing, ringing with the accents of menace and defiance; and abruptly Presley saw again, in his imagination, the galloping monster, the terror of steel and steam, with its single eye, Cyclopean, red, shooting from horizon to horizon; but saw it now as a symbol of a vast destruction in its path; the leviathan, with tentacles of steel clutching into the soil, the soulless Force, the iron-hearted Power, the monster, the Colossus, the Octopus.

Again, the inexorable malignancy of the Railroad is symbolized by a map of its lines:

It was as though the state had been sucked white and colorless, and against this pallid background the red arteries of the monster stood out, swollen with life-blood reaching out to infinity, gorged to bursting; an excrescence, a gigantic parasite fattening upon the life-blood of an entire commonwealth.

The more significant differences between Zola's and Norris's use of symbolism will be discussed later in this chapter.

A further similarity, and a basic one, between *The Octopus* and *Germinal* is that both depend for their structure on the operation of an economic institution upon the lives of a social group who struggle for existence under or within it. To ruminate upon and digest the intellectual implications of this great struggle, both authors provide a number of commentators who interpret condi-tions from their particular points of view. Zola has three: a socialist, an anarchist, and the hero, Lantier, an average thinking man who is turned into a reformer by the evils he sees. In *The Octopus* Caraher is an anarchist — a saloon keeper — who, like Zola's anarchist, has been converted into a passionate hater of monied power by his wife's death at the hands of Pinkerton strikebreakers. Again it must be observed that if these similarities represent an influence of Zola upon Norris it is a literary influence, a matter of method, of storytelling, that has no necessary relation to the philosophy of naturalism.

More interesting and fruitful are the dissimilarities between these novels, for it is through them that Norris's position in the naturalistic movement may be explained. The most important problem in the consideration of any panoramic naturalistic novel is the relation between the characters and the external forces that oppress or control them, the amount of will displayed, and the extent to which such "will" is explained in terms of the forces which the novel presents. In *Germinal*, it will be recalled, the mine has made the miners what they are, has determined their economic situation and physical characteristics from generation to generation. During the action of the novel it pervades and directs their thoughts. It is the object against which they struggle even while it is responsible for having made them what they are. No two characters can affect each other without the mine's having some part in their activity. Physically and spiritually ubiquitous, it is a force with amazing power and scope of operation.

In *The Octopus* conditions are otherwise. The characters begin their struggle with the Trust as free, ethical, and independent men who have achieved a high degree of prosperity upon the frontier. They have struggled with nature and triumphed. And the struggle of such titans with the Octopus is Homeric in conception rather than a pathetic illustration of determining forces controlling helpless and insignificant automata. Annixter is the most striking example of an heroic frontiersman. He is a despiser of "feemale girls," a distruster of marriage, hot-tempered, contentious, gruffly generous. He calls his enemy a *pip*, eats quantities of dried prunes, and re-reads *David Copperfield* constantly. He is college educated, and his ranch is a model of efficiency and modern brightness. Considerable attention is given to his romance with Hilma Tree, who works for him: "Annixter turned into the dairy-house . . . Hilma stood bathed from head to foot in the torrent of sunlight that poured in upon her from the three wide-open windows.

She was charming, delicious, radiant of youth, of health, of well-being." He intrudes upon her innocence by a clumsy attempt to kiss her, is properly mortified at his own gaucherie, and stamps off in a rage. But the seed is planted, the hater of women is trapped. It is some time before he can accept the idea of love, and, above all, marriage. Finally he drives her from him, but an all-night vigil under the stars shows him the way:

By a supreme effort, not of the will, but of the emotion, he fought his way across that vast gulf that for a time had gaped between Hilma and the idea of his marriage. Instantly, like the swift blending of beautiful colours, like the harmony of beautiful chords of music, the two ideas melted into one, and in that moment into his harsh, unlovely world a new idea was born. Annixter stood suddenly upright, a mighty tenderness, a gentleness of spirit, such as he had never conceived of, in his heart strained, swelled, and in a moment seemed to burst. Out of the dark furrows of his soul, up from the deep rugged recesses of his being, something rose, expanding . . .
"Why . . . I *love* her," he cried.

These activities enhance Annixter's personal independence. They add "spiritual" elements to his character that defy explanation in terms of heredity and environment. His stature is further increased by a duel which he has with a discharged farm hand who dashes on horseback into the dance that Annixter is giving in honor of his new barn. Firing blindly through the smoke, Annixter is astonished to discover that he has hit his opponent in the hand:

"Well, where did *you* learn to shoot *that* way?" someone in the crowd demanded. Annixter moved his shoulders with a gesture of vast unconcern.
"Oh," he observed carelessly, "it's not my *shooting* that ever worries *me*, m'son."
The crowd gaped with delight. There was a great wagging of heads.

Such offhanded, humorous bravado takes us out of the feeling of a confined, determined life. This same freedom becomes headstrong defiance when the Railroad serves, an hour later, its notice of the new land prices. The ranchers' league is formed in an explosion of defiance. Knowing the power of the Railroad, the reader will regard this event as tragic irony rather than as an illustration of economic determinism. Annixter's death at the climax is tragically wasteful but also heroic. It is almost a glorious death.

A further instance of what I have termed the heroic character of the struggle is to be found in the presentation of Magnus Derrick, chief of the ranchers and president of the league. Talking to his son — the one who is expected to aid the league by reducing rates on wheat — he reveals a tragic flaw:

"I know you will be fair to the Railroad. That is all we want. Fairness to the corporation is fairness to the farmer, and we won't expect you to readjust the whole matter out of hand. Take your time. We can afford to wait."

"And suppose the next commission is a railroad board, and reverses all our figures?"

The one-time mining king, the most redoubtable poker player of Calaveras County, permitted himself a momentary twinkle of his eyes.

"By then it will be too late. We will, all of us, have made our fortunes by then." . . .

Magnus was by nature a public man, judicious, deliberate, standing firm for principle, yet upon rare occasions, by some such remark as this, he would betray the presence of a sub-nature of recklessness, inconsistent, all at variance with his creeds and tenets.[21]

Such an analysis raises the conflict to Homeric levels. Frontier heroics we see, battles waged with lives and fortunes at stake — and on one side at least the actors are responsible for their deeds even though they are faced with a fairly impossible choice. On the other side — the villainous side of the Octopus — the supposed economic forces receive such concrete embodiment in characters of inhuman viciousness that all idea of economic determinism is forgotten in the reader's moral indignation at their brutal deeds. S. Behrman, symbol of the Railroad's greed, "was a large, fat man, with a great stomach; his cheek and the upper part of his thick neck ran together to form a great tremulous jowl, shaven and blue-grey in colour; a roll of fat, sprinkled with sparse hair, moist with perspiration, protruded over the back of his collar." Throughout the story he is motivated, apparently, by an unchanging resolve to crush the farmers by fair means or foul. His actions could be explained only by a deep-seated hatred which he is not shown to harbor. In *Germinal* the mine owners are almost as helpless as the miners. Economic forces are clearly portrayed. In *The Octopus* Behrman's villainy is a thing apart from economic forces. It makes excellent material for the story, it adds to the passion of the conflict, but it also obscures whatever forces Behrman is meant to represent. Lyman Derrick's betrayal of the ranchers, similarly, is presented as a piece of personal baseness, motivated doubtless by the lure of railroad gold, but possible only in a man devoid of loyalty and decency.

The same difference of conception between the *Octopus* and *Germinal* extends to the very symbols which the two authors employ. The Octopus, as we have seen, is an actively evil and malignant force. Adjectives like "inexorable," "iron-hearted," and "pitiless" are constantly applied to it. It is cruel and villainous — a thing to be hated. Compare with this the mine buildings and the black tower of the Voreux in *Germinal*. Gloomy, black, immobile, they stand as a symbol of oppression. But no false attempt is made to have them reach out and devour the miners. Instead they squat there as gaunt and horrible symbols of the forces which the miners cannot evade. Their immobility makes them ideally representative of the economic forces which dominate the book. No moral values can be attached to them; they do not indulge in active evil for which they can be hated. They represent the nature of deterministic forces — inescapable, unchanging, destroyed only by the earth-shaking catastrophe of revolution or the destructive anarchy of Souverine who lets in the water that floods the mine and swallows up the buildings. Zola's symbol carries philosophical as well as dramatic significance. Norris's is almost solely dramatic.

A Homeric conflict between free agents and a fatal but malign institution raises more questions than it answers about the workings of the cosmic mechanism which it is presented as illustrating. What natural laws are demonstrated? What processes are explained? What scientific insights are achieved? And what do we discover about man's relation to nature? The answer takes us into a new

145

set of symbols and related ideas, which I should designate generally by the label natural dynamism. Under this concept nature is presented as a conscious, living, benign force — as in the description of the plowing, where rows of horse-drawn plows, as far as the eye can reach, turn the rich earth:

It was the long stroking caress, vigorous, male, powerful, for which the Earth seemed panting. The heroic embrace of a multitude of iron hands, gripping deep into the brown, warm flesh of the land that quivered responsive and passionate under this rude advance, so robust as to be almost an assault, so violent as to be veritably brutal. There, under the sky, the wooing of the Titan began, the vast primal passion, the two world-forces, the elemental Male and Female, locked in a colossal embrace, at grapples in the throes of an infinite desire . . .

A second expression of this theme is the story of Vanamee. He became a solitary when his fiancée, having been mysteriously assaulted in the night, died in childbirth. During the course of the novel he frequently appears, experiencing a mystical call that reaches to him out of the night in answer to his conscious willing for his dead love. The experience grows sharper with each repetition, until finally She comes to him — the daughter of his dead Angele — and with the morning he finds that the wheat has appeared above the ground; stretching as far as the eye can see: thus the Vanamee motif is related to the wheat, symbol of fruitfulness and benign natural force. Vanamee achieves the same affirmation of life which the reader is expected to recognize in the constant bountiful pressure of growth in the nourishing grain:

There it was. The Wheat! The Wheat! In the night it had come up. It was there, everywhere, from margin to margin of the horizon. The earth, long empty, teemed with green life. Once more the pendulum of the seasons swung in its mighty arc, from death back to life. Life out of death, eternity rising from out dissolution. There was the lesson. Angele was not the symbol, but the *proof* of immortality. The seed dying, rotting and corrupting in the earth; rising again in life unconquerable, and in immaculate purity — Angele dying as she gave birth to her little daughter, life springing from her death, the pure, unconquerable, coming forth from the defiled. . . . So Angele, so life, so also the resurrection of the dead . . . It is sown in weakness. It is raised in power. Death was swallowed up in Victory.

Annixter, too, relates his newborn love to the benign natural compulsion which produces the first shoots of wheat on the morning of his long vigil:

There it was, the Wheat! The Wheat! The little seed long planted, germinating in the deep, dark furrows of the soil, straining, swelling, suddenly in one night had burst upward to the light. . . . The earth, the loyal mother, who never failed, who never disappointed, was keeping her faith again. Once more the strength of nations was renewed. Once more the Titan, benignant, calm, stirred and woke, and the morning abruptly blazed into glory upon the spectacle of a man whose heart leaped exuberant with the love of a woman, and an exulting earth gleaming transcendent with the radiant magnificence of an inviolable pledge.

The most striking and adventitious illustration of this natural dynamism is the famous scene in which S. Behrman, gloating over a ship that is being filled with wheat, falls into the hold and is smothered under the rushing stream of grain. One feels that this is the very wheat that was stolen from the ranchers, when their lands were taken just at the time of harvest, and that the wheat is taking revenge upon the villain who presumed to interfere with its growth and distribution.

Such invocations of the wheat abound in *The Octopus*. Presley goes out to look at it after the painful scene in which Lyman Derrick's perfidy is revealed, and his thoughts provide a convenient transition to the economic ideology underlying the action:

Ah, yes, the Wheat — it was over this that the Railroad, the ranchers, the traitor false to his trust, all the members of an obscure conspiracy, were wrangling. As if human agency could affect this colossal power! What were these heated, tiny squabbles, this feverish, small bustle of mankind, this minute swarming of the human insect, to the great majestic, silent ocean of the Wheat itself! Indifferent, gigantic, resistless, it moved in its appointed grooves. Men. Lilliputians, gnats in the sunshine, buzzed impudently in their tiny battles, were born, lived through their little day, died, and were forgotten; while the Wheat, wrapped in Nirvanic calm, grew steadily under the night, alone with the stars and with God.

Here are forces intelligent, benign, purposeful, leading the world and its people into the felicity of God's love. Economic determinism is a mere incident in the cosmic enterprise. Zola, to continue our comparison, makes it clear that both his miners and the mine owners are caught up in the strangling grip of the capitalistic system: they are destined to clash, but neither can profit by winning the battle within the framework of capitalism, for if the miners' wages are raised the owners will be ruined. The only answer is world revolution. Zola's theory is explicit and coherent without being unduly obtruded upon the story. It emerges as the only possible meaning of the action.

Norris presents his situation in various ways. At one point the economic struggle results from the moral laxness of the public: "Every State has its own grievance. If it is not a railroad trust, it is a sugar trust, or an oil trust, or an industrial trust, that exploits the People, *because the People allow it.* The indifference of the People is the opportunity of the despot." Elsewhere the Railroad is said to be operated by the blackest of villains. As Presley shouts: "They swindle a nation of a hundred million and call it Financiering; they levy a blackmail and call it Commerce; they corrupt a legislature and call it Politics . . . they prostitute the honor of a State and call it Competition." The Railroad is cursed and the people are exhorted to action, always against a *responsible* evil force which moral rightness demands should be curbed. But when Norris thinks of the wheat his love of great forces and resounding phrases impels him to body it forth, again and again, as a positive, God-sent, benign force which will triumph in spite of temporary conflicts waged over the enjoyment of wealth to be derived from its control. In Presley's thought, already quoted, it is a "colossal power" containing apparently within itself the ability to bring about its own distribution and consumption. It wills to be the feeder of nations. Nothing can stop its movement. Stated in less rhapsodic language this conviction comes forth as a blind and outmoded form of utilitarianism — which Shelgrim, head of the Railroad — expounds with the author's approval:

"Believe this, young man . . . try to believe this — to begin with — *that railroads build themselves.* Where there is a demand sooner or later there will be a supply. Dr. Derrick, does he grow his wheat? The Wheat grows itself. What does he count for? Do I build the Railroad? You are dealing with forces, young man, when you speak of Wheat and the Railroads, not with men. There is the Wheat, the supply. It must be carried to feed the People. There is the demand. The Wheat is one force, the Railroad another, and there is the law that governs them — supply and demand. Men have only little to do in the whole business. Complications may arise, conditions that bear hard on the individual — crush him maybe — *but the Wheat will be carried to feed the people* as inevitably as it will grow."

Such language condones the evils of competition because through it the wheat reaches the people. The fact that it is finally eaten, we are told, makes it a symbol of truth, a concrete proof that good triumphs in the end, that nature works for human betterment through the economic system:

Greed, cruelty, selfishness, and inhumanity are short-lived; the individual suffers, but the race goes on. Annixter dies, but in a far distant corner of the world a thousand lives are saved. The larger view always and through all shams, all wickedness, discovers the Truth that will, in the end, prevail, and all things, surely inevitably, resistlessly work together for good.

Here, then, is where the fabric of reason is thinnest in *The Octopus*. The wheat as an incarnation of natural dynamism, of an inherent desire in nature to be bountiful, is equated with the prevailing social arrangements for buying and selling. Laissez-faire economics is treated as if it were an aspect of nature's dynamic urge to reproduce herself and feed her children. We are told that *how* the wheat is distributed does not matter; we are almost persuaded that the manner of its distribution is a part of nature's larger plan. One does not of course question a novelist's right to accept laissez-faire economics. But we must note that these conclusions do not satisfactorily answer the *problem as posed* in the novel. That problem is not whether the wheat will finally be eaten (it always was in those days) but whether the railroads must and will continue to swindle and oppress the less powerful American citizens whom, if the will of our democracy is to find expression, it is supposed to serve in a free market. The question is whether the people must or should stand for such criminal injustice, whether our social order must countenance a condition in which a corporation controls the press, the banks, and the courts and so becomes a law unto itself in defiance of democratic process. This problem is not solved. It is simply evaded, while a vaguely religious affirmation of ultimate good is offered to appease the emotions aroused by the action.

When Behrman, the immediate individual object of the reader's dislike, is smothered in the hold of the wheat ship, pent-up emotions are released. The reader is made to feel, by this poetic fusion of disparate elements, that the wheat as a force has answered the social and economic problem of the novel, the problem of monopoly and coercion. Of course it has not, and the thoughtful reader is bound after a time to feel that it is he who has been swindled of a solution. Conditions in the American West differed essentially from those in the coal mines of *Germinal* where there was no answer for either miner or owner. Zola was true to his materials and wove a consistently dark tragic pattern — leaving at the end a single bright thread in the suggestion that revolution must inevitably come. Norris copies this tragic pattern for a conflict that did not have to end tragically. The democratic process could still work in America, where there were natural resources in abundance and relatively few people. Not revolution but a safer legal basis for trade was indicated. The tragedy of the story speaks magnificently for itself. It is the attempt to explain it that does irreparable harm to the novel. Only once is there a strong expression of the new naturalistic philosophy, when Presley ponders the idea of a mechanistic universe, indifferent and unchangeable, which pursues its way not toward the utilitarian goal of prosperity but toward no goal at all, operating merely because motion is the law of the cosmic mechanism:

Nature was, then, a gigantic engine, a vast Cyclopean power, huge, terrible, a leviathan with a heart of steel, knowing no compunction, no forgiveness, no tolerance; crushing out the human atom standing in its way with nirvanic calm, the agony of destruction sending never a jar, never the faintest tremor through all that prodigious mechanism of wheels and cogs.[22]

One is tempted to perceive a close relationship between the incoherence of Norris's philosophy and the steadily growing orotundity of his style. In *The Octopus* there is an endless accumulation of sonorous adjectives. The rolling periods throb and rumble. Sometimes they produce superb effects; at other times they seem rather to be giving voice to a love of power and size which, an end in itself, sweeps careful ratiocination aside. Norris's development thus far shows a steady movement toward this love of high-sounding words. As the style inflates, the conviction of his books diminishes. *McTeague,* though better built, carries less final conviction than *Vandover. The Octopus,* still better constructed, has less than *McTeague.*

But in the last analysis *The Octopus* is one of the finest American novels written before 1910. It towers immeasurably far above the sickly sentiment of Norris's contemporaries. Its chief weakness can be traced to a certain feebleness of intellectual grip, and this feebleness is reflected in the inadequacy of his grasp on the ideology — naturalism — through which he chose to work. It must be emphasized that he does not fall short merely because he was not a perfect naturalist, but because of the intellectual softness which prevented him from completely mastering the set of ideas he adopted. We may assume that he would have similarly failed in the comprehension of another philosophy that required the same sharpness of perception. We may, further, conclude that the naturalistic philosophy provided a much-needed discipline for Norris's creative exuberance — a discipline which aided him wonderfully in directing his genius toward expression in significant form. As the tonic effect of this discipline abated, Norris went over toward the trifling contemporaries whom he had previously condemned.

Although *The Pit* (1903) bears only traces of having been influenced by the naturalistic movement, it seems to be a logical culmination of the tendency apparent in Norris's books up to and including *The Octopus,* and we may therefore welcome it, intellectually, as the "probable" culmination of a tendency that has been identified already. The story contains three distinct elements. There are first the adventures of Curtis Jadwin, who attempts to corner the Chicago wheat market, holds tremendous power for a time, but is crushed when a new crop of wheat comes on the market faster than he can buy. The second strand is Jadwin's private life; and this is really the story of his wife Laura, who is the emotional center of the struggle between love and business that goes on within the hero. The third element is the wheat, the life force which Norris had taken as the great central theme of his trilogy.

In the descriptions of the wheat — which is curiously remote as a force because there is no way that it can enter the story except as an unseen force — Norris carries still further the tendency which reached its previous high point in *The Octopus* — the tendency to pile up booming, thunderous periods with the intention of conveying directly, as well as intellectually, a feeling for the majesty of the wheat. Such a description as the following shows to what lengths he carries the device:

Thus it went, day after day. Endlessly, ceaselessly the Pit, enormous, thundering, sucked in and spewed out, sending the swirl of its mighty central eddy far out through the city's channels. Terrible at the center, it was, at the circumference, gentle, insidious and persuasive, the send of the flowing so mild, that to embark upon it, yielding to the influence, was a pleasure that seemed all devoid of risk. But the circumference was not bounded by the city. All through the Northwest, all through the central world of the Wheat the set and whirl of that innermost Pit made itself felt; and it spread . . . and spread till grain in the elevators of Western Iowa moved and stirred and answered to its centripetal force, and men upon the streets of New York felt the mysterious tugging of its undertow engage their feet, embrace their bodies, overwhelm them, and carry them bewildered and unresisting back and downwards to the Pit itself . . .

It was as if the Wheat, Nourisher of the Nations, as it rolled gigantic and majestic in a vast flood from West to East, here, like a Niagara, finding its flow impeded, burst suddenly into the appalling fury of the Maelstrom, into the chaotic spasm of a world-force, a primeval energy, blood-brother of the earthquake and the glacier, raging and wrathful that its power should be braved by some pinch of human spawn that dared raise barriers across its courses.[23]

The Pit as an agent of economic force is presented with a moderately coherent thesis. One Cressler, an operator, explains "officially" how the poor grower and consumer of wheat are both cheated and ruined by the Chicago dealer who fixes the price. He fails to consider that supply and demand, even in his own system and on his own terms, have a great deal to do with the price, and that the speculator is not the only price fixer. On the other hand there is presented the opposite side of the coin: the speculators who get the fever in their blood and become possessed and ruined by the idea of making a fortune at one stroke. The intent of denouncing the Pit as an unsocial social force represents the idealistic branch of the divided stream of naturalism — its reforming zeal, its passionate belief in a moral law which *ought* to prevail. The novel's presentation of economic forces which should embody the materialism and determinism of naturalism is spectacularly neglected. In place of theoretical (or scientific) explanation we find an increased reliance on the mystical natural dynamism by which the wheat crushes those petty fools who would interfere with its distribution and consumption.

A further obstacle to a disinterested evaluation of forces is the fact that Curtis Jadwin is another of Norris's red-blooded heroes. His battle with the wheat becomes a heroic clash between superman and super-force. Jadwin is beaten at the end, but his powerful will has never been questioned, nor has anything but his driving gambler's aggressiveness been shown as the cause of his decisions. The great game that he plays does not seem to take place within an immovable system. It is so individual a struggle that nothing is proved but the irresistible power of the wheat:

He had laid his puny human grasp upon Creation and the very earth herself, the great mother, feeling the touch of the cobweb that the human insect had spun, had stirred at last in her sleep and sent her omnipotence moving through the grooves of the world to find and crush the disturber of her appointed courses.

The most disturbing influence of all upon the structural unity of *The Pit* is the intrusion of Jadwin's home life and the personality and problems of Laura into the story. She is both important and unimportant. Though she seems real enough at times, her character is nevertheless intellectually rather than emotionally apprehended. One feels that Norris thinks of new things to do with her as he proceeds with the story: he makes dialectical discoveries of ways to write pages of reasoning about how she should feel and act at particular times. These reasoned pages do not make her come to life. Her whole role, to be sure, is vitiated by the supreme importance of Jadwin's fight over the wheat. Obviously she is there merely as a foil to set off the great struggle in the Pit, to show the other side of Jadwin's public failure. Thus the story breaks completely in two when Norris devotes considerable time to her connection with Sheldon Corthell, the understanding artist to whom she goes for comfort when Jadwin is deserting her more and more for the Pit. The division between romance and economics anticipates Winston Churchill and his *Coniston*.

The demands of the story as story, the need of any novel to be an artistic whole, are constantly at odds with the problem of the wheat. Thus the presumably naturalistic use of actual, living material fails because it is not made the material and setting of the whole story. The forces, in short, do not affect everything they should. In *Germinal* the setting of the mines does not seem to be imposed upon the plot; far from it — it is the story. Everything grows directly from the mines and the life which they produce. The people who work the mines are part of how the mines work. In *The Pit,* however, the love story of Laura is her own story; it is a romantic, individual story of a single beautiful woman's great problem. And from the point of view of Laura, the whole workings of the Pit and Jadwin are important only insofar as they bring about changes in her situation and feelings. Thus the soul and theme of the book, the wheat, becomes much of the time only an incidental force acting upon Laura in a way that any number of other diversions or passions of Jadwin's might act upon her. He might as well be pursuing other women, or absorbed in an invention, as caught up in the whirlpool of the Pit. And one must further emphasize the romantic nature of the conception: a beautiful and spirited woman living in the greatest luxury — and wanting love. In *Germinal* the story, the setting, and the characters are always perfectly fused and interdependent; social significance and personal experience are integrated. In *The Pit* there are two stories, and the "naturalistic" setting applies to only one of them.

Norris was led astray by two elements. There was the public demand for love interest; and there was the fact that the Pit does not, apparently, provide a setting for a story that takes in all sides of a man's life. The farmers in *The Octopus* lived with their wheat. They could never act apart from its background and influence. But Jadwin is not always in the Pit; and the story is his story rather than a story absolutely about the Pit. To achieve structural unity Norris might either have written entirely about a great wheat operation and its consequences — a story that never moved out from under the shadow of the Pit and in which all human actions were portrayed in close relation to the central fact of the operation — or else he might have composed a story about a woman's inner life and her love, in which the wheat market never pretends to enter except as an incidental force. He has fallen between the two stools. Fully two thirds of *The Pit* is devoted to Laura. The rest is an individual's colossal gamble. All that remain of Norris's essentially literary naturalism are the Zolaesque descriptions of the swirling, sucking Pit and a vague feeling for the irresistible power of the wheat.

— —

To *Vandover, McTeague,* and *The Octopus* the naturalistic impulse brought newness and vigor — enough newness to distinguish them utterly from the work of Norris's genteel contemporaries; enough vigor to blow the new candor like a mountain wind into stuffy Victorian parlors. But Norris did not think through to any fundamental conclusions about the relations between naturalism (i.e., materialistic monism) and the conventional universe of free will and moral responsibility. He was attracted by the sensational aspects of naturalism (which he considered "romantic"), and he imitated the spectacular effects of Zola without much thought for the underlying implications. (Zola too was more interested in effects than in abstract theories, but with characteristic French lucidity he was able to make his abstractions play a consistent part in his works.) Norris's minor novels are monstrosities, deformed by the fantastic overgrowth of some aspect or motif of naturalism. The wheat books, magnificently conceived, fail structurally because they contain conflicting and contradictory sets of ideas all of which Norris apparently was trying to prove through the action of his story. It would be ungracious not to remark in conclusion that most of Norris's contemporaries and successors have failed more completely than he in their search for a form that would integrate the free-will world of our experience, the moral order of our convictions, and the naturalistic world of our theory. Most of his contemporaries never strayed from purely romantic and sentimental patterns in their fictions. His successors have, generally, avoided coming face-on to the issue of will versus determinism. If they are not as reckless as Norris, neither are they as powerful. Today we have floods of novels that are merely trivial, whimsical, timely, or reportorial and which often have no form at all because their writers do not even try to make a significant pattern appear through a contrived action. They are satisfied to be interesting.

VII

The Romantic Compromise of
Winston Churchill

Winston Churchill's novels were prodigious best
sellers from 1900 to 1917. They were emotionally powerful. They
were considered highly intellectual. Any list of distinguished contemporary novelists would have had Churchill's name near the
top. Yet since World War I he has seldom been mentioned, no one
has dealt with his work at any length, and he is remembered only
because so many people still living read him when they were
young.[1]

If Churchill had written only romances like *Richard Carvel*
(1899), *The Crisis* (1901), and *The Crossing* (1904), he would now
be classed with Francis Marion Crawford and Lew Wallace. But it
was at once his fortune (in two senses) and his misfortune to become
aware of the "new science" and of the new ways of thinking about
personal and social problems which it implied. It was his good
fortune because he then wrote a series of problem novels which
were also romantic love stories; he retained his romance audience,
he attracted thousands of new readers with his problems, and his
sales jumped to more than a quarter of a million copies for each of
several books. His misfortune was that, when he dealt with social,
economic, and moral problems, he moved into an area of larger
significance — an area in which he might have written novels that
were important in addition to being readable. But the intellectual
assumptions underlying his romances constituted a closed system.
It was, simply, a system of ethical optimism in which choices are
free and justice is invariably done. I think it will appear in the

ensuing descriptions of these novels that it is a fatuous system. Introducing new and incompatible ideas into this closed system led Churchill into confusion, contradiction, and, it appears, mental travail. For whereas the conventional designs of his early chronicles and romances were perfectly adequate for their purposes, the introduction of issues depending upon a scientific outlook complicated his technical problems to a point where he was incapable of solving them. This chapter will attempt to show the elements of that complicatedness, to explain why it was so difficult to reduce them to order, and to interpret what happened in Churchill's later novels as he struggled with technical problems that he did not understand.

Churchill is of special interest because he stands at the very point where the old verities crumbled under the pressure of new ideas. Before him, and in his early work, we have romance and sentiment, adventure and ethical conflict. After him came the variety and the vitality of twentieth-century experimentation. Not that he caused that new trend; nor did his work mark an exact chronological division between the old and the new; but no other American novelist offers at once so rich and typical a pudding of nineteenth-century thought and so incongruous a sauce of twentieth-century materialism and social consciousness. If this dish is not successfully blended, there is all the more to be learned from tasting it carefully.

Most of the writers treated in this volume were trying to slough off their outworn romantic ideas and finding it difficult or impossible to do so. Churchill is on the other side; he wants to use the new ideas without disturbing the romantic morality to which he seems by temperament and literary genius to be attached. Thus where other writers in the naturalistic tradition seem to be confused by tradition, Churchill is put to rout by the scientific and radical ideas he tries to use in his romances.

In 1906 Churchill's most famous novel, *Coniston*, appeared. Although no idea of determinism appears in the plot structure or in the author's comments, it is a story about the social system. The evils of boss politics, succeeded by the greater evils of railroad control, are its setting and substance. The action revolves around Jethro Bass, an uncouth political boss, whose beautiful ward, Cynthia Wetherell, falls in love with the upright son of Isaac Worthington, a corrupt but genteel and well-bred railroad tycoon who plans to gain control of the state. A struggle for power between the fathers is settled when Bass agrees to withdraw from politics on condition that Worthington will consent to the marriage of his son and Cynthia.

For the modern reader, the moral of this astonishingly immoral book is that to bring genteel social ideas into politics is to sacrifice social and political justice for the merely nominal good of preserving genteel appearances. Only a basic snobbishness could have led Churchill to allow Jethro (a rascal, but with a heart of gold) to give in to the wicked and hypocritical Worthington. The beautiful Cynthia must marry "well," and the social issues are forgotten completely.

Mr. Crewe's Career (1908), although somewhat more complicated, deals with the same general subject as *Coniston* and suffers from the same weaknesses. It deals with the efforts of Humphrey Crewe, a wealthy eccentric, to enter politics and wrest from the powerful railroad interests their control of the state. But Churchill remains on the level of romance and gentlemanly intercourse. He treats the weightiest issues in a mock epic style, as if he were afraid to face them squarely, as if a gentleman must escape into irony from the sordid rapacities of politics.

The grand action of the story is the campaign for governor. Here old Hilary Vane, the political operator, is fighting his last battle for the railroad; Crewe is gaining strength as a reform candidate, which means he is anti-railroad; and young Austen Vane, with a large following of the best people, is torn between his desire to bring honest government to the state, his love for the beautiful Victoria Flint, daughter of Hilary Vane's boss, and his loyalty to his aging father. Austen can be elected; of this there is no doubt. But he holds back while Crewe goes gallantly (and somewhat blindly) forward into mock-epic strife. In the end Crewe is defeated by the crooked agents into whose hands he had put his campaign, Hilary wins his last fight, father and son are reconciled, and Austen wins the girl. There are various speeches in which homage is paid to the moral order, and the reader is assured that railroad control of politics is seeing its last days regardless of the outcome of a single campaign.

The action of the story, then, settles nothing. Crewe is outwitted and defeated because he engages in the shady political practices at which the railroad is much more skillful than he, for his own corrupt agents betray him. He is also something of a comic, a fact which makes his defeat a highly personal matter. Austen represents righteousness, and could win, but he does not enter the race, partly from filial devotion but largely because of his love for Victoria Flint. That a young man like Austen could, without any effort, defeat the powerful railroad machine belies the very conditions of the story. Yet that is what we are told; supporters come to him unsought because he is an honest man. Again, the economic question is transformed from a harsh struggle for power into a moral issue because all the main characters are on the same social level. Hence the outcome depends upon their intimate personal relations — not upon the interaction of the sociopolitical forces which are supposed to underlie the story.

Although the action deals with the corruptness of the rich railroad people, the characters who carry the action are presented in a way that equates social status and goodness. The president of the railroad, for example, is father to the divine Victoria. So he withdraws from action and leaves the dirty work to Hilary Vane, who chews snuff to indicate his social position. His son, Austen, is a gentleman, marked to marry Victoria; so he too refuses to join the forces of reform against her father.

This means that social position, gentility, integrity, and income develop *pari passu*. At the top of the social scale one has an abundance of all three. But the thesis of the novel rests upon precisely the opposite assumption, namely, that wealth is the greatest political malefactor. We are urged to trust the enlightened public, but in the movement of the story the cause of reform depends upon the powerful leadership of a strong man with social standing. In practice, then, the enlightened public is impotent. These examples help to show why the demands of the romantic plot constantly interfere with the writer's consistent development of the themes and movements implicit in his problem.

The next novel, *A Modern Chronicle* (1910), goes into the problem of the modern woman. The beautiful and gifted Honora Leffingwell marries a successful stockbroker, then divorces him to ascend the social ladder by way of a marriage with Hugh Chiltern, who is not merely wealthy but also possesses ancestral acres in Pennsylvania, where Honora settles down to enjoy a life of tradition and responsibility. Her sensibilities have been badly scraped by the divorce proceedings, not because she has withdrawn from an unpleasant bargain or because divorce offends some ethical or religious standard, but because of the social stigma and unpleasantness involved. She despises society and was willing to defy it in her great love for Chiltern, but at the same time her high spirit is uncomfortable in a sense that taste or dignity has been offended. Churchill implies that a heroine as exalted as Honora must have wealth, beauty of setting, and status; and indeed it presently transpires that her craving for tradition and responsibility cannot be satisfied on Chiltern's ancestral acres because the estate has been run for decades without her. Her soul yearns for a more substantial *raison d'être*. Churchill extricates his heroine from her difficulties by suddenly revealing that Chiltern is a dissolute villain and by bringing him to a violent death in falling from a horse. Honora withdraws from the world for four years and returns, her soul cleansed, to marry her childhood sweetheart who has become famous and wealthy and who will be the perfect husband.

One cannot ascribe the structural failure of this novel to stupidity, ignorance, or mere lack of craftsmanship in the author. The answer lies, as usual, in the contradictory traditions with which he dealt: on one hand, the sacred institution of marriage and the social stigma branded on divorce; on the other hand, an individual somehow in opposition to this code. If the author accepted the social code absolutely, he could have the sinner destroyed, with auctorial approval, for her sins. If he quite denied the validity of the code, while recognizing its power, he might have a superior individual — superior intellectually, in talent, and by virtue of an independent moral integrity — flout the code and either triumph over it or be destroyed by it. Either course would be consistent and possible and would lend firmness and coherence to the whole novel. With such a scheme, furthermore, the novelist could devote himself to the study of his characters, as they developed and worked out their destinies under the conditions in which they lived. The heroine of *A Modern Chronicle* does not enjoy this freedom to live and grow. As the writer's ideas shift, she must change from a designing climber to an ambitious girl who has made an error she regrets, to a fine soul carried away by ignorance and susceptibility, to a noble soul compelled by overpowering love to flout the codes of society, to a noble, noble soul suffering for her sin, to a noble and now enlightened soul being at length richly rewarded (financially!) for the good that was always in her.

In simplest terms, the conflict is between the need for a thrillingly perfect romantic heroine who must be right because she is charming, and a problem in which there is no right but only groping among choices all more or less unsatisfactory. Churchill is willing for his heroine to despise the values of Mammon, but he is not willing for her to be poor. Hence she must realize and display her beauty of spirit through luxury. He cannot see a fine individual with anything but fine clothes and sophisticated manners. Yet he shows again and again that wealth almost invariably involves some dirtying of the hands that make and keep it. He despises those who grub for it, but he portrays grace, goodness, and beauty always in terms of it. The romantic world of absolute values faces a relative world wavering among God, Mammon, and tradition. Trying to see reality in all three of these glasses more or less at once, Churchill multiplies variety in a wilderness of mirrors, and the form of his novel is chaos.

The next problem was religion. *The Inside of the Cup* (1912–

1913) presents a young minister's struggle to preach the Christian ethic to a materialistic society and drive the money changers from the temple. Mr. Hodder, the young rector, discovering that his wealthy parishioners own slums and brothels, determines to cleanse "the inside of the cup." In true Churchillian fashion he has fallen in love with Alison Parr, daughter of the greatest pillar of the church and greatest robber of the poor. After a heroic vestry meeting at which Hodder denounces Parr, who in turn insists that Hodder is insane or, even worse, a socialist, Hodder proposes to Alison and is accepted. The gigantic struggle between Hodder and the embattled forces of Mammon comes to nothing; instead the climax comes in personal terms.

Hodder asks Alison Parr to marry him.

If this were *Coniston,* we should look for an evasive action beginning with Hodder's asking Alison Parr to marry him. But Churchill has outgrown such patent artifices. Instead of meeting his issue, or of confusing or falsifying it, in this novel he starts so far back that he never reaches it. By the time Hodder has abandoned his ironbound authoritarian orthodoxy, plunged into and emerged from agnosticism (almost atheism!), seen and studied Christ incarnate in a modern humanitarian, reinterpreted Christian dogma, and won the lady of his heart, there is no time for the great conflict between Christianity and capitalism that was clearly foreshadowed in the vestry meeting when Parr had the rector's salary cut off. For four hundred and fifty pages we have been backing up, like the hero of a melodrama, for a forward rush that does not take place.

The substituted climax in personal terms does not genuinely represent the forces in question; Parr's dissolute son dies of apoplexy and alcohol, and Parr has to come to the home of a man he has ruined and to face a girl whom his son had seduced but whom old Parr would not allow him to marry — an act by which Parr ruined both the girl and his son. Here is retribution with a vengeance. The old sinner resists stoutly, but his spirit is broken, and he is presently convinced that he must devote his declining years to restoring his ill-gotten gains. Even here there is more bickering than illumination as Hodder and Parr quibble over how the money is to be returned without its going to imposters.

Generalizations scarcely seem necessary. The unresolved conflict could end only in tragedy, unless Churchill lowered or, if the reader chooses, raised his argument to the level of expediency and showed that Hodder must stay in the church in order to be where he could have contact with the people who exert the greatest control over society. Perhaps his own concern, as we have seen from the earlier novels, is too exclusively with the financial aspects of American life; he identifies wealth and prowess and decency so closely that he is unable actually to entertain other values. No hero in his novels can turn his back on the standards of polite society, even though he may try slightly to alter them. One cannot be good unless he is also genteel. Romance runs a close second through most of this novel, but she comes home a winner, though perhaps in this instance by default rather than by her own speed, for the race does not really end.

～　～

The purpose of *A Far Country* (published in 1915) is to show the fruits of capitalism turning to ashes in the mouth of a highly successful lawyer, because he is a man whose finer feelings ultimately lead him to see the right. There is a good deal of persuasive talk about socialism — and the usual romance, which in this instance parallels the hero's reaction to his socioeconomic situation. On the business side of the action we see Hugh Paret work up and up until he is running for the Senate as the candidate of the exploiting corporate interests. He is opposed by a socialist named Krebs, whom he knew at college and who slowly gains the ascendency over Paret both by presenting more convincing arguments and by being a nobler person. A climax occurs when Paret suffers a nervous collapse brought on in part by his growing conviction that Krebs is right. Thereafter he goes to California, recuperates physically, and "finds" himself spiritually. What he finds is the new science of biology, by which man will control his environment:

"Here indeed was another sign of the times, to find in a strictly scientific work a sentence truly religious! As I continued to read these works, I found them suffused with religion, religion of a kind and quality I had not imagined. The birthright of the spirit of man was freedom, freedom to experiment, to determine, to create — to create himself, to create society in the image of God! Spiritual creation the function of cooperative man through the coming ages, the task that was to make him divine. Here indeed was the germ of a new sanction, of a new motive, of a new religion that strangely harmonized with the concepts of the old — once the dynamic power of these was revealed."

It is not easy to comment seriously on this passage. It is a starry-eyed Spencerianism that finds biological evolution toward spiritual beatitude a law of nature, which man has merely to watch and applaud, with now and again a kindly scientific push to help it on its blessed way. It assumes that God himself is watching over the scientist's benevolent management of Destiny. It is naturalism softened into a sentimentalized and genteelized New Humanism.

The romantic action concerns Hugh's love for Nancy Durrett, a woman of beauty, character, and breeding who turned away from Hugh when his early idealism was soiled in the contest for material power. Both married unsuccessfully, Nancy a worthless rich man and Hugh a girl whose depth of character was not garnished with social poise and who could not bring herself to understand his political maneuvers. When they have separated from their respective spouses, their old love revives. Being free from conventional moral inhibitions, Hugh, the aggressive capitalist, wants to seize happiness immediately; but Nancy discovers grave doubts which seem somehow to correspond to the better nature of Hugh that is presently to appear and make him withdraw from political corruption.[2]

Churchill allows this romance to flower, with the appropriate love scenes, but its physical consummation is forestalled by an accident to Nancy's husband which causes his mind to deteriorate slowly. She returns to care for him, the call of duty enabling her to understand and so to resist an "unworthy" passion. We are familiar with such adventitious resolutions of problems in Churchill's novels. One dwells upon them not maliciously but, rather, because they are crucial proofs that the ideas are not operative in the structure of these novels. Or, more accurately, the novels contain two or more incompatible sets of ideas, one of which controls the form to the confusion of the others.

Three such sets of ideas can be distinguished here. First there is a good deal of Marxian socialism flavored with institutionalism. The radical Krebs, for example, says:

"All this talk of political and financial 'wickedness' was rubbish; the wickedness they complained of did not reside merely in individuals: it was a social disorder, or rather an order that no longer suited social conditions . . . What we still called 'sin' was largely the result of lack of opportunity, and the active principle of society as at present organized tended more and more to restrict opportunity."

The institutionalism lies in the belief that the social system has become a force which operates regardless of the desires of the people who compose it. A second idea pattern is the scientific optimism already noted which undoubtedly reflects Spencer's evolutionary philosophy; it finds a sublime order in creation, an order whose tendency is always upward. The third pattern relies on the inner check of New Humanism to control the old Adam of man's dual nature. The confusion among these ideas is most sharply manifested in Churchill's continual romantic, admiring preoccupation with the very rich people whose greed has brought about the social dislocation that he deplores. It is unreasonable to suppose that hearts which sink to the nadir of greed and selfishness should also rise to the zenith of enlightenment.

This gap is bridged by the silken cable of the genteel tradition — as strong as it is soft — introduced when Nancy explains the weakening of values which has caused the evils of industrialism:

"We have raised up a class in America, but we have lost sight, a little — considerably, I think — of the distinguishing human characteristics. The men you were eulogizing *are* lords of the forest, more or less, and we women, who are of their own kind, what they have made us, surrender ourselves in submission and adoration to the lordly stag in the face of all the sacraments that have been painfully inaugurated by the race for the very purpose of distinguishing us *from* animals. It is equivalent to saying that there is no moral law; or, if there is, nobody can define it. We deny, inferentially, a human realm as distinguished from the animal, and in the denial it seems to me we are cutting ourselves off from what is essential — human development. We are reverting to the animal. I have lost and you have lost — not entirely, perhaps, but still to a considerable extent — the bloom of that fervour, of that idealism, we may call it, that both of us possessed when we were in our teens."

Here is no proof, but a plain assumption that the possessors of good manners (the wealthy) are also the latent possessors of the ideals which will save society from greedy barbarism. It is a working-class man like Krebs who presents the arguments for social justice which ultimately convert Hugh. Yet Krebs is not the hero of the story; he dies conveniently while the latent nobility in Hugh's soul flowers. Not Krebs, who would not be accepted in polite society, but Hugh will guide men out of the wilderness.

~ ~

The Dwelling-Place of Light (published in 1917) opens with an extended presentation of the home life and ideals of a family which has fallen in income and status. The Bumpuses are of old New England stock. Heirs to the Puritan tradition, they retain their ingrained reverence for the American past. But at fifty-five Edward Bumpus, the father, finds himself gatekeeper of a huge spinning mill in a town near Boston. We see him bewildered and ineffectual, crushed by the forces of industrial change, consoling himself with his ancestors. He holds himself aloof from the alien millworkers, but he is as poor as they, and his family lives in a miserable flat that resembles their tenements in squalor. His wife is bedraggled and resentful. His two daughters are struggling in the abyss with their jobs as clerk and stenographer. They are of the white-collar proletariat whose last clutch at gentility causes them to work for less than the millworkers receive. The younger, Lise, has been shaped by the tawdriest elements of modern civilization — tabloids, advertisements, movies, cheap dance halls. Janet, the other daughter, is of finer stuff. "She was one of the unfortunates who love beauty, who are condemned to dwell in exile, unacquainted with what they love. Desire was incandescent within her breast. Desire for what? It would have been some relief to know." [3] The early pages of the novel create a fairly convincing impression of her eagerness for knowledge and beauty, her utter ignorance of where to seek it — since she does not know just what she wants — and of the richness of her personality. She is the individual with a lust for life who may appear on any level and who is sure to affect the destinies of those about her. She works as a stenographer in the mammoth Chippering mill for which her father is gatekeeper.

Claude Ditmar, manager and director of the mill, is a powerful businessman, aggressive, dominating, efficient, and single-minded. Without the background of the New England aristocracy, he has nevertheless risen high in the social scale, as high, perhaps, as he could. [4] Although cynical toward women, he recognizes the fire in Janet and makes her his private secretary so that he may have her near him. The situation between Ditmar and Janet is developed with some subtlety. He is powerful and fortunate, a glamorous figure to a working girl, and he has many admirable qualities; but he does not have the finer sensibilities which Churchill assumes come only from leisure and tradition. Janet, on the other hand, though completely untutored, is able instinctively to discredit her sister's shabby ideals and to see through the falseness of modern life. She has, furthermore, by the same instinct, a sense of the past and of the finer beauty of traditional things. Such perception in one who has had no training to prepare her for it is sentimental and romantic. It is, further, incongruous and inconsistent with the author's genteel attitude toward Ditmar, who lacks taste *because* he lacks money and family.

Janet resists Ditmar's growing attachment for her because she knows it can bode her no good; but she also welcomes it because, for one thing, she responds to it, and, for another, because he holds out to her rebellious and passionate spirit the promise of escape. She does not want money; nor — so great is her vitality — does she shrink from overstepping conventional moral scruples; but she possesses an integrity and pride which raise her above ordinary morals to a high plane of ethical awareness, and from this high plane she resents being promoted because of "certain dynamic feminine qualities." The setting also includes a social situation. In modern business, we are told, may be studied "one phase of the evolution tending to transform if not disintegrate certain institutions hitherto the cornerstones of society." We expect the action to turn upon this situation, and indeed the love affair develops through Janet's and Ditmar's relations to the great mill. It presently transpires that a law has been enacted reducing the working week from fifty-six to fifty-four hours — just when Ditmar has landed the biggest order the mill has ever had. He exclaims, "All this union labour talk about shorter hours makes me sick — why, there was a time when I worked ten and twelve hours a day, and I'm man enough to do it yet, if I have to." He does not intend to recognize the union. The social implications are heightened when Janet is taken through the mill and sees the terrible conditions of the laborers — terrible even though Ditmar is genuinely concerned with making his operatives as comfortable as possible. She realizes for the first time that these alien toilers are human beings. At the same time Ditmar's control over them heightens her interest in him and in the adventure of her situation.

The glitter of Janet's adventure is tarnished when her sister, Lise, comes home drunk. Lise, after her sordid and cynical fashion, is searching for the same escape that Janet wants. Again and again Lise's vulgar gold digging reminds Janet that her attraction for Ditmar and his for her are based, perhaps, on lust and the desire for escape. We are never quite sure. At one moment their physical attraction seems to bind them in a noble romantic love. At another the author seems to intend that a man like Ditmar is incapable of love that is free from the desire for conquest and sensual gratification. But at this stage Churchill confounds those who would accuse him of Victorian prudishness by hinting that the physical and "spiritual" aspects of love are not to be distinguished — as when he writes that "we may some day arrive at a saner meaning of the term [spiritual] and include within it the impulses and needs of the entire organism." [5] Churchill's discernment does not remain uniformly thus remarkable; and when the romancer lets himself go in the description of passionate love scenes the reader is apt to feel that his subtlety has passed over the fine boundary into confusion.

An integration of the personal with the industrial conflict occurs when a reformer attempts to interest Ditmar in improving the housing of his workers. To his assertion that they are living worse than cattle, Ditmar replies, "Isn't it because these people want to live that way? . . . They actually like it, they wouldn't be happy in anything but a pigsty — they had 'em in Europe. And what do you expect us to do? Buy land and build flats for them? Inside of a month they'd have all the woodwork stripped off for kindling, the drainage stopped up, the bathtubs filled with ashes. I know, because it's been tried." As Janet listens to this interview she realizes that Ditmar's arguments are specious, feels a sympathetic kinship with the downtrodden, and even takes a malicious pleasure in seeing Ditmar confounded. At the same time Churchill makes it clear that the problem is not one that could be solved simply. As Ditmar says, "When you're in my position, you're up against hard facts. We can't pay a slubber or a drawing tender any more than he's worth, whether he has a wife or children in the mills or whether he hasn't. We're in competition with other mills, we're in competition with the South. We can't regulate the cost of living." Nor does he blame Ditmar for his attitude, and even Janet understands that it is the result of Ditmar's training and environment. Yet Churchill's sympathies are with the underprivileged, although he ascribes their misfortunes to the capitalistic system rather than to the wickedness of individual exploiters.

For the reasons given above Janet resists Ditmar's importunities until he proposes marriage. Even then she understands that his proposal is dictated by his desire for her and will doubtless be regretted later, but Ditmar sweeps these objections aside. So far both the plot and the development of character have been consistent and, with the exception noted, fairly good. An arresting problem has been set forth. We shall presently begin to observe that Churchill is straying from the social and economic point of view which has so far guided him, and it will be most interesting to see whether he can alter his ideas without losing his grasp on his characters. In this issue are concentrated all the contradictions of Churchill's intellectual career.

The affair becomes increasingly idyllic and passionate — Churchill's apprenticeship to romance serving him magnificently — until finally Janet becomes, in a scene of exalted passion, a willing accomplice to her own seduction. For the time being the romancer triumphs; lust is transmuted into love, and Janet is borne aloft in a veritable apotheosis of body and spirit.

In the meantime the other strands of the plot have been drawn closer to the main one. Ditmar revels in his power as a member of the ruling class. Janet is intoxicated by her contact with it through him. "If you could get the power, and refused to take it, the more fool you! A topsy-turvy world, in which the stupid toiled day by day, week by week, exhausting their energies and craving joy, while others adroitly carried off the prize; and virtue had apparently as little to do with the matter as fair hair or a club foot." She is also aware that there are "higher" things in life which money cannot buy (a theme which we shall see developed later), that the workers *are* exploited horribly, and, by her frequent contact with Lise, that of the men who pursue women those with money most frequently get what they want. On the morning after the consummation of her "love" with Ditmar, Janet finds that Lise, thinking herself with child by a married man, has gone to Boston for an abortion. The need for it turns out to have been a delusion, and Lise hereupon fades from the story; but Janet wonders whether she hasn't been a dupe like Lise.[6]

At this point the fifty-four-hour law becomes effective, the mill-owners decide to cut the workers' pay, and the workers retaliate with a strike. Then I.W.W. organizers come to town, and violence breaks out. In her hatred of Ditmar Janet realizes her kinship with the oppressed. "Their anger seemed to embody and express, as nothing else could have done, the revolt that had been rising, rising within her soul; and the babel [of strikers] to which she listened was not a confusion of tongues, but one voice lifted up to proclaim the wrongs of all the duped, of all the exploited and oppressed. She was fused with them, their cause was her cause, their betrayers her betrayers." As it is represented, this realization of her kinship with the proletariat is natural and right. Churchill presents the strikers' side with complete sympathy. Ditmar damns himself by saying, "By God, I'll fix 'em for this — I'll crush 'em. And if any operatives try to walk out here I'll see that they starve before they get back — after all I've done for 'em." Janet bitterly sums up the situation — personal and industrial:

"Love me!" she repeated. "I know how men of your sort love — I've seen it — I know. As long as I give you what you want and don't bother you, you love me. And I know how these workers feel," she cried, with sudden passionate vehemence. "I never knew before, but I know now. I've been with them, I marched up here with them . . . and I wanted to smash your windows, too, to blow up your mill."

As Ditmar imports strikebreakers and corrupts the courts, Janet joins the I.W.W. and throws herself into the fight.

Churchill's sympathies are clearly with the strikers. But whether he sympathizes with, or even understands, their program of syndicalism is questionable. Analyzing the situation, he says, ironically, that the strike should not be considered an act of God.

Let us surmise, rather, that a decrepit social system in a moment of lowered vitality becomes an easy prey to certain diseases which respectable communities are not supposed to have. The germ of a philosophy evolved in decadent Europe flies across the sea to prey upon a youthful and vigorous America, lodging as host wherever industrial strife has made congenial soil.

The irony in his use of "respectable" is patent; but are "decadent Europe" and "prey" also used ironically? It is not easy to tell. Churchill nowhere explains the dilemma of capitalism; and as the story proceeds he allows moral considerations and a sort of moral indignation to disrupt his presentation of economic fact. The leader of the I.W.W. is depicted as a splendid and courageous general; but the traditional notion that radicals are atheists, loose livers, and free lovers, a notion which he at first presents ironically, comes to dominate his own outlook, and the man for whom Janet works, who harangues the strikers so eloquently, is described as a sensualist who associates every crusade with a new love affair and whose political addresses must be inspired by a woman. The revolutionaries he depicts are actuated largely by hate and a desire for revenge — motives certainly not calculated to produce a better social order — but he does not do full justice to the forces that produce these motives. One sensualist cannot invalidate liberalism. On the other hand, Churchill shows that the members of the militia, which is called out, are laborers who are duped into opposing members of their own class. Drawing a sympathtic picture of strikers freezing and starving in the winter, he shows that the mill operators consider themselves above the law and are, indeed, beyond the reach of the civil authority.

This mixture of ideas is perfectly reflected in the state of Janet's mind as it is presented to us. At one moment she hates Ditmar passionately and sees herself aligned with the workers against him. The next she is uncertain whether she does not love him after all. In short, we have realism on one hand and romance on the other. In the former, Janet is presented as a part of her environment. In the latter, she is a free spirit to whom the industrial conflict is merely an incident. Vacillating between these two conceptions, she begins to lose reality as a character. Yet, in spite of this uncertainty, the story is fairly coherent to this point; the stage is set for a climax and denouement that would grow out of the interaction of the forces already set in motion.

But another element has been introduced. On a walk Janet has been deeply moved by the tradition and the serenity of a private academy near the mill town. Passing it, she meets an author whom she takes for a carpenter because he is building a fence. Now he and a lady of the college, Mrs. Maturin, appear in the town to run a free-soup kitchen for the children of the strikers. They are described as embodying the richest cultural development of our country — urbane, intelligent, also generous and public-spirited. They are said to be liberals, but in the present crisis they think only of feeding the children. This motive is admirable, and what they do is useful, but when Churchill sets them up as the finest type of Americans he implicitly approves of their opinions. In their eyes both sides of the conflict are wrong.[7] Businessmen never see the significant things in life. Strikers are to be pitied. Such an attitude evades the urgencies of the economic crisis by ignoring them — or by seeing in them inevitable results of the evil in man. It is an attitude that resembles the most superficial and irresponsible sort of New Humanism, proposing that hungry people forget sordid worldly problems and develop their "inner checks." Indeed, it denies the possession of light to more than a favored few, and it urges those few to develop it for themselves rather than to spread it or to work for the production of social conditions under which it may spread naturally. The charity of the author, Insall, and of Mrs. Maturin springs from noble motives, but it serves to protect rather than to eliminate the industrial evils which Churchill has so vividly presented. The New Humanism cannot resolve an industrial conflict. For Churchill suddenly to adopt it is for him to abandon the problem *he has set for himself.* For Janet to partake of this philosophy is for her to be removed into another world — entirely apart from the conditions which have formed her character, controlled her life, and made her story real to the reader.

Yet that is what happens. Janet is attracted to these two people and frequently drops in at their kitchen. As the strike approaches its climax, Janet, who has not seen Ditmar for a month, finds she is with child. She goes to his office armed and with murderous intent but, of course, cannot bring herself to shoot. As long as he thinks she is a suppliant he shrinks from the possible burden of helping her, but when he finds that she wants nothing from him, he suddenly decides that he loves her and wants to marry her. She spurns him and flees into the night, dazed and broken. Whereupon the story takes wings to fairyland. She struggles to the author's kitchen and faints, regaining consciousness in the sunny hospital of the beautiful old academy. Mrs. Maturin reads poetry to her and inducts her eager soul into Culture. We are incidentally informed that Ditmar has been shot and killed by angry strikers (he had planted dynamite in their homes and made false charges against them) and that the strike was finally won by the I.W.W.; but these matters are no longer important, for Janet is another person by now. Mrs. Maturin learns Janet's secret and promises to care for her. All is serene until Insall proposes to Janet. Then she must tell him her secret too. He disappears for a time, she accompanies Mrs. Maturin to the Canadian wilds to have her child, and ten days after its birth there comes a letter from Insall saying he still wants to marry her. On the last page, wonder of wonders, Janet calmly announces that she knows she is going to die, and Mrs. Maturin promises to adopt the child. Janet is now confident that Ditmar really loved her.

The interesting aspect of this resolution is, of course, its evasion of the problem which the author set out to study. It scarcely need be remarked that the Janet who serenely gives up her ghost in the Canadian woods bears no resemblance to the Janet whose exploitation by Ditmar was a symbol of the exploitation of labor by capital. The great virtue of the early part of the story was that an individual's activities were a representative, typical part of the setting and situation. It was a story of class struggle, a story which under the conditions of that time could end only in tragedy for a member of the working class. Escape from the struggle is certainly conceivable, for a single individual, but it is not *probable*; and the individual who escapes by making cultured friends ceases to be typical of her class.

As the plot changes, so does the philosophy. When Churchill earlier remarked that "spiritual" activity should be thought of as including the entire organism, he was a materialist. The same philosophy underlay his frank statement of Janet's moral outlook and of the insufficiency of the old moral orthodoxy in the face of new conditions. Now as an advocate of self-realization through tradition and culture he becomes a humanist and, hence, a dualist. From this new outlook Mrs. Maturin, oblivious to the evils of class warfare, can explain to Janet, with the author's approval, how the cloistered academy,

indifferent to cults and cataclysms, undisturbed by the dark tides flung westward to gather in deposits in other parts of the land, had held fast to the old tradition, stood ready to do her share to transform it into something even nobler when the time should come.

Simplicity and worth and beauty — these elements at least of the older Republic should not perish, but in the end prevail.

One's charge against Churchill does not rest on a belief in violence. It is not claimed that the class struggle will produce beneficial results, for there is much historical evidence to show that violence in the long run usually leads to more violence, debasing both winner and loser. The point is that neither the evils of our business system considered as a means of producing and distributing wealth, nor the dislocation resulting from poverty, unemployment, and, finally, violence, can be corrected by fleeing to the ivory tower of genteel Culture.

This novel represents a third stage in Churchill's growth. First he wrote pure romance. Then came problem novels with a sociological bias that did not deny individual freedom and that represented economic and political evils as caused by *men*. In them he could *blame* people and institutions, like the clergy, and he did so. The third stage embodies his attempt to get behind personalities to the determining forces that control them. Here he is even more urgently required to abandon the ethical presuppositions that brought confusion to the novels of the second stage. He comes nearer to doing so, because he sees that the problem is no longer a moral one; but he cannot face it through to the end. Hence his evasion in this last novel is his most conspicuous failure. He could not carry his study through to the conclusions which were so plainly indicated by his presentation of the problem.

～ ～

Discussing the question of *intention,* a number of critics have maintained in recent years that the artist discovers his meaning as he works with his medium rather than, as had been supposed, sets about his work with a clearly conceived idea and plan which he merely had to transfer into a permanent form. Croce held that creation took place in the artist's mind and that the labor of converting this creation into paint, stone, or words was merely "extrinsication." The later critics [8] have argued persuasively that the meaning is inseparable from the medium or, to put it differently, that the meaning grows in the form and cannot exist before or apart from it. Whatever a poem or a painting "says" does not exist until the work has been completed.

These formulations may perhaps help us to imagine how Churchill's novels grew into their ambiguous patterns. He knew that he must have a romantic love story, and every novel begins with the presentation of two challenging characters who are clearly destined to fall in love. These characters are endowed with ideas, attitudes, and values — and there the trouble begins, for the concern with intellectual problems which gives depth and reality to the characters produces conflicts that cannot be resolved without doing great violence to the social values involved with romantic love. Thus the romantic hero or heroine (usually both) is invariably on both sides of the conflict. In *Coniston* Cynthia Wetherell's superb honesty brings her into conflict with her guardian, Jethro, whom she rejects because he lives by corrupt political practices. This is noble of her, we are assured; it heightens the loveliness of spirit for which Bob Worthington adores her. When it appears that the elder Worthington, trying to control the state legislature in order to make more dishonest money from his railroad, is more lavishly dishonest and corrupt than Jethro, it follows that the social position and charm of Bob are tainted. If the characters and the conflict are to be consistent, someone must either change or be defeated. Cynthia, having rejected Jethro, must also reject Bob, or Bob must reject his father's dirty gold, or the Worthington fortune must be destroyed. But Churchill at this point finds himself with one hand tied so that he cannot grapple with this issue. No, the hand is not tied — it is busy with the other values: love, loveliness, and the need to win for Cynthia a social status "worthy" of her exquisite self. So the grand contest for control of the state legislature becomes no more than a means to Jethro's end of humbling the elder Worthington so that he will allow his son to marry Cynthia. This romantic consummation is bought at the expense of nearly every respectable value that Churchill has introduced — a point which I believe is too obvious to require further elucidation.

The form which the novel assumes thus becomes one in which the love story dominates and the liberal social values are of no real importance.

And so with the other novels: in every one the intellectual interests and the social issues which make the rising action both important and exciting have to be cast aside somehow because the conflict of the rising action leads toward disaster for the hero and heroine. Honora Leffingwell (*A Modern Chronicle*) cannot reasonably sell herself again and again, each time to a higher bidder, and rise by this means through levels of taste, refinement, gentility, and beauty of spirit. Yet she does, and Churchill shows no awareness of the irony of his tale. The appalling hypocrisies of a system in which the teachings of Jesus, the apostle of poverty and humility, are owned and administered by millionaires lead toward a crisis in the life of the Reverend Mr. Hodder that must bring disaster. In that novel, we have seen, the issue is developed at such length that there is no time for a denouement. The action simply stops. No one is hurt. Nothing is resolved. In the last two novels discussed here Churchill evades his intolerable issue by translating it into a new set of terms: in effect he abandons his issue. Hugh Paret moves to California (A Far Country indeed), forgets the financial and political evils which harried his implicated conscience into a nervous collapse, and finds an "answer" in the new science. This is no answer to the issues of the rising action. The complete abandonment of the conflict of *The Dwelling-Place of Light* is, I trust, fresh in the reader's mind.

It becomes apparent from this examination of Churchill's novels how dependent the structure of a work of fiction is upon the author's philosophy. Whether he thinks himself a philosopher or not, whether, indeed, he is aware that he has any basic assumptions, the novelist builds his work as an expression of the cosmology he accepts. It is easy to imagine that in ages of strong belief the problem which we have set forth in these chapters would not arise: the artist would speak for his people and his time; there would be for him no choice among assumptions, for he would be unaware that more than one view of reality existed. The unity and integrity of artistic expression in the world's great ages bear unceasing testimony to this truth. In a period of fundamental change in thought, such as that from 1859 to the present, the writer who deals with man in society finds himself confused not only in what he believes but also by the medium, the artistic tradition, with which he works. Impressed and startled by the findings of materialistic science, clinging, perhaps in confusion, to the idealism of the transcendentalists, he is also oppressed by the moral traditionalism which we have come to associate with the word Victorian. This confusion of thought patterns is thrice confounded when his traditional medium — the well-made dramatic novel — offers a form for which he has no ready alternative. If he accepts this traditional form, or any parts of it, he will find his ideas modified by it; and yet he has problem enough to cling to his new ideas without the added burden of devising a new artistic medium through which to express them. Small wonder that a half-hearted pioneer like Churchill failed! He might as well have tried to carry a nine-room Victorian mansion, complete with furniture, over the Rockies in a prairie schooner.

Churchill's dilemma is interesting because it is so open. While he reverenced gentility, social position, old homes, and fine manners, he strongly believed in social justice and a good life that depended on finer things than material decorations and snobbishness. The constant reality of these two attractions in his novels is astonishing now as we reach the middle of this great century; for today we have learned, not indeed to resolve the dilemma or to integrate the duality of an outlook like Churchill's, but to refrain from posing such questions so baldly and openly and revealing so clearly that we do not dare to face them.

VIII

Theodore Dreiser: The Wonder and Terror of Life

THEODORE DREISER (1871–1945) drank his inspiration from both branches of the divided stream. He has been described as a pessimist, a socialist, a communist; he has been said to embody the antithesis of American transcendentalism; he has himself acknowledged beliefs in the meaninglessness of life, in the moral autonomy of the superman, in the ultimate value and dignity of the individual. In his later works he has placed mind above matter. And even while he was writing his early books he believed in a mystical Cosmic Consciousness that one would hardly have suspected from reading those books. His mixture of despair and idealism, of wonder and fear, of pity and guilt, of chemistry and intuition has given us the most moving and powerful novels of the naturalistic tradition. Examined chronologically, they reveal naturalistic ideas struggling to find a structure by which the novel could move without turning upon crucial ethical choices. They also reveal a continuous *ethical* questioning of tradition, dogma, received morality, and social "justice." Thus they always contain the antithesis of their materialistic premises. Between the poles of this tension is Dreiser's "naturalism." It moves, during his literary career, through phases of objectivity, resignation, and protest toward the groping affirmation of spirit that presides over and, oddly, defeats his final work.

Psychologically, Dreiser is himself a divided stream of pity and guilt, of wonder and terror, of objectivity and responsibility. He

observes a world without meaning, yet he also responds to a compelling need to believe. Misery in any form moved the young
Dreiser to tears. Of his brother, to whom he does not appear to
have been especially close, he wrote: "A—— always seemed more
or less thwarted in his ambitions, and whenever I saw him I felt
sad, because, like so many millions of others in this grinding world,
he had never had a real chance. Life is so casual, and luck comes
to many who sleep and flies from those who try." [1] And one sees
that to him his brother was a symbol of all human sorrow and
thwarted potentiality.

Elsewhere he remarked: "I was never tired of looking at the hot,
hungry, weary slums." [2] "I was honestly and sympathetically interested in the horrible deprivations inflicted upon others, their
weaknesses of mind and body, afflictions of all sizes and sorts, the
way so often they blundered or were driven by internal chemic
fires." [3] Again, he was so moved by these words in a letter from a
girl he had abandoned that he used them almost verbatim in *The
"Genius"* more than twenty years later: "I stood by the window
last night and looked out on the street. The moon was shining and
those dead trees over the way were waving in the wind. I saw the
moon on that little pool of water over in the field. It looked like
silver. Oh, Theo, I wish I were dead." [4]

Throughout *A Book about Myself* one of the dominant notes
is Dreiser's wondering sympathy for the pain which life inflicts in
the form of hunger, weariness, and uncertainty on those whom
poverty and suffering have already rendered inarticulate. He was
ever "sensitive to the brevity of life and what one may do in a given
span." [5] In Pittsburgh he was curious about the captains of industry, but "It was the underdog that always interested me more than
the upper one, his needs, his woes, his simplicities." [6] "Indeed," he
writes, "I could never think of the work being done in any factory
or institution without passing from that work to the lives behind
it, the separate and distinct dramas of their individual lives." [7] A
less sensitive and sympathetic man would have either fled from
such painful sights or, if flight were impossible, developed a cynical indifference and saved his pity for more gratifying exercise. He

had, furthermore, experienced no little of the poverty for which he pitied others. His autobiography is full of the poignancy of his hungry craving for comfort, travel, finery, and the leisure to know sophisticated men and glamorous women.

Dreiser's repeated references in his early books to the "chemical compound which is youth," the "chemic force" within the mind, "the chemic formula which works to reproduce the species," show that he believed in a sort of mechanistic psychology. He did not pretend to comprehend the workings of the mind, but he was, *apparently*, sure that there is nothing transcendental in it. This real but as yet unexplained phenomenon of human thought and vitality he deprived of some of its mystery by naming it "chemic." The notion that mental activity is a chemical reaction is not, of course, a full explanation of that activity, and nowhere does Dreiser suggest that it does constitute such a full explanation. He still recognized some wonderful mystery, some all-important force, which gives life its wonder and terror and meaning. Again and again in his autobiography he broods over the impermanence of life and his conviction that only living is of absolute value:

I could see the tiny sands of my little life's hourglass sifting down, and what was I achieving? Soon the strength of time, the love time, the gay time, of color and romance, would be gone, and if I had not spent it fully, joyously, richly what would there be left for me, then? The joys of a mythical heaven or hereafter played no part in my calculations. When one was dead one was dead for all time. Hence the reason for the heartbreak over failure here and now; the awful tragedy of a love lost, a youth never properly enjoyed. Think of living and yet not living in so thrashing a world as this, the best of one's hours passing unused or not properly used. Think of seeing this tinkling phantasmagoria of pain and pleasure, beauty and all its sweets, go by, and yet being compelled to be a bystander, a mere onlooker, enhungered but never satisfied! [8]

This yearning is everywhere in his books; it is a part of his temperament which we must feel in order to understand the peculiar qualities that he brought to his writing. As a materialist, then, he recognized that man is not in control of his destiny:

Most of these young men [reporters] looked upon life as a fierce, grim struggle in which no quarter was either given or taken, and in which all men laid traps, lied, squandered, erred through illusion; a conclusion with which I now most heartily agree.[9]

In this connection the account he gives of his first acquaintance with the works of Herbert Spencer, in about 1893, is worthy of extended quotation:

At this time I had the fortune to discover Huxley and Tyndall and Herbert Spencer, whose introductory volume to his *Synthetic Philosophy* (*First Principles*) quite blew me, intellectually, to bits. Hitherto, until I had read Huxley, I had some lingering filaments of Catholicism trailing about me, faith in the existence of Christ, the soundness of his moral and sociologic deductions, the brotherhood of man. But on reading *Science and Hebrew Tradition* and *Science and Christian Tradition,* and finding both Old and New Testaments to be not compendiums of revealed truth but mere records of religious experiences, and very erroneous ones at that, and then taking up First Principles and discovering that all I deemed substantial — man's place in nature, his importance in the universe, this, too, too solid earth, man's very identity save as an infinitesimal speck of energy or a "suspended equation" drawn or blown here and there by larger forces in which he moved quite unconsciously as an atom — all questioned and dissolved into other and less understandable things, I was completely thrown down in my conceptions or non-conceptions of life.

Up to this time there had been in me a blazing and unchecked desire to get on and the feeling that in doing so we did get somewhere; now in its place was the definite conviction that spiritually one got nowhere, and there was no hereafter, that one lived and had his being because one had to, and that it was of no importance. Of one's ideals, struggles, deprivations, sorrows and joys, it could only be said that they were chemic compulsions, something which for some inexplicable but unimportant reason responded to and resulted from the hope of pleasure and the fear of pain. Man was a mechanism, undevised and uncreated, and a badly and carelessly driven one at that.

I fear that I cannot make you feel how these things came upon me in the course of a few weeks' reading and left me numb, my gravest fears as to the unsolvable disorder and brutality of life eternally verified. . . . There was of course this other [note the dichotomy] matter of necessity, internal chemical compulsion, to which I had to respond whether I would or no. I was daily facing a round of duties which now more than ever verified all that I had suspected and that these books proved. With a gloomy eye I began to watch how the chemical — and their children, the mechanical — forces operated through man and outside him, and this under my very eyes . . . and when I read Spencer I could only sigh. All I could think of was that since nature would not or could not do anything for man, he must, if he could, do something for himself; and of this I saw no prospect, he being a product of these selfsame accidental, indifferent and bitterly cruel forces.[10]

Science did not appeal to Dreiser. He had had so much experience with human misery that it did not seem to him possible to achieve any reasoned explanation of the riddle of life. On the contrary he was endlessly impressed by the instances he saw of life's steady and purposeless flux: "What a queer, haphazard, disconnected thing this living was!" ". . . life is haphazard and casual and cruel; to some lavish, to others niggardly." "But as I wandered about I realized . . . that life was a baseless, shifting thing, its seeming ties uncertain and unstable and that that which one day we held dear was tomorrow gone, to come no more." "The tangle of life, its unfairness and indifference to the moods and longings of any individual, swept over me once more weighing me down far beyond the power of expression." [11] This wonder at the ceaseless, confusing flux of life is elaborated in his book of "philosophy," the very title of which — *Hey Rub-a-Dub-Dub; A Book of the Mystery and Terror and Wonder of Life* — is an expression of his characteristic attitude toward cosmic forces:

But these [justice, truth, etc.] have been assumed, in an absolute and not a relative sense, to be attributes of a Supreme Being who is all-just, all-truthful, all-merciful, all-tender, rather than as mechanic or, if one accepts the created theory of life, as an intelligently and yet not moralistically worked-out system of minor arrangements, reciprocations and minute equations, which have little to do with the aspects and movements of much larger forces of which as yet we know nothing and which at first glance hinder rather than aid the intellect in perceiving the ultimate possibilities of the governing force in any direction. Indeed the rough balance or equation everywhere seen and struck between element and element, impulse and impulse . . . really indicates nothing more than this rough approximation to equation in everything — force with matter, element with element — as an offset to incomprehensible and, to mortal minds, even horrible and ghastly extremes and disorders; nothing more. For in face of all the schemes and contrivances whereby man may live in harmony with his neighbor there is the contrary fact that all these schemes are constantly being interfered with by contrary forces, delays, mistaken notions, dreams which produce inharmony. This can mean nothing if not an inherent impulse in Nature that makes for change and so rearrangement, regardless of any existing harmonies or balances, plus the curious impulse in man and Nature (inertia?) which seems to wish to avoid change.[12]

The combination of his observations with his philosophy could produce only moral and ethical agnosticism; and indeed if his autobiography is to be relied upon Dreiser had lost faith in conventional moral codes long before he had come upon the writings of Spencer. We find him declaring that

The world, as I see it now, has trussed itself up too helplessly with too many strings of convention, religion, dogma. . . . Is it everybody's business to get married and accept all the dictates of conventional society — that is, bear and rear children according to a given social or religious theory? . . . And, furthermore, I am inclined to suspect that the monogamous standard to which the world has been tethered much too harshly for a thousand years or more now is entirely wrong. I do not believe that it is Nature's only or ultimate way of continuing or preserving itself. Nor am I inclined to accept the belief that it produces the highest type of citizen.[13]

And not only did he distrust the unthinking Christian repression of sex — he was concerned with the importance of the sexual urge in normal human life and with the impossibility of giving an authentic or rounded picture of human activity without taking full cognizance of its ubiquitous pressure and stimulation:

While it is true that some of the minor professors of psychoanalysis are offering what they are pleased to term the "sublimation of the holophilic (or sex) impulse" into more "useful," or, at any rate, more agreeable fields of effort via suppression or restraint, this in my judgment is little more than a sop, and an obvious one, to the moralists. What is actually true is that via sex gratification — or perhaps better, its ardent and often defeated pursuit — comes most or all that is most distinguished in art, letters and our social economy and progress generally. It may be and usually is "displaced," "referred," "transferred," "substituted by," "identified with" desires for wealth, preferment, distinction and what not, but underneath each and every one of such successes must primarily be written a deep and abiding craving for women, or some one woman, in whom the sex desires of any one person for the time being are centered. "Love" or "lust" (and the one is but an intellectual sublimation of the other) moves the seeker in every field of effort.[14]

A warm, boundless human sympathy; a tremendous vital lust for life with a conviction that man is the end and measure of all things in a world which is nevertheless without purpose or standards; moral, ethical, and religious agnosticism; contact with the scientific thought of the late nineteenth century which emphasized the power and scope of mechanical laws over human desires; belief in a chemical-mechanistic explanation of the human machine; plus a constant yearning for faith — these are the elements which Dreiser brought to the writing of his novels. Determinism as a working hypothesis did not attract him because he was more interested in the mystery and terror and wonder of life itself than in tracing those forces which might account for and so dispel the mystery.[15]

By knowing Dreiser's life and character one avoids the pitfall of assuming that his naturalism is derived primarily from other writers. Of literary "influences" it is sufficient to indicate that Dreiser had been urged to read Zola[16] but had not read him when he wrote *Sister Carrie*,[17] although he had been considerably impressed by a Zolaesque novel composed by one of his friends on a Chicago newspaper.[18] On the other hand, he had devoured Balzac as early as 1893–1894.[19] If literary influences were to be pursued, they would obviously point toward realism; but our concern here is to analyze the form which the naturalistic impulse received in his novels, rather than to search out the exact sources of that impulse in his reading.

Dreiser's "naturalism" found expression in four distinct stages. Different ideas about the body of theory just presented appear in succeeding novels and give them different significant forms — until we come to his last novels, where the predominance of materialistic, non-teleological theory has gone, and in its place appears a solid affirmation of tradition and moral restraint as the values capable of resisting the deteriorating effects of modern society.

～ ～

In the first stage Dreiser was expounding his conviction of the essential purposelessness of life and attacking the conventional ethical codes which to him seemed to hold men to standards of conduct that had no rational basis in fact, while they condemned others without regard to what Dreiser thought might be the real merits of their situations. The first half of this program — expounding the purposelessness of life — is the backbone of his first novel, *Sister Carrie,* published in 1900. Through a queer juxtaposition of incidents, and with only small regard for the worthiness of their impulses, one character achieves fame and comfort while another loses his wealth, social position, pride, and finally his life.

Into this novel Dreiser has brought all the vivid reality of his own experience with the dreary, beaten, downtrodden life of those who have no money, no background, no sophistication, and no especial talent. With a deep compassion that never assumes the right to pass moral judgment upon the actions of his characters, he shows Carrie Meeber coming to Chicago from the country, drearily passing from one ill-paid and health-breaking job to another, and at length, jobless and depressed by the thought of having to return defeated to the country, setting up housekeeping with Drouet, a "drummer" whom she had met on the train as she first entered the city.

At this crucial instance begins Carrie's rise in the world. As a "fallen woman" she is in no wise judged; and even more astonishing, Drouet is shown to be flashy, crude, essentially shallow, but nevertheless at the antipodes from villainy. He is goodhearted and generous; in fact he has every intention of marrying Carrie. With this social and financial advance over the miserable narrowness that characterized the home life of the sister with whom she had been living, Carrie begins to recognize class differences, to long for "better" things, even to sense Drouet's limitations. Drouet's friend

Hurstwood represents the next higher level of culture and wealth. He is manager of a prosperous saloon, he owns a fine house, and his family is eagerly climbing the social ladder. When he meets Carrie he falls desperately in love with her and, in what almost amounts to an abduction, abandons his family, steals $10,000 from his employers, and flees with her through Canada and into New York.

From this point the fall of Hurstwood and the rise of Carrie are depicted in antiphonal relationship. Hurstwood's degeneration is a remarkable representation of the meaningless, almost unmotivated sort of tragedy that art had, until then, conspired to ignore. His wife's grasping jealousy and pettiness impel him toward Carrie, and his being seen with her gives his wife grounds for a divorce action. It is by the merest chance that he finds the safe open on the very night when he had planned to disappear. His theft of the money results from a frantic impulse which he is too weak to resist. When he tries to return the cash to the safe, he finds that the lock has clicked shut. So the theft is consummated by an accident. He is later forced to return the money, but he never recovers his self-esteem. In New York he takes a half interest in a second-rate saloon and after a time loses his investment. Then he dawdles, first looking for jobs, finally sitting in hotels instead of looking; at length he stays home, reading newspapers endlessly and hoarding the little money he has left. The change in his character from an affluent good-fellow to a seedy miser is convincing and pathetic.

Some men never recognize the turning in the tide of their abilities. It is only in chance cases, where a fortune or a state of success is wrested from them, that the lack of ability to do as they did formerly becomes apparent. Hurstwood, set down under new conditions, was in a position to see that he was no longer young.[20]

Carrie stays with him as long as she can; but when she gets a place in a stage chorus she leaves him in order to room with a girl who is dancing in the same chorus. Hurstwood goes down and down — to poverty, destitution, begging, starvation, and finally suicide.

Carrie, on the other hand, rises rapidly from the moment she leaves Hurstwood. She graduates from the chorus to a minor role:

Evidently the part was not intended to take precedence as Miss Madena [Carrie] is not often on the stage, but the audience, with the characteristic perversity of such bodies, selected for itself. The little Quakeress was marked for a favourite the moment she appeared, and thereafter easily held attention and applause. The vagaries of fortune are indeed curious.

The last sentence of this newspaper account of Carrie's first step forward on the stage emphasizes the major theme of the book — how curious are the vagaries of fortune. As Hurstwood is drawing nearer to his sordid death, Carrie climbs rapidly until she is earning what is to her an unheard-of salary, living in one of the finest hotels in the city, and receiving proposals and attentions from men as far superior to Hurstwood at his best as he had been to the flashy Drouet. "Even had Hurstwood returned in his original beauty and glory, he could not now have allured her." The book ends on a note of uncertainty. Carrie is not to be thought of as having attained any final goal. She is still longing and wondering, "an illustration of the devious ways by which one who feels, rather than reasons, may be led in the pursuit of beauty. Though often disillusioned, she was still waiting for that halcyon day when she should be led forth among dreams become real."

Shocking to contemporary readers — or reviewers, for there were few readers at first — was the amoral attitude from which *Sister Carrie* was written.[21] Nowhere is a moral pointed. There is no inevitable punishment for transgression, no suggestion that there ought to be. In one passage Dreiser even appeals to nature as against conventional moral standards and intimates that the only evil in what is ordinarily considered sinful comes from the codes which call it evil, because they introduce elements of guilt and hypocrisy into conduct:

He [Drouet] could not help what he was going to do. He could not see clearly enough to wish to do differently. He was drawn by his innate desire to act the old pursuing part. He would need to delight himself with Carrie as surely as he would need to eat his heavy breakfast. He might suffer the least rudimentary twinge of conscience in whatever he did, and *in just so far he was evil and sinning*. But whatever twinges of conscience he might have would be rudimentary . . .[22]

What is perfectly natural or spontaneous is good: the brooding mind makes it sin. Conventional morals may thus be rigid and unrealistic; but they do reflect a reality that transcends (while it includes) simple mechanism. This is what the transcendentalist called spirit. Dreiser's feeling for this transcendental reality appears clearly in the following passage, where morals are not denied even though conventional morality has been rejected:

> For all the liberal analysis of Spencer and our modern naturalistic philosophers, we have but an infantile perception of morals. There is more in the subject than mere conformity to a law of evolution. It is yet deeper than conformity to things of earth alone. It is more involved than we, as yet, perceive. Answer, first, why the heart thrills; explain wherefore some plaintive note goes wandering about the world, undying; make clear the rose's subtle alchemy evolving its ruddy lamp in light and rain. In the essence of these facts lie the first principles of morals.[23]

Dreiser has been shown to distrust the concept of purpose or ethical design in the universe; yet such passages as that just quoted betray him in the characteristically naturalistic action of substituting the compelling, vital mystery of Nature for the failing God of orthodox religion.

Here the transcendental roots thrust boldly up, showing that the apparent line separating the spiritual tree from the natural earth is only apparent: the tree of spirit grows from the earth. Yet the confidence that nature reveals spirit and design is not as strong with Dreiser, who has come to see the impossibility of reducing all phenomena to orderly laws, as it was with those earlier devotees of science who transferred their religious zeal directly to Nature, never doubting that the answers to all men's problems were to be found by patient searching through her spacious domain. For them Nature was perfect meaning; for Dreiser the Design is perpetually tantalizing and elusive.

A consciously scientific use of detail appears when Dreiser brings chemical physiology to the explanation of Hurstwood's mental condition as he is beginning his final downward plunge:

Constant comparison between his old state and his new showed a balance for the worse, which produced a constant state of gloom or, at least, depression. Now, it has been shown experimentally that a constantly subdued frame of mind produces certain poisons in the blood, called katastates, just as virtuous feelings of pleasure and delight produce helpful chemicals called anastates. The poisons generated by remorse inveigh against the system, and eventually produce marked physical deterioration. To these Hurstwood was subject.[24]

This, in small compass, is a clear-cut instance of the influence of science upon Dreiser's method: he is approaching his problem with a new set of instruments. The chemical explanation of mental conditions is of a piece with the amoral outlook and the change of focus away from ethical plot-conflict toward the dispassionate *observation* of life. This latter problem brings one to the heart of what is new in the form of *Sister Carrie*.

Structurally the novel consists of the two life cycles which are opposed to each other in studied balance. What *Sister Carrie* exhibits that is most characteristically naturalistic is the complete absence of ethical plot-complication. The movement of the novel does not depend upon acts of will by the central figures. There is no suspense waiting to be resolved by a decision which will be judged in terms of absolute ethical standards. The movement is the movement of life — skillfully selected and represented by the artist, to be sure, but still a movement which has little resemblance to the typical plot that begins with a choice or a crucial action and ends with the satisfaction of the forces and the passions set in motion by that choice. The difference is fundamental. The novels of such writers as Thackeray and Trollope have complication, climax, and denouement in every instance. *Sister Carrie* has no such movement. There is no suspense created because the art of the novelist is directed by an entirely different motive. Dreiser is not manipulating a portion of life; he is observing it. It is the quality of the lives represented that moves the reader, not the excitement of what the characters do. Here Dreiser reflects the impressionism of Crane and strikes a note that we hear later in the work of Sherwood Anderson, where a very different sort of writer has in a different way presented the qualities of experience instead of choices and results. Having deprived his novel of the conventional structure, Dreiser supplies the two cycles — Carrie's rise and Hurst-wood's descent. These two cycles embody the principle of change which Dreiser finds fundamental to all life and all natural process. In a naïve mechanist's novel they would pretend to embody social laws. Not so with Dreiser.

Dreiser is primarily a novelist, a student of humanity, and only incidentally a philosopher. Human values are never subordinated to philosophical implications. *Sister Carrie* is more important as a story than for the ideas it contains. The reader is interested in Carrie as a person who faces problems comparable to his own; and if the reader is not to be offended by the course of the story, the successes and failures of the characters must in some way answer to the reader's notion of their worth as human beings. Because of this fact, ethical standards can hardly be eliminated from any novel. Carrie's rise, even though accidental and not, by conventional standards, "deserved," is welcome because she is an appealing character; and Hurstwood's degeneration, distressing though it may be, is not unbearably offensive because Hurstwood has qualities which cause him to lose some of the reader's sympathy. The philosopher in Dreiser makes concessions to the novelist because his heart is in league with humanity. This is another way of saying that what happens in a piece of fiction must be probable, and probability includes the satisfaction, to some degree, of the moral sense. Hardy's *Return of the Native* appears to turn upon the cruelest coincidences, and yet each character in it experiences a morally probable fate. So with Dreiser. One cannot write stories in which, just as the crisis is approaching, the villain is killed by a falling meteor. Such things occur in life, but they cannot in novels, which in their design and organization depict a truth free from the outrageous accidents of actuality. With these reservations, which return us to the fact that the novelist cares more for human suffering than for demonstrating the principle of cosmic indifference, we may return to the assertion that *Sister Carrie* is organized to depict the essential purposelessness of life. The plot structure of conventional fiction is abandoned for the new organization that answers to Dreiser's view of life.

But though he recognized the operation of external force he is not, in *Sister Carrie*, concerned with an experimental demonstration of the nature of that operation. Rather he is concerned with the pathos of human life and with the constant inscrutable change that attends it. We come, in the last analysis, to a matter of emphasis: one may study the way external forces operate upon man, attempting to lay bare the secrets of their action; or one may see life through the eyes of the objects of these forces, with the wonder and terror of the changes unexplained. Dreiser does a little of both: he shows clearly enough how Hurstwood and Carrie change as they do; but mostly he is concerned with bringing out the shifting, uncertain, mysterious nature of life as it appears when being acted upon by forces which it cannot fathom and which — most terrible truth — have no purpose that can be related to the purposes of men.

Dreiser believes in a determinism which destroys or modifies the moral view of conduct. He is, further, impressed by the inscrutability of fortune, the lack of meaning and purpose in the action of external force. Between these two smothering convictions flourishes his affirmation — his belief in the vitality and importance of life. It is upon the latter that one's attention is directed in *Sister Carrie*. The inscrutable variations of fortune serve chiefly to underline the positive quality of living. Throughout the book it is this quality of life — shifting, elusive, unaccountable — that holds our attention, rather than the spectacle of carefully analyzed forces operating under "experimental" conditions. Dreiser's affirmation of the human spirit is in the transcendental tradition.[25]

The generalizations applied to *Sister Carrie* are also true of *Jennie Gerhardt* (1911). The difference between the two books which is of importance to this study is a difference of emphasis. In *Sister Carrie* conventional ethical codes are assumed to be invalid or at least impractical for evaluating life as it is, while the story is largely pointed toward demonstrating the unpredictable purposelessness of all things. In *Jennie Gerhardt* this emphasis is reversed. Ceaseless and unintentioned change has become an accepted hypothesis with Dreiser, while the story is devoted to a consideration of the moral and ethical standards according to which society (supposedly) operates. The previous assumption that they are unreal here becomes the point at issue, the substance of Dreiser's thesis. He shows how the life of a "kept woman" is blighted by society's treatment of what it considers her immorality. The criticism is pointed by the heroine's being a rich and lovely character (which illustrates again the contention that Dreiser is primarily a novelist, in league with humanity), and the effect of the story is to show how utterly inadequate are standard Christian ethics for the judgment or guidance of conduct in a world that does not, as Dreiser sees it, correspond to the notion of reality upon which that ethical code is based.

Jennie Gerhardt is the daughter of a stupidly devout German glass blower. She is one of a large family which lives in the poor district of Columbus, Ohio, at a bare subsistence level. She is not a semi-moron (as one critic has said) but a girl rich and direct in feeling — the sort of person whose feelings take the place of thoughts:

There are natures born to the inheritance of flesh that come without understanding, and that go again without seeming to have wondered why. Life, so long as they endure it, is a true wonderland, a thing of infinite beauty, which could they but wander into it wonderingly, would be heaven enough. . . . From her earliest youth goodness and mercy had molded her every impulse.[26]

At the hotel where she scrubs floors, Senator Brander is impressed by her beauty, decides to marry her, and presently seduces her.

The Senator dies suddenly, before he is able to carry out his intention of marrying Jennie, leaving her pregnant. After the child is born, the disgraced family moves to Cleveland where Jennie presently meets the man who is to be the center of her thoughts for the rest of her life. Lester Kane comes from a wealthy Cincinnati family of carriage makers. He is generous, forceful, direct, and the slightest bit coarse-grained. In spite of his wealth and good breeding, the reader is made to feel that he is, emotionally, less beautifully constructed than Jennie, though he is capable of appreciating her fine nature and is, indeed, worlds beyond her culturally. Most of the book is devoted to their changing relations.

He keeps her in various apartments, supplying her liberally with money, always half intending to marry her but never quite making up his mind to disturb the comfortable *status quo*. Jennie's most pressing concern, after her love for Lester, is to keep her little girl near her without having Lester, whom she has foolishly kept in ignorance, learn of the child's existence. She is happy in her love for him and in being able to help her impoverished family with money. Lester's discovery of the child precipitates a crisis, and he thinks of leaving her. But he has become so attached to her goodness that he cannot bear the thought of separation. When his family discovers the connection and tries to break it off he defiantly installs Jennie in a large house in Chicago, and a period of precarious happiness follows.

Then forces conspire to take Lester away from her. His father dies, leaving Lester's inheritance contingent upon his abandoning Jennie. His family brings all its persuasive force to bear. And, to sweep aside the last hesitation, Lester is attracted by a cultivated and wealthy widow who is deeply in love with him. As always, Jennie is wholly unselfish in wanting Lester to do what is best for himself — and it is he who is uncertain which way to turn, drawn at once by loyalty to Jennie, fascination for Mrs. Gerald, the desire to retain his accustomed wealth and to be active in his father's business, and the influence exerted by his family and the polite society which wants him to become finally "respectable."

But he did not want to do this. The thought was painful to him — objectionable in every way. Jennie was growing in mental acumen. She was beginning to see things quite as clearly as he did. She was not a cheap, ambitious, climbing creature. She was a big woman and a good one. It would be a shame to throw her down, and besides she was good-looking. . . . It is an exceptional thing to find beauty, youth, compatibility, intelligence, your own point of view — softened and charmingly emotionalized — in another.

The reader cannot entirely blame Lester when he finally gives Jennie up, for he understands the many subtle pressures — which Dreiser so fully presents — that condition his exercise of volition. Lester could choose readily enough if he knew exactly what he wanted. What makes the influence of external forces credible is the wealth of careful documentation that Dreiser presents so that the reader may actually see all the influences that work upon Lester and paralyze his will. Social ostracism and the loss of a large part of his independent fortune, which makes his need for a share in his father's estate more pressing, finally turn the balance against Jennie — though it is she who urges him to go.

At a subsequent meeting he tries to explain his feelings:

"I was just as happy with you as I ever will be. It isn't myself that's important in this transaction apparently; the individual doesn't count much in the situation. . . . All of us are more or less pawns. We're moved about like chessmen by circumstances over which we have no control. . . .

"After all, life is more or less of a farce," he went on a little bitterly. "It's a silly show. The best we can do is to hold our personality intact. It doesn't appear that integrity has much to do with it." [27]

Stricken with a fatal illness, he calls her to his deathbed, where he tells her,

"I haven't been satisfied with the way we parted. It wasn't the right thing, after all. I haven't been any happier. I'm sorry. I wish now, for my own peace of mind, that I hadn't done it. . . . It wasn't right. The thing wasn't worked out right from the start; but that wasn't your fault. I'm sorry. I wanted to tell you that. I'm glad I'm here to do it."

The story ends with Jennie at the station for a last glimpse of the coffin. Nowhere has Dreiser matched the pathos of these closing lines:

Before her was stretching a vista of lonely years down which she was steadily gazing. Now what? She was not so old yet. There were those two orphan children to raise. They would marry and leave after a while, and then what? Days and days in endless reiteration, and then — ?

A novel with a "kept woman" for its central figure was somewhat unusual in 1911, but when that kept woman is presented as good and admirable, as possessing positive virtues which raise her quite above the general run of socially minded people, then we recognize a novel in which conventional values are challenged, in which the approach that is taken to the problem of man in society is not an ordinary one.

This approach constitutes the philosophy. As in *Sister Carrie,* it can be stated as a belief in determinism accompanied by a conviction that the appointed course of events has neither purpose nor an order that is accessible to man's intellect. What strikes the reader again and again is the unreasonable way in which events pile up to direct the lives of the characters. Luck is more important than careful planning, and "goodness" does not necessarily appeal to the unknown or nonexistent controllers of destiny. The evidence shows that a thousand circumstances enfold man in their invisible garment of steel; no one is capable of seeing the pattern according to which the garment is woven; one only feels the pressures which check or direct him in particular movements. Conventional moral standards constitute one part of this garment; they control Jennie's life and prevent her from achieving happiness.

The same kind of thinking is extended to Dreiser's idea of the human will. He recognizes will as a function of what he might call personality. His people act from apparently autonomous impulses. Jennie's goodness, for example, he regards as something which need not and indeed cannot be accounted for. But at the same time, by the approach outlined in the preceding pages, Dreiser shows that the will is not free to operate independently, that it has not the power to bring its impulses to fulfillment. Thus instead of attempting to go behind the will and identify the components of its apparently free volitions, he follows these impulses into the world and shows us precisely why and how they are thwarted by social and economic forces. We might say that he admits free will with reference to volition but denies it with reference to action. One can wish freely, but one cannot freely carry out one's wishes.

In a world so envisaged, good intentions do not necessarily bear good results. Nor is what is conventionally called evil punished. Hence standard ethics are discredited because they do not represent a realistic interpretation of social relations. They do not constitute the genuine forces which make for social cohesion and regulate the conduct of civilized man. It would be useless to blame someone for conditions beyond his control. This assumption is fundamental in *Jennie Gerhardt*. As the hero says, "The best we can do is to hold our personality intact." Jennie's goodness is valued more highly than the society which destroys her chance for happiness. Dreiser does not show that there may be extenuating circumstances to pardon the sinfulness of the "fallen woman." He denies that she is sinful; he deplores the moral codes which, failing to restrain her first slip, inflict a consciousness of guilt upon her ever after; he considers her good and beautiful, and the reader is led to conclude that Lester Kane was foolish (or very unlucky) not to have married her. These conclusions show that Dreiser believes in a spiritual truth which exists above the flux and error of actuality. He does not account for it, but he affirms its presence in Jennie and he deplores through his novel the social conditions which blight its growth and free expression.

All these abstract notions depend for their conviction upon the emotional weight which Dreiser is able to attach to the personality of Jennie. That he succeeds with his message is due to his success in making of her a rich and lovely woman, a creature who is all good and whose simple heart is capable of endless devotion. Jennie is undoubtedly his richest creation. The reader's sympathies are entirely with her. Her sufferings are so real that the reader is not aware of an auctorial "message," for he reaches the conclusions here described through his emotional response to the events of the story. This point is important, for it shows that the pathos of Jennie's life is the outstanding fact of the novel, the fact upon which depend any ideas that the reader may gather. As a work of art *Jennie Gerhardt* is highly successful, the ideas upon which it is based serve first of all to create a certain aesthetic effect and do not obtrude themselves in the way of that effect. It is too bad that Jennie should suffer, and the system is to be deplored for making her suffer, but that is not tantamount to saying that the institution of marriage, for example, should be rejected. It would indeed detract from the pathos of Jennie's situation if the author were crusading for change. The conditions which crush her must, for the purposes of the novel, be regarded as unchangeable.

~ ~

In the second stage of his development Dreiser added the idea of the superman to the two main ideas which I have described. When one had found that life was meaningless and morals absurdly in-adequate, the next step was to conclude that the only good lay in exercising one's will to power. The philosophy of the superman was conveniently available to enable Dreiser to take this step; and he wrote four novels about the activities of supermen in the modern business world. Nietzsche's philosophy saw in the superman the only hope for the betterment of mankind. Dreiser may have known this aspect of Nietzsche's thought, he may even have begun *The Financier* with the intention of demonstrating some such idea, but his study of the activities of one of the Robber Barons of the late nineteenth century seems finally to have drawn him away from the notion that the financial superman was an indispensable agent in the development of a capitalistic society.

Dreiser's "Trilogy of Desire," composed of *The Financier* (1912), *The Titan* (1914), and *The Stoic* (1947), represents his effort to set forth the life of a modern financial superman. Although written from the point of view of the superman and begun as a celebration rather than an indictment of him, these novels virtually accom-plish Jack London's avowed but unfulfilled purpose in writing *The Sea-Wolf* — to show that "the superman cannot be successful in modern life . . . he acts like an irritant in the social body." [28] This cannot be called Dreiser's purpose, however, for he never arrived at that degree of conviction which would permit him to organize a portion of the social scene and write about it as if he had thought his way through to a final conclusion about its mean-ing. It is the planlessness and inconclusiveness of life that inter-ested Dreiser. On the other hand, nearly all critics have ceased ac-cusing him of being merely a patient recorder who copied his books tediously from newspaper records. The organizing hand of the artist is always present, but its purpose is not to reduce the complexity of life to a prettily simplified pattern that answers all one's questions about cause and effect, design and purpose.

The Financier and *The Titan* contain perhaps the greatest mass of documentation to be found in any American novels in the naturalistic tradition. They are records of an epoch of American life. The career of Charles T. Yerkes, traction magnate of Philadelphia and Chicago, supplied Dreiser with the materials for his two books. Yerkes is transformed into Frank Algernon Cowperwood, and the novels record his economic and amorous affairs in minutest detail. *The Financier* takes Cowperwood from boyhood up to the panic of 1873. A "superman" devoid of ethical restraints, he goes from business to business, gaining control of the Philadelphia street-railway network, and buying cooperation from the politicians. He becomes a millionaire and is laying plans to make a billion when the Chicago fire of 1871 causes a panic which wipes out his fortune. Because he seduced the daughter of the political boss, he is at this time abandoned by those in control and made a scapegoat to appease an indignant populace. After thirteen months in prison he is pardoned just in time to regain his fortune by selling short in the panic of 1873. Here ends *The Financier*.

The Titan is longer and more detailed. It tells how Cowperwood moves to Chicago and, through bribes and cleverness, gains a number of franchises for the distribution of suburban gas. After this coup he launches into a long fight to gain control of all the Chicago street railways. The novel presents the great struggle in all its complexity, showing how banks, local politicians, legislators, governors, and newspapers are drawn into the vortex of the conflict — and how Cowperwood is finally defeated in his efforts to buy or control the entire state legislature and obtain from them a fifty-year franchise on Chicago street-railway transportation. The details of these transactions are given so fully that the reader is convinced of their authenticity: he comes from the books feeling that he has seen the whole picture, presented more minutely — and far more effectively — than it could have been presented in the best historical or economic treatise available. The facts are all there, vividly realized and brought to life. And since the affairs of Cowperwood are part and parcel of this vast economic complex, the recording of its intricacies is documentation in the closest natural-istic tradition. It is as intimately united with the story as the docu-mentation in Zola's *L'Assommoir* or *Germinal*. It is setting, condi-tion, and material for the novel; none of it is extraneous, none gratuitous, because it is all a part of Cowperwood's career.

Intermingled with Cowperwood's business dealings throughout the two novels are his amorous intrigues and domestic difficulties. One critic described *The Titan* as a "huge club-sandwich com-posed of slices of business alternating with erotic episodes," [29] and the description is an apt one, although it gives less attention than it might to the close relationship between the two sides of Cowper-wood's life that Dreiser is continually bringing out. Cowperwood's amorous escapades round out his "business" personality; they also cause violent repercussions in his various business transactions, for the women he knows quite naturally are connected with the men with whom he deals in the world of politics and finance.

It has been shown in the discussion of both *Sister Carrie* and *Jennie Gerhardt* that Dreiser's determinism is determinism *after the fact*. That is, he does not pretend to go behind an act of so-called will and show all the conditions and pressures of which it is composed. He does not pretend to set down a perfect chain of causal relationships that account for the fiction known as free will; but, admitting its existence, he does show how in its actions it is swayed and guided by "deterministic" forces beyond it — so that in effect it is relatively helpless.[30]

In *The Financier* and *The Titan* there is the same attitude toward man and society, but the situation is greatly altered by a change in one of the factors of the problem. That factor of course is Frank Algernon Cowperwood. Instead of being relatively weak like Carrie, Hurstwood, Jennie, and Lester Kane, Cowperwood is endowed with tremendous energy and ability. He is born to conquer, and he knows it. At the age of eighteen he receives a five-hundred-dollar Christmas bonus from the grain brokers to whom he has been apprenticed without salary to learn the busi-ness. Already he is indispensable — and perfectly confident:

On his way home that evening he speculated as to the nature of this business. He knew he wasn't going to stay there long, even in spite of this gift and promise of salary. They were grateful, of course; but why shouldn't they be? He was efficient, he knew that; under him things moved smoothly. It never occurred to him that he belonged in the realm of clerkdom. Those people were the kind of beings who ought to work for him, and who would. There was nothing savage in his attitude, no rage against fate, no dark fear of failure.[31]

He is selfish because his own concerns are paramount with him. In another paragraph his nature is carefully described:

Cowperwood was innately and primarily an egoist and intellectual, though blended strongly therewith was a humane and democratic spirit. We think of egoism and intellectualism as closely confined to the arts. Finance is an art. And it presents the operations of the subtlest of the intellectuals and of the egoists. Cowperwood was a financier. Instead of dwelling on the works of nature, its beauty and subtlety, to his material disadvantage, he found a happy mean, owing to the swiftness of his intellectual operations, whereby he could, intellectually and emotionally, rejoice in the beauty of life without interfering with his perpetual material and financial calculations. And when it came to women and morals, which involved so much relating to beauty, happiness, a sense of distinction and variety in living, he was but now beginning to suspect for himself at least that apart from maintaining organized society in its present form there was no basis for this one-life, one-love idea.[32]

Toward the end of *The Titan* he is still strong: "he seemed a kind of superman, and yet also a bad boy — handsome, powerful, hopeful . . . impelled by some blazing internal force which harried him on and on.[33] He is the apotheosis of individualism, the man who moves the mass, which "only moves forward because of the services of the exceptional individual." He answers to the wish "that the significant individual will always appear and will always do what his instincts tell him to do." [34]

At the end of *The Financier* Cowperwood has asserted himself stupendously, made and lost a great fortune, complicated the life of every banker and politician in Philadelphia, and yet, like Jennie and Lester Kane and Hurstwood, has been swept back and

forth by environing forces more powerful than even his intelligence and resolution. Being a larger figure, he moves in a more
elaborate complex of forces; but the forces elude his foresight and
generalship and temporarily strip him of freedom and fortune.

At the end of the great struggle related in *The Titan*, when
Cowperwood is temporarily defeated by the enmity his power
has evoked (a situation which is a better example than London
could produce of how the financial superman "acts like an irritant
in the social body"), Dreiser expatiates upon the spectacle of his
superman's career:

Rushing like a great comet to the zenith, his path a blazing
trail, Cowperwood did for the hour illuminate the terrors and
wonders of individuality. But for him also the eternal equation —
the pathos of the discovery that even giants are but pygmies, and
that an ultimate balance must be struck. Of the strange, tortured,
terrified, reflection of those who, caught in his wake, were swept
from the normal and the commonplace, what shall we say? Legislators by the hundreds were hounded from politics into their
graves; a half-hundred aldermen of various councils who were
driven grumbling or whining into the limbo of the dull, the
useless, the commonplace.

These sentences repeat the philosophy outlined earlier in connection with *Sister Carrie* and *Jennie Gerhardt*. The action of the
books involves the same wondering uncertainty, the same vision of
life as purposeless and unpredictable, the same denial of ethical
codes, the same recognition of external pressures which determine
the courses of our lives. What distinguishes *The Financier* and
The Titan from the two previous novels is, as we have seen, the
different weight given in them to the human factor in Dreiser's
equation of change. Cowperwood is a greater force than Dreiser's
earlier characters, but his position in the cosmos is essentially
the same.

In conclusion we may consider the ethical import of these books.
Hearing about them, one's reaction is that Dreiser must have
composed them as an indictment of the business methods of the
Robber Barons — to show that they were social menaces who
should have been extirpated. Doubtless some such conclusion

comes to the reader after he has finished the novels; but so long as he is reading them Cowperwood is the hero. His morals may not be held up as exemplary for American society, but his intelligence and energy make him the center of attention and concern. The reader sees the struggle though Cowperwood's eyes; he cannot avoid lending his sympathy to the owner of those eyes. He is attracted, as people always are in reality, to a man with the personal force to affect the lives of thousands of people. Further than this, Dreiser is frequently at pains to cast doubt upon the judgments which condemn Cowperwood. Early in *The Financier*, young Cowperwood gets his first lesson in the law of tooth and fang by watching a lobster devour a squid that was placed in a tank with him in a store window. The same novel ends with a parable about the black grouper, a fish which survives by virtue of its ability to change color and so deceive enemy and prey alike. We are asked,

What would you say was the intention of the overruling, intelligent, constructive force which gives to Mycteroperca this ability? To fit it to be truthful? To permit it to present an unvarying appearance which all honest life-seeking fish may know? Or would you say that subtlety, chicanery, trickery, were here at work? An implement of illusion one might readily suspect it to be, a living lie, a creature whose business it is to appear what it is not, to simulate that with which it has nothing in common, to get its living by great subtlety, the power of its enemies to forefend against which is little. The indictment is fair.

Would you say, in the face of this, that a beatific, beneficent, creative overruling power never wills that which is either tricky or deceptive?

The conclusion is that Christian ethics are illusory, that people should not be blamed for disobeying a code which, if followed, would render them unfit to survive. Indeed, he found, as Burton Rascoe writes, "an epic quality in the rise of individuals to merciless and remorseless power through the adaptation of their combative instincts to the peculiar conditions of the American struggle for existence." [35] In the same spirit Dreiser interpolates a disquisition on monogamy, his point being that Christian moral standards do not answer human needs.[36] Again, he questions the idea of divine guidance and the relation of man to nature:

How shall I explain these subtleties of temperament and desire? Life has to deal with them at every turn. They will not down, and the large, placid movements of nature outside of man's little organisms would indicate that she is not greatly concerned. We see much punishment in the form of jails, diseases, failure, and wrecks; but we also see that the old tendency is not visibly lessened. Is there no law outside of the subtle will and power of the individual to achieve? If not, it is surely high time that we knew it — one and all. We might then agree to do as we do; but there would be no silly illusions as to divine regulation.[37]

It does not follow from this denial of conventional ethics that a Cowperwood is a boon to society. He may "move the mass," but Dreiser's own story shows that he does not move it to any good end. There is no paradox here. The point is that Dreiser is thinking in terms of the individual without sufficiently considering his social function. He is condemning "Divine Law" without apparently realizing that it often corresponds to natural law. Cowperwood cannot reasonably be condemned to hell-fire for following his natural bent, and it is natural for him to strive for power; but his social value is another matter. Dreiser denies a beneficent guiding Purpose, and so removes moral blame; but he does not investigate the social function of Cowperwood. If he did, he would unquestionably recognize society's need to restrain such individuals. And he has done so since then.

The "Genius" (1915) is cut from the same block as *The Financier* and *The Titan*. Both in form and thesis it resembles those novels so closely that an extended analysis of it is unnecessary. Eugene Witla, the hero of *The "Genius,"* is a superman like Cowperwood. He is an artist rather than a financier, but otherwise he is much the same sort of person. Like Cowperwood, again, he is set loose in the turbulence of modern life and permitted to exercise his superior cunning and resourcefulness untrammeled by moral restraints or inhibiting consideration for others. Like Cowperwood he has his successes and his failures, the forces which thwart his intentions frequently being the combination of weaker people who unite in defiance of his superman self-assertion. And again, Witla's amours occupy a large portion of the story, represent the superabundance of his artistic "genius," and are responsible for several of his misfortunes. Like *The Financier* and *The Titan, The "Genius"* consists of a loosely connected sequence of events related by chronology and by the fact that Eugene Witla participates in them all. The book, furthermore, ends upon a note of wonder and uncertainty which we have found to be characteristic of Dreiser's attitude toward life at this stage. And finally, the superman hero is the center of reference and attention throughout the story. His effect upon society is not considered, for Dreiser is still brooding over the place of the individual in his meaningless cosmos. *The "Genius"* is probably also the most personal of Dreiser's books. Revelation replaces theory to a considerable degree.

The third stage in Dreiser's naturalism is marked by his conversion to socialism. Here the ideas that signalized his first stage remain, but instead of advocating individual anarchy, as he tended to do under the aegis of Nietzsche, he has come to believe that something can be accomplished toward the amelioration of social evils if men will unite in a concerted attack upon those evils. *An American Tragedy* (1925) is founded upon this point of view, although we must remember that this, like Dreiser's other novels, is first of all a human story.

An American Tragedy recounts the life of Clyde Griffiths. He is first seen in Kansas City, the child of itinerant street preachers, singing on a corner with them. He becomes a bellhop in a large hotel and there acquires a longing for the luxuries which his family cannot provide. He soon goes to Chicago where, still working as a bellhop, he meets his rich uncle Samuel, a collar manufacturer in Lycurgus, New York. The uncle later has Clyde come to Lycurgus and starts him at the bottom of his business, with every opportunity to work his way to the top. But Clyde is not accepted socially by his wealthy relatives until the fascinating Sondra Finchley takes him up — out of spite — and introduces him to the highest social set of Lycurgus. In the meantime Clyde had been sharing his loneliness with Roberta Alden, a simple country girl who was working under him in the factory. Now when he sees a promising future before him, he learns that Roberta is pregnant. In desperation, after weeks of torturing worry, he plans to take her boating in the country and "accidentally" drown her. At the final moment he lacks courage to overturn the boat, but chance — or the situation produced by the two personalities in their particular relation — completes the design in another way: seeing his despairing and horrified expression, Roberta comes toward him in the boat. He strikes out desperately to fend her off and unintentionally hits her with a camera. The boat capsizes, striking Roberta as she falls into the water, and Clyde refrains from saving her.[38]

The rest of the story is devoted to the apprehension, trial, conviction, and execution of Clyde for the murder of Roberta. As the passage referred to above indicates, Clyde himself is not perfectly sure whether or not he is guilty. Before Roberta arose and came toward him in the rowboat, he had certainly decided that he would not commit the crime he had planned. On the other hand, he instituted the expedition with murder in his heart — a fact which exerted great influence upon the final decision of the jury. The prosecution brings dozens of witnesses and traces Clyde's movements minutely. Clyde's only defense is his last-minute change of heart, for which there is no evidence and which is easily counterbalanced by the absolute proof of his murderous intentions.

The peculiar way in which the "murder" of Roberta occurred is one of the most important facts in the novel. Clyde's inability to commit the deed in cold blood is indicative of his general weakness of will. But when some kind of chance (which might be described by an omniscient psychologist as the inevitable reaction of Roberta to Clyde's horrified expression) enters the action and the boat is capsized, Clyde is given a shock which enables him to allow her to drown. The effect of this careful decription of the incident is to show that Clyde is not the master of his fate, that only under particular conditions is he able to "choose" the "evil" course that he desires to carry out. He does not really "choose" to abandon Roberta; it would be more accurate to say that he is conditioned by his weeks of planning so that when the situation enables him to overcome his scruples (equally the product of long training) he is carried along by the impetus of this conditioning to commit the act he has planned. Thus from an objective point of view one can hardly blame Clyde for an action in which he was largely a weak and helpless participant. Clyde did not willfully produce the dilemma which called forth his attempt to resolve it. His craving for wealth and social position can be understood — like his complementary lack of ethical standards — in the light of his upbringing. His weakness is contemptible to some readers, but Dreiser certainly does not contemn it. Clyde has a certain power of choice, to be sure, which Dreiser does not reduce to its ultimate chemical constituents as the first naïve naturalists thought they might finally be able to do; but that power of choice, though accepted as a factor in the problem, is shown to be conditioned by the many forces among which it exists. Jennie Gerhardt and Lester Kane had "wills" that were impotent, because of external pressures, to fulfill their desires. The same generalization holds for Clyde. In both books Dreiser's attitude toward the relation between personal will and conditioning pressures is the same, and that attitude has been sufficiently described in the preceding pages.

In *An American Tragedy,* however, there is a difference of emphasis which is intimately associated with the structure of the novel. To begin with, Clyde is doubtless the weakest of Dreiser's heroes; he has least of the inexplicable inner drive which makes a commanding personality. He begins, further, with a pitifully meager background and a narrow view of life. He is no Cowperwood or Witla superman — he has not even the charm of Carrie or Jennie. And as the novel proceeds there is so careful an attention to detail and so complete a delineation of the various experiences which add to Clyde's miserable store of ideas and ideals that the reader seems to be gaining a full insight into the forces which account for Clyde's personality.

This statement involves a good deal of oversimplification — for indeed Clyde has a certain amount of personality from the beginning which is never explained as the product of any known forces. It is, further, only a literary convention which permits the novelist to appear to be presenting all the facts of a situation. Dreiser, to be sure, presents more documentation perhaps than any other novelist has ever gathered about a comparable problem; and so the illusion of completeness achieved is less "illusory" than in any other novel which seeks to create the same illusion. The effect on the reader is to make him understand the Clyde who commits the crime in terms of the growth through which Dreiser has conducted him in the first half of the novel. Clyde is more fully accounted for by the nature of his environment than any other character of Dreiser's. The characters in *Sister Carrie* and *Jennie Gerhardt* begin, so to speak, in mid-career; they enter the story with attributes the sources of which Dreiser has not time to explore. Only a suggestion of their previous experiences is recorded, and the reader has no feeling that he has seen their minds grow or watched the important influences which have molded their personalities. They have, further, more of that charm or individuality which creates the impression of free will and ethical independence. Thus we illustrate the truism that only with simple characters — who usually live under sordid conditions — can the naturalistic method succeed in appearing to present the external pressures which control the characters' lives and account for what they are as well as what they do. It is because of the simplicity of Clyde's character and the narrowness of his initial outlook that Dreiser is able to go so much further behind the phenomenon of his will and explain its constituents.

This is a striking difference between the naturalism of *An American Tragedy* and that of Dreiser's earlier novels. But even so it is a difference only in degree, for Dreiser still gazes at the wonder and mystery and terror of life and is unable to find purpose or organization in its ceaseless ebb and flow. His American tragedy contains so much detail that one is aware of the hundreds of independent pressures, working at odds or in complete indifference to each other, that produce the simplest event. The reader is impressed with the futility of trying either to control or to comprehend any event in all of its ramifications. Dreiser, to repeat, pretends to explain Clyde's character more fully in terms of heredity and especially milieu than he has done before — but he is still bound to the conviction that the changes of fate are too inscrutable ever to be finally revealed by man.

Having offered these generalizations, I must hasten to qualify them in another respect. *An American Tragedy* differs greatly in structure from the earlier novels. In all of them we have discerned a formlessness which seemed to answer to Dreiser's conception of reality. Carrie was left in mid-career with a question. Lester and Jennie were buffeted about, but not through any sharply articulated dramatic sequence of events. Cowperwood and Witla, likewise, moved through a long series of incidents which were not integrated into a single action. The structure of *The "Genius"* and *The Titan* is Dreiser's assertion that real life is not made up of beautifully organized patterns but of ceaseless fluctuations about a norm which is hidden or even nonexistent. *An American Tragedy*, however, is completely unified by the fact that every event in the novel is related to the central crisis of Roberta's murder.

Book One presents Clyde's early years and his development. Book Two deals with his life in Lycurgus, his affair with Roberta, and the complications brought about by his love for Sondra Finchley — ending with murder. Book Three contains the apprehension, trial, and execution of Clyde. What would have been a tawdry and wandering life is given meaning and centrality by the great event of the murder. By making the last two books of the novel specifically the story of the murder Dreiser is able to have his action single and unified. Doubtless this unity is characteristic of tragedy, which can occur even in a naturalist's world and give a principle of organization to what might otherwise be a dreary, meaningless, and tangled life. This change in structure, then, arises from a change in the content of the novel, not from a change in Dreiser's ideas.

There is, on the other hand, a difference between the philosophy of *An American Tragedy* and that of the earlier novels which justifies the assertion that it marks a third distinct stage in Dreiser's naturalism. In *The Financier, The Titan,* and *The "Genius"* he saw life through the eyes of a superman, to whom it appeared as a welter of forces among which he must try somehow to work out his individual salvation. The damage to society in the career of a Cowperwood may be discovered in the books; but the purpose of those books is not to dwell upon the social evil of his career. Similarly Eugene Witla's career is seen as an individual's struggle, without particular social implications. In Clyde Griffith's progress, on the contrary, social implications abound. Dreiser had been converted to socialism since writing *The "Genius";* his American tragedy is a tragedy brought about by the society in which we live. That society is responsible, as the immediate cause, for Clyde's actions. This social consciousness marks the third stage of Dreiser's naturalism. This is not to say that *An American Tragedy* is an indictment of our social order. It is first of all a work of art, the tragedy of Clyde Griffiths, a picture of a life that is tragic because the protagonist is at once responsible (as any human being feels another to be) and helpless (as the philosopher views events). Clyde's tragedy is a tragedy that depends upon the American social system. It shows the unfortunate effects of that system more, for example, than did the defeat of Cowperwood at the end of *The Titan.* In the latter instance a "superman" was battling the opposition aroused by his will to power. In Clyde's case the whole of the American social order, in its normal activity, is brought into the picture.

An American Tragedy is naturalistic because normal social pressures make Clyde's downfall inevitable. The reader's being led to wonder about the rightness of the social order is, like his doubts about the social value of Cowperwood, an activity subsequent to the aesthetic experience of the tragedy itself. Dreiser the artist deals with things as they are. Dreiser the socialist demonstrates the evils of our society in a way that may lead the reader sometime to think about correcting them. But this socialistic purpose — if it may be called a purpose — does not become part of the movement of the novel; it does not contaminate the tragedy; it does not, in short, prevent Dreiser from being, still, a naturalist.

~ ~

I have deferred discussion of *The Stoic* because, although it completes the "Trilogy of Desire," taking up Cowperwood's career after the Chicago debacle, it was not published until 1947, thirty-three years after *The Titan*. Dreiser had most of the book written shortly after publication of *The Titan,* but he kept it by him because he could not, apparently, work out a satisfactory conclusion. In the meantime he wrote new sorts of novels which took him into new spheres of thought where it became increasingly difficult to carry through the implications of ideas which were still growing while he wrote the two earlier volumes.

The opening chapters discover Cowperwood taking stock after his expulsion from the Chicago scene. Love and business as usual are interwoven, on this occasion when Berenice Fleming, whom he has supported through her adolescence and who is now in the bloom of young womanhood, gives herself to him and persuades him also to undertake a new and grander venture in the world of finance. Renewed by the consummation of his love for Berenice, the most charming and talented woman he has known, he lays plans to invade the traction business of London; and this project creates the problems which occupy the reader through the volume. In the first place, Cowperwood must somehow dispose of Eileen, his wife, whose uncontrollable jealousy will lead her to create a scandal if she learns that Berenice has traveled to England and is to be established in a country house where, passing as Cowperwood's ward, she will by her poise and beauty help him into the select circles without whose support it is impossible for a foreigner to break into the world of British finance. To this end he employs an indigent American socialite named Tollifer who pursues Eileen, takes her to Paris, introduces her into a circle of aristocratic waifs and strays, and altogether gives her the happiest days she has known for more than a decade. Meanwhile Cowperwood makes his usual startling impression on British financiers and aristocrats and very soon has set in motion a gigantic scheme to unify and modernize the London Underground system.

Complications appear by virtue, as usual, of the impingement of sex upon business. Lord Stane, who is to launch Cowperwood socially as well as bring his large Underground holdings into the financial pool, falls in love with Berenice. On a money-raising trip to America, Cowperwood enters a brief but intense affair with a young dancer, which gets into the papers. When Eileen reads of this she sends the clipping to Berenice whose relation to Cowperwood she believes to be innocent. Presently Eileen learns why Tollifer has been taking such good care of her and she returns to New York in a fury, threatening to expose Cowperwood in a scandal that will ruin his British operations. But now, when the elements of a highly dramatic involvement are set before us, the story comes to an abrupt and inconclusive ending: Cowperwood dies of Bright's disease.

Following his death, his fortune of some $12,000,000 is quickly eaten away by taxes, litigation, assessments, litigation, and more litigation. His great house and art collection are auctioned off to pay claims. There is no money to build the hospital he had arranged to leave to the city of New York. Eileen is put out of her house, forced to take an absurdly small settlement, and dies of pneumonia without ever adjusting herself to the uncertainties of living in the shadow of continual litigation. We hear nothing of what happens to the great London Underground unification. Cowperwood is treated somewhat unkindly by the press, as his enormous fortune and influence evaporate when he is no longer present to maintain them. If he has been a "superman," he has made no permanent impression on society, and his material contribution of street railway systems will not provide alms for oblivion. Any larger significance of his demise is lost because Dreiser devotes most of his attention to the sordid vanity of Eileen, who deserts Cowperwood on his deathbed when she learns that Berenice is seeing him.

But most striking and extraordinary of culminations is the

turning of Berenice to Yogi in the concluding chapters. Here the divided stream of American transcendentalism does astonishing things. Wandering in a chaos of pure materialistic flux, Dreiser allows his heroine in these closing chapters to leap to pure spirit, to Brahma, and to the contemplation and realization of Divine Love. And Dreiser too seems to make this leap, because it appears beyond any question that Berenice carries his thought and conviction. She is the most sensitive and intelligent of his characters; she is the only one who makes significant discoveries about the folly and selfishness of even the most cultivated materialistic life; her four years of study with a Guru in India are presented with what I can read only as utter seriousness on the part of the author. This leap of Dreiser's from pure matter to pure Spirit invites various speculations and comments. The philosophical abysses of Brahmanism, with its concepts of unknowable mysteries and endless cosmic cycles of repetition, are psychologically not unrelated to the abysses of purposeless flux which terrify the devoted materialist. Nor has it ever been possible to say that Dreiser denied the existence of mysteries. Always in league with humanity, he from his earliest book presented the mazes of the human quest as pathetic and compelling. He sought through his love of man to express the sense of an ideal pattern for which he had sought vainly in nature.

Viewed in artistic terms, however, Dreiser's conclusion of *The Stoic* must be considered grotesque. Berenice is too utterly brilliant and dazzling to be quite real. Her love of fine things, her absorption with herself, her whimsical intelligence, and her courageous defiance of convention in becoming Cowperwood's mistress — these are too many traits to fuse into a convincing personality. In India she ascends through all the levels of Yogi to a direct experience of the supreme Reality — a level from which it is hardly probable that she would return to New York, make the amazing discovery that there is poverty there just as in India, and so devote herself to building and working in the hospital that Cowperwood had planned. The birth of a social consciousness comes naïvely twinned to the discovery of Brahma.

Another false start occurs when Berenice finds herself drawn by the culture and charm of Lord Stane. He seems to have the background that Cowperwood lacks. His interests, too, are much broader. And Cowperwood, after swearing his undying love for Berenice, has just been revealed as having a new love affair in New York. But nothing comes of this potential conflict (a favorite in American fiction, by the way), for Berenice decides that Cowperwood's attraction is irresistible. We see her at one moment shrewdly calculating a liaison of vengeance but at the next giving in to pure passion and fascination. After Berenice returns from India to discover that Cowperwood's fortune has vanished into the pockets of lawyers, she "was filled with sorrow as she inwardly viewed the wreckage of all of his plans." Now Cowperwood's plans were largely predaceous and materialistic. After her years of study with the Guru, Berenice would have known that Cowperwood's desire to perpetuate his name by leaving a hospital was not to be confused with the charity which suffereth all. Yet this is what she appears to do. These are all indications of Dreisers' failure to adapt his materials into an effective pattern. Too many ideas wander about the borders of his action without actually being drawn into it.

What finally identifies the structural weakness of this book is Dreiser's failure to manage the problem of *scale*. He begins by describing financial transactions with an attention to detail that would have carried the volume to 600 pages, but these are abandoned without remorse in the midst of the barest beginnings of the great London venture. The love entanglements, likewise, are given here and there chapters of such minute detail that they create the expectation of an exhaustive presentation; but these turn out to be only samples of a whole that does not take shape. The point of view shifts loosely from person to person at least a dozen times during the story. Minds are invaded and then abandoned with little regard for the values of a controlled point of view. We have no sense of exhaustive documentation, of the patient methodical accumulation of all the facts needed to understand a great personal and social condition. The tired and grainy fragments of the story fall apart. The architectonics of naturalism have disappeared. Instead of liberating Dreiser's talent, naturalism left him with a cumbersome technique which he could not use for his newer ideas.

An example of this weakness is the fact that although Cowperwood is, in the title, called a stoic, there is no indication in the book that he is one. He has changed only physiologically, age making it somewhat more difficult for him to be consumed with zeal for an enterprise. But his restless seeking cannot be considered stoical. He comments on the new venture:

"There's a lot of nonsense to all this, you know. . . . Here we are, you and I, both of us getting along in years, and now running around on this new job, which, whether we do it or not, can't mean so much to either of us. For we're not going to be here so much longer . . . neither of us can do much more than eat a little, drink a little, play about a little longer, that's all. What astonishes me is that we can get so excited over it." [39]

Some time later he speculates with wonder and resignation on morality and human motives:

Was any man noble? Had there ever been such a thing as an indubitably noble soul? He was scarcely prepared to believe it. Men killed to live — all of them — and wallowed in lust in order to reproduce themselves. In fact, wars, vanities, pretenses, cruelties, greeds, lusts, murder, spelled their true history, with only the weak running to a mythical saviour or god for aid. And the strong using this belief in a god to further the conquest of the weak.

A page later he muses on "the mystery and meaninglessness of human activity." Cowperwood has not changed except that he has tired somewhat and therefore occasionally questions the hustle and striving of life. After he is stricken with his fatal illness we are told almost nothing of his thoughts, even though he lives for several months.

If Dreiser's novel appears wooden, it is because the mixture of new ideas and old is grotesque; the style and the techniques of characterization have not accommodated the new ideas. His characters are introduced and described formally — background, occupation, financial status, followed by a few words of generalization about personality or character. For example:

Also present were Lord and Lady Bosvike, both young and smart and very popular. They were clever at all sports, enjoyed gambling and the races, and were valuable in any gathering because of their enthusiasm and gaiety. Secretly they laughed at Ettinge and his wife, though at the same time they valued their position and deliberately set themselves out to be agreeable to them.

This writing has not made use of modern techniques of characterization or modern concepts of personality. It illustrates rather Dreiser's consistent use of the formal Victorian categories, like honesty, diligence, and piety. This made *The Stoic* seem old-fashioned in 1947; the startling "newness" of early naturalism was not one of its characteristics. Where the newness does appear is in Dreiser's treatment of love. This is anything but Victorian, for to him love is dependent upon all the social, financial, and personal forces that operate at any moment. It is a tension of lust, ambition, vanity, insecurity, and hate; an alteration in any of these elements will unbalance the tension and set it moving toward a new relationship. Dreiser is not able to exhibit this idea dramatically, but it appears again and again in the thoughts of his characters. Anyone making a new acquaintance of the opposite sex wonders what it would be like to be in love with him and adds up the various financial and social complications. Even in their moments of passion, lovers are busy assessing the *status* of their relation, for nothing is permanent and every action initiates irreversible changes. This fragment of the old Dreiser struggles rather feebly in *The Stoic* with Yogi, traces of socialism, and the writer's weariness. The return to spirit, although it completes the broken arc of the transcendental tradition, does not furnish here a pattern for coherent fiction.

～ ～

Dreiser's final novel, although published only a year before *The Stoic*, was conceived many years earlier and most of it was written long before *The Stoic* was begun. In its published form *The Bulwark* (1946) appears to represent a transitional stage between the materialism of his earlier work and the Brahminism which ap-

pears in the closing pages of *The Stoic*. It deals with three generations of Quakers in Pennsylvania. They go from piety to prosperity to perdition. The protagonist is Solon, of the middle generation, who gets rich, clings to the Inner Light, but sees his children
drawn away into various forms of vice and vanity because they
cannot resist the material attractions of fine clothes and automo-
biles or the physical attractions of sex.

The novel has a double theme. Sociologically, it shows that the
control exercised by a religion of simplicity like Quakerism is
powerless against the lures of American materialism. Within
Solon it shows the same conflict: Solon contributes to the downfall of his children because he thinks he can serve both God
and Mammon. By serving Mammon he makes a lot of money,
which opens up the world of ostentation and vice to his children.
If they had all lived in poverty, they would not have been tempted.
Yet, paradoxically, it is Solon's Quaker background that makes
him sober, industrious, and trustworthy — so that he can rise to
affluence as a banker. (I do not know what to say about the unquestioned fact that there have been and still are many Quaker
families where wealth and simplicity do go together without difficulty, even through several generations. They do not appear in
the argument of *The Bulwark*.)

The Bulwark does not reveal the mixture and confusion of
socialism and Yogi that appear in *The Stoic*. When Solon becomes
a successful banker, rich enough to give his children the luxuries
they crave, it is not suggested that he is exploiting the poor or living on the unearned increment of usury. His rise is presented as
the reward of diligence and devotion. It appears in time that he
has erred in believing that the moral sobriety of Quakerism could
carry him through financial maneuvers unscathed; but his error
is, depending upon how one regards it, either a fatal error that
was inescapable under the circumstances or the error of judgment
of a man who could not foresee where his commercial involve-
ments would take him. Any Marxian analysis of his experience
must be supplied by the reader. The frivolous outlooks of his
children are not attributed to the class struggle but are presented

sub specie aeternitatis; here, he seems to say, are children growing up with false human values — values that do not call for the good of which these children are capable. Their lives are wasted in ostentation and frivolity.

The early Dreiser would have stressed the idea that they were not responsible for their standards; he would have implied that any standards were relative and therefore questionable. In 1946 he hurried past these old and easy assumptions to consider what values are good and where they can be found. The Inner Light of Quakerism is not said to be the perfect guide, but it is a guide which made the old people strong and which sustained Solon until he meddled with such powerful gods as Mammon and Moloch. Although Quakerism is not contrasted with Buddhism or Yogi or Platonism, it is clearly presented as a way which made strong Americans; and its strength lies in its qualities of tradition and myth. These compel belief, fidelity, and discipline — without which it would appear that man is not capable of leading a coherent life. The whole book asserts that man must be guided — that is, man in modern America — by powerful attachments to an Authority that he accepts on faith. The rigid morality of Quakerism dampens spontaneity and snubs impulse. To the early Dreiser such repression was bad. Now it is good, for it is a discipline that strengthens the will and quickens the spirit. Dreiser has turned from materialistic monism to Christian dualism, from impulse to control, from nature to spirit, from iconoclasm to traditionalism, from flux to myth.

This is the first novel in which Dreiser has been confronted with the problem of advancing four or five separate actions, instead of concentrating on one person, as in his early novels, and the result is not fortunate. It is, to begin with, difficult for a writer of Dreiser's diffuseness to deal with the birth, early education, adolescence, and "end" of five children and their parents in fewer than 400 pages. He has performed this task as it were through the small end of a telescope: occasional incidents are dramatized, but most are recounted hastily, in a bewildering succession of two- and three-page chapters. Characters are developed only to be dropped;

some live and die without ever coming to life; others are introduced, forgotten, and then embarrassingly revived for a new occasion. This failure of form reveals a literary artistry that could
not keep pace with changing times. In the historical context of
1900, a straight-line presentation of one incident after another was
striking and powerful. Given a prevailing notion of form in the
novel, the denial of it becomes a form. The movement of Dreiser's
early novels had such a form. But without the foil of that-from-
which-it-revolts the same work would be either chaotic or commonplace. Here the latter is true, for there is, in this matter, a
dialectic at work; whereas in 1900 Dreiser expressed a powerful
antithesis, in 1946 the same kind of form is irrelevant because
several new syntheses have nullified the tension in which it formerly participated. Nor, in view of the confusion of its plots, can
we say that *The Bulwark* is as well constructed as *Sister Carrie*.
Today it will be asked, with genuine bewilderment, whether *The
Bulwark* is naturalistic. The question would not have been asked
in 1900, when it would have struck the pious reader that here was
a shockingly detached presentation of moral issues: a boy who
strays into vice because he has been repressed at home, who commits suicide rather than bear the shame of having been in jail, who
has, in fine, not been equipped to judge wisely and so is not judged
by the author. To the world of 1900 this would have seemed an
attack upon the very concept of moral responsibility. Today it is
old-fashioned.

As I have already said, Dreiser's greatness as a novelist cannot
be accounted for by his naturalism. His greatness is in his insight,
his sympathy, and his tragic view of life. Although *The Bulwark*
reveals major shifts in his beliefs, and although it is very clumsily
contrived, it could still have all the power and greatness of *Jennie
Gerhardt* or *An American Tragedy* if Dreiser had succeeded, to use
James's term, in "rendering" his idea. I would not suggest that *The
Bulwark* fails because Dreiser abandoned some of his old theories.
Not at all. Much the same view of life is there. Dreiser has always
been seeking solid foundations for social and personal order. His
characters have always been bewildered because the world was too

complicated and they were not equipped to understand it. Sister Carrie seeks a meaning in her experience which she cannot find. Solon Barnes has a meaning but he cannot live by it, and at the end of the book he is not unlike Carrie in wondering why events have happened as they have.

Thus the fourth stage of Dreiser's naturalism is not naturalism, after all, and it is indeed most instructive to see how easily the style, the method, and the attitudes of the early Dreiser are entirely converted in these final novels to the uses of Authority and Spirit. Having brooded long and sadly over the materialist's world, he turns away from it at the end without greatly changing his tone.

IX

Sherwood Anderson: Impressionism and the Buried Life

SHERWOOD ANDERSON (1876–1941) was less than ten years younger than Stephen Crane, but his productive period came a generation later than Crane's. Whereas Crane wrote in the 1890s and died in 1900, Anderson began writing after 1915 and published his first outstanding work, *Winesburg, Ohio,* in 1919. I mention them together because I believe Anderson's work shows what Crane's might have developed into if he had lived another twenty-five years. It also shows how a certain quality of the naturalistic impulse finds expression after twenty years of literary experimentation have altered and enriched the technical resources upon which it can draw.

In an earlier chapter I called Stephen Crane an impressionist — a writer particularly concerned to render with a new vividness the feel and flavor of experience. He uses fantastic metaphors to convey the incredibleness of being under fire; he communicates shock, outrage, and fright with a sensuous density that was brand-new to American literature in 1895. He takes bold strides, furthermore, along the way of altering the Victorian notions of character and personality. His people are not types; nor are they presented to us as a collection of moral traits (loyalty, honesty, thrift) by which they can be judged. Crane takes us inside his people and shows the impingement of experience upon their minds. This is impressionism. This is writing that is particularly concerned with the life of the mind — particularly but not exclusively, for Crane has definite moral convictions around which his stories are constructed. *Maggie* asserts that a girl of the streets is spiritually too poor to be capable of moral conduct. "The Blue Hotel" asserts that responsibility is so intricate a matter that it is in fact impossible to hold any single individual responsible for an event. *The Red Badge of Courage* asserts that bravery is not a characteristic that one has or has not and for which one can be praised or blamed; bravery is nothing, but a man can know something of himself through a series of battle experiences, learn a sort of discipline, and if he survives emerge with some knowledge of his capacities and limitations. *The Red Badge* asserts the futility of "judging" a "coward," although it does not deny that there may be rich satisfaction in achieving what is called courage.

This inwardness of experience cannot be reached by a writer who recognizes conventional standards and judges his characters according to them. But in Crane's day these traditional norms could not be ignored. To question them in the America of 1895 was to defy the orthodox (if not *épater les bourgeois*), and much of Crane's work includes a conscious and formal attack upon the accuracy and validity of the accepted measuring stick. "The Blue Hotel," as I have suggested, takes its shape around a formal attack on the notion of responsibility. *Maggie* likewise attacks the norms that measure sexual morality. *The Red Badge* is as concerned with attacking the Fourth-of-July idea of bravery as it is with exploring the inwardness of fear and hysteria. Crane's attacks on these problems imply a philosophical position which can be defined as anti-supernaturalism, anti-abstractionism, and anti-orthodoxy.

If we took the genius and the energy that Crane devoted to these social and philosophical considerations and used them instead on his explorations of the inwardness of the mind we might approach perhaps the quality of Sherwood Anderson's exquisite insight. Writing a generation later and therefore freed from the compulsion to fight ideological battles, Anderson renders qualities of personality and dimensions of experience beyond anything in the work of Crane, Norris, London, or Dreiser. He is far freer from taboos than they; he works on smaller areas; he does not condescend to his characters nor does he feel obliged to defend them. As a result he has laid bare an American heart which had not been known until it was caught and felt in his stories. Whereas by the severest standards Dreiser is ponderous, Norris turgid, Crane staccato and tense, and London often close to ridiculous, Anderson is mellow, lyrical, controlled, and glowing with sonorous warmth. Paul Rosenfeld, who has written the best appreciation of Anderson's work,[1] likens it to field-flowers: "Flowing rhythmically as it does, made like them with zest, it has the freshness of clover, buttercups, black-eyed Susans. It has their modesty, their innocence. . . . No personal interest, neither desire for display or prestige, money or applause, motivated these writings. They are the uninduced, naive consequences of a simple need for understanding and the communication of that understanding, fulfilled by an extraordinary imagination."

~ ~

Anderson's naturalism may be considered on three planes: his exploration of character without reference to the orthodox moral yardsticks; his questionings, and his quiet, suppressed conclusions as to what orders our cosmos and what is man's place in it; and his social attitudes, which are left-wing and increasingly critical, as the years pass, of American business enterprise. After briefly discussing these aspects of Anderson's work, I shall try to show how his naturalism, while making possible his exquisite insights into personality, confronts him with a later version of the problem of structure that baffled Hamlin Garland: Anderson's medium is the short story or sketch; in the novel he is baffled by the problem of form.

Understanding naturalism as a result of the divided stream of American transcendentalism enables us to account for many confusions and contradictions which appear in the tradition. Does the appeal to nature, for example, commit us to reason or unreason? Is truth to be found in the study of the scientist, the insight of the mystic, or the simple reactions of the folk? In short, is reason or impulse to be more respected? These are old questions, indeed, but they seem no less confusing now than they have ever been, for never have the poles of order and frenzy whirled more bewilderingly around an unknown center. Respect for reason seems to be a part of modern naturalistic thinking, but so does respect for instinct. How can it be that these two contrary notions exist in the same general pattern of ideas? The answer is that the dichotomy between order and frenzy, between reason and instinct, is not the important or major one. In a larger scheme, Authority goes at one pole, and at the other stands Nature whose two children are order (or reason) and instinct. Under the orthodox dispensation man was to be enlightened by revelation and controlled by the rule of Authority. Under the new, he is to find the truth in himself. Since the emotions have been most severely distrusted under the aegis of orthodoxy, it is natural that, in the revolt against it, the rationalism of the eighteenth century should precede the emotionalism of the nineteenth, and that the scientific materialism of the late nineteenth century should precede the second return to emotion that we see in the psychology of Freud and the fiction of Sherwood Anderson. In each trend the return to reason comes as the first rebellion against orthodoxy, the return to emotion the second. Anderson, in almost everything he writes, searches out the emotional values involved in an experience. He seeks to render the actual flow of life to people in small towns and on farms who are struggling with all their *natural* ardor against the confines of tradition or the inhibitions of Puritanism.

Anderson explores two major themes. One is discovery, the other inhibition. These themes correspond with the demands of the two branches of the divided stream of transcendentalism. The theme of discovery is the recognition of spirit, the unfolding of the world and its perception by the intuition, the secret insight by which a man's life is suddenly revealed to him. It comes when George Willard sits in the dark over the fairground with Helen White; when the adolescent narrator of "The Man Who Became a Woman" (in *Horses and Men,* 1924) after a night of extraordinary adventures, culminating in the illusion that he has turned into a woman, breaks through the veil of ignorance and confusion and goes forth to a new life; when Rosalind Westcott of "Out of Nowhere into Nothing" (in *The Triumph of the Egg*, 1921), who has gone home from Chicago to ask her mother's advice and has found only a complete lack of sympathy, walking through the night comes into possession of a delicious confidence in her powers: "She found herself able to run, without stopping to rest and half-wished she might run on forever, through the land, through towns and cities, driving darkness away with her presence."

The theme of inhibition appears in almost every story of Anderson's, and it relates to three general areas of cause and experience. The first is the problem of growing up. Every youth finds himself baffled, inarticulate, frustrated because he does not know what he wants out of life. He wants to be loved, more than anything else, perhaps, but he also wants to express himself and to communicate with others, and these needs cannot be answered until they are clearly recognized. Childhood and youth are therefore characterized by bottled-up yearnings, unformed desires, and wild resentments. Second is the frustration which comes from the absence of a tradition of manners that could lend graciousness and ease instead of the rawness and harshness that grow when people express themselves through broad humor, scurrility, and cruel pranks. Third is the problem of social opportunity which becomes increasingly important in Anderson's later work. People without education, mill workers in *Beyond Desire*, all the countless Americans who have not even a meager share of the opportunities which constitute the democratic dream of a full life for all — these live in endless spiritual privation, and passages which appear with increasing frequency in the later books suggest that Anderson shared the hatred of the oppressed for the vapid plutocrats who deprive them. This theme of inhibition obviously reflects the materialistic branch of the transcendental stream when it identifies spiritual and material privation. If Anderson ever suggested that all we need in America is a tradition of manners and devout observances to control the wildness of the yokel, he would be returning to orthodoxy and dualism. This he never does.

Rather he evolves the concept of the *grotesque* to indicate what small-town life has done to its people. The grotesque is the person who has become obsessed by a mannerism, an idea, or an interest to the point where he ceases to be Man in the ideal sense. This condition is not the single defect referred to by Hamlet:

> these men —
> Carrying, I say, the stamp of one defect,
> Being Nature's livery, or Fortune's star —
> Their virtues else — be they as pure as grace,
> As infinite as man may undergo —
> Shall in the general censure take corruption
> From that particular fault.

It is, rather, the state wherein the defect has become the man, while his potentialities have remained undeveloped. Anderson describes it thus:

That in the beginning when the world was young there were a great many thoughts but no such thing as a truth. Man made the truths himself and each truth was a composite of a great many vague thoughts. . . .

And then the people came along. Each as he appeared snatched up one of the truths and some who were quite strong snatched up a dozen of them.

It was the truths that made the people grotesques. The old man had quite an elaborate theory concerning the matter. It was his notion that the moment one of the people took one of the truths to himself, called it his truth, and tried to live his life by it, he became a grotesque and the truth he embraced became a falsehood.[2]

Again and again the stories of Anderson are marked by a union of surprise and insight. What was apt to be merely shocking or horrendous or sensational in the work of Zola and Norris acts in Anderson's stories as a key to a fuller grasp of the extraordinary range of "normal" reality. He has got into the heart of bizarre, even fantastic experiences which are nevertheless also universal.

"Godliness: A Tale in Four Parts," in *Winesburg, Ohio*, presents the effects on children and grandchildren of the zeal for possessions and godliness that dominates the simple heart of Jesse Bentley. Jesse has the simplicity and power of a prophet; with these go the blindness of a fanatic and the pitiful ignorance of a bigot. When his grandson, David, is twelve, he takes him into the forest and terrifies him by praying to God for a sign. The boy runs, falls, and is knocked unconscious on a root, while the old man, oblivious to the boy's terror, thinks only that God has frowned upon him. When David is fifteen, he is out with the old man recovering a strayed lamb when Jesse conceives the notion that, like Abraham, he should sacrifice the lamb and daub the boy's head with its blood. Terrified beyond measure, the boy releases the lamb, hits Jesse in the head with a stone from his sling, and, believing he has killed the old man, leaves that part of the country for good. As for old Jesse, "It happened because I was too greedy for glory," he declared, and would have no more to say on the matter. Here Anderson is, on the surface, studiously objective, presenting only the cold facts; but the delicacy and sweetness of his style invest this harsh tale with a rare quality of understanding and love. The hidden life has never been more effectively searched out. Here there is no judgment either of the fanatical old man or of the terrified boy whose life he nearly ruins. Pity, understanding, and insight there are, made possible by the naturalistic impulse to seek into the heart of experience without reference to the limits or prepossessions of convention.

Winesburg, Ohio is full of insights into the buried life, into the thoughts of the repressed, the inarticulate, the misunderstood. Most frequently frustrated is the desire to establish some degree of intimacy with another person. A tradition of manners would accomplish just this by providing a medium through which acquaintance could ripen into intimacy. Small-town America has wanted such a tradition. In place of it, it has had joking, backslapping, and buffooning which irk the sensitive spirit and make him draw ever more secretly into himself. The concluding paragraph of "The Thinker" shows these confused and constricted emotions working at a critical moment in the life of a boy who wants to get away. He has told a girl whom he has long known rather at a distance that he plans to leave Winesburg, and she has offered to kiss him:

Seth hesitated and, as he stood waiting, the girl turned and ran away through the hedge. A desire to run after her came to him, but he only stood staring, perplexed and puzzled by her action as he had been perplexed and puzzled by all of the life of the town out of which she had come. Walking slowly toward the house, he stopped in the shadow of a large tree and looked at his mother sitting by a lighted window busily sewing. The feeling of loneliness that had visited him earlier in the evening returned and colored his thoughts of the adventure through which he had just passed. "Huh!" he exclaimed, turning and staring in the direction taken by Helen White. "That's how things'll turn out. She'll be like the rest. I suppose she'll begin now to look at me in a funny way." He looked at the ground and pondered this thought. "She'll be embarrassed and feel strange when I'm around," he whispered to himself. "That's how it'll be. That's how everything'll turn out. When it comes to loving some one, it won't never be me. It'll be some one else — some fool — some one who talks a lot — some one like that George Willard."

In another story he speaks of "the quality of being strong to be loved" as if it were the key to America's need.

These ideas are all in the naturalistic tradition in that they are motivated by the feeling of need for their expression of the "inner man." Anderson assumes that this inner man exists and is good and "should" be permitted to fulfill itself through love and experience. The need is alive and eager; it is the social order that prevents its satisfaction.

Patterns emerge in *Winesburg, Ohio* through the growth of George Willard, who may be considered the protagonist of what connected story there is. George appears frequently, sometimes in an experience and sometimes hearing about another's. An extraordinary pattern emerges when George receives, late at night in the newspaper office where he works, a hint he cannot yet interpret from the minister, who enters brandishing a bloody fist, exclaiming that he has been "delivered." "God," he says, "has appeared to me in the person of Kate Swift, the school teacher, kneeling naked on a bed." The minister has been peeping at her through a small hole in the colored window of his study. This night as his lustful thoughts were running wild, Kate, naked, beat the pillow of her bed and wept, and then knelt to pray, and the minister was moved to smash the window with his fist so that the glass would be replaced and he would no longer be tempted. The turmoil in the schoolteacher's bosom resulted from a mixture of interest, desire, enthusiasm, and love. Earlier the same evening she had been thinking of George Willard, whom she wanted to become a writer, and became so excited that she went to see him in the newspaper office, and for a moment allowed him to take her in his arms. George was only a youth at this point, and the schoolteacher's interest in his talents was perfectly genuine and unselfish. But she was also a passionate and unsatisfied woman in whom interest and desire interacted. When George put his arms around her she struck his face with her fists and ran out into the night again. Some time later the minister burst in, and it seemed to George that all Winesburg had gone crazy. George goes to bed later, fitting these puzzling incidents together and thinking that he has missed something Kate Swift was trying to tell him.

All the gropings and cross-purposes of these grotesques and semi-grotesques reveal the failure of communication in Winesburg. The mores impose a set of standards and taboos that are utterly incapable of serving the pent-up needs in the hearts of the people. They regard themselves with wonder and contempt while they study their neighbors with fear and suspicion. And the trouble, which begins with the gap between public morality and private reality, extends finally into the personality of a rich and good person like Kate Swift. Because her emotions are inhibited she acts confusedly toward George; is desperate, frightened, and ashamed; and fails to help him as she had wanted to do.

The climax (perhaps it should only be called the high point in George's life to then) of the book occurs when George Willard and Helen White reach a complete understanding one autumn evening, sitting up in the old grandstand on the fairgrounds, rapt and wordless. "With all his strength he tried to hold and to understand the mood that had come upon him. In that high place in the darkness the two oddly sensitive human atoms held each other tightly and waited. In the mind of each was the same thought. 'I have come to this lovely place and here is this other,' was the substance of the thing felt." It is most significant that this experience is almost entirely wordless. The shared feeling, indeed, is of seeking and wondering. It is inarticulate because it occurs in a world without meaning. Such incidents suggest that men's instincts are good but that conventional morality has warped and stifled them. Interpreted in terms of the divided stream of transcendentalism, they show that the spirit is misdirected because its physical house is mistreated. When Whitman wrote

> Logic and sermons never convince,
> The damp of the night drives deeper into my soul
> Only what proves itself to every man and woman is so

he was making the same plea for the liberation of body and spirit together that we infer from *Winesburg, Ohio*. I say infer, because Anderson does not precisely declare this; one might indeed infer that he regards these repressions as inseparable from life — that he takes the tragic view of man — but I think not entirely so. The pains of growth are probably inevitable, but the whole world is not as confining as Winesburg, and Anderson seems to say that people *should* be able to grow up less painfully to more abundant lives. His protagonist does, and gets away from Winesburg, though he endures torments of misunderstanding and unsatisfied love which cannot be laid to Winesburg so much as to the condition of youth in this world.

But George Willard, who will escape, is different from Elmer Cowley, who is literally inarticulate with frustration and the conviction that everyone in Winesburg considers him "queer"; from old Ray Pearson, who runs sobbing across a rough field through the beauty of an autumn evening in order to catch Hal Winters and tell him not to marry the girl whom he has got in trouble — not marry like himself and be trapped into having more children than he can support and living in a tumble-down shack by the creek, working as a hired hand, bent with labor, all his dreams come to naught. Those buried lives are disclosed with heartbreaking insight. And as we reflect upon them we sense the aptness of the "naturalistic" view of life that the author puts into the mind of George Willard and also presents as his own thought. "One shudders at the thought of the meaninglessness of life while at the same instant . . . one loves life so intensely that tears come into the eyes."

If the universe here seems meaningless. the needs and emotions of men are intensely meaningful. Anderson feels love for them and pity for their desperate and usually fruitless questing. It is not therefore surprising that he should turn increasingly in his later works toward emphasis on the social and institutional causes of their frustration. Like Hamlin Garland, however, Anderson does not master the structure of the novel. His poignant sketches, which contain some of the best and most memorable writing in our literature, do not "connect" naturally into the sustained expression of the longer form. Perhaps the scale is too narrow or the feeling too intense and special. Perhaps Anderson could not achieve the necessary objectivity. Certainly the patterns of protest and socialism do not provide the sort of frame upon which he could weave.

～ ～

Impressionism involves two or three attitudes and literary modes which can be related to naturalism only by careful definition. To begin with, impressionism attempts to render the *quality* of experience more closely, more colorfully, more delicately than it has been rendered. To this end it presents the mind of a character *receiving* impressions rather than judging, classifying, or speculating; and because it attempts to catch the experience as it is received, that experience will not have a reasonable order but a chronological or associational one. The order in Anderson's work is one of its most striking qualities, for he shows people thinking of several things at once, combining incidents in the past with present experience which now makes those incidents relevant, and having at the same time emotions which they cannot understand while they entertain thoughts which do not do any sort of justice to their emotional states. As a device of presentation he tells his stories through the minds of ignorant — or certainly unstudied — narrators who have no sense of selection and arrangement and so give a story that has the tone and flavor of free association. Here in the mixture of impressionist rendering of experience and the device of the story told by a disorderly narrator we find the heart of Anderson's form. He makes a virtue of beginning a story at the end and ending it at the middle. He gives away information which would create suspense of the conventional sort and yet contrives to produce a surprise and a satisfaction at the end of his story by a psychological revelation or a sharing of experience that suddenly becomes coherent out of the chaos of the narrator's apparently objectless rambling. Often what begins as incoherence emerges as the disorder caused by emotion which the story discloses and which indeed turns out to be the cause of its telling.

Such a story is "I'm a Fool," in *Horses and Men* (1922). Its indignant narrator, who is all mixed up about money, horses, and girls, tells about a day at the races and his meeting with a truly nice girl who is strongly attracted to him. He tells her a pack of fantastic lies in order to impress her and of course comes too late to the realization that he loves her and can never go back to her and endure the shame of admitting to all the lies he has told. The rambling story represents the ignorant and disorganized character of the narrator. It reveals his naïveté and his ludicrous confusion of values. It also shows a fundamental goodhearted sincerity in a fellow who keeps repeating that he is a fool. It shows how the absence of "manners" makes it impossible for him to establish an easy intimacy with the girl. And finally it represents the universal in this provincial story — the tendency of all young men to brag before girls and be ashamed of themselves afterwards. The "disorderly" arrangement of the details in the story finally appears quite orderly, for it is perfectly suited to the kind of experience that it renders.

In addition to identifying new flavors of experience and providing a new order for storytelling, Anderson's impressionism quite obviously questions the established social and moral orders. It asks, "What *is* reality?" and repeatedly shows that the telling experience, the thing at the heart of life, is not what is ordinarily represented. Things do not make the kind of sense they are "supposed" to make. They are more complicated and more subtle than the public moralists have heart to see or words to express. This is the theme of *Winesburg, Ohio* and *The Triumph of the Egg*: what appears on the surface, what is commonly described, is not the true and inward reality. But what the true reality is remains a mystery. Characters continually discover that the world is complex, that evil and good are inseparable, and that their simple ideals are inadequate. But this discovery is pathetic because its bewilderment does not pass.

The theme of *Beyond Desire* (1932) is, still, inhibition, but the attempt to make a novel out of the same materials and the same attitudes that were so successfully integrated into *Winesburg, Ohio* does not come off. *Beyond Desire* is bare of movement. Instead of an action or plot it flows in and out of the sensibilities of various characters and develops their feelings about life, the incidents which have shaped or scarred them, and the ways in which they are dominated by the forces of American social inequality. Now in Winesburg the people are so boldly and so poignantly dealt with that the reader is made vividly aware of their privations, of the way they are fenced in by ignorance, fear, and insecurity. When Anderson reaches out into the dimension of the novel in *Beyond Desire,* he accumulates his added material by dealing with somewhat more complicated characters and, instead of contenting himself with their *plights,* showing how their minds react in a variety of situations.

A long opening section presents the character of Red Oliver, a member of the better class of people in Langdon. He has been north to college, has thought about socialism, and yearns for a woman. He differs from other townspeople in being less sensitive to the differences between whites and Negroes, and in being willing to work in the cotton mills on terms of equality with the "lint-heads." He is presented almost entirely in terms of his strange poetical thoughts, his feeling of strangeness in Langdon, and his confusion as to the meaning or purpose of life.

The second part takes us into the twilight minds of the mill girls. Some of these girls have imagination and spirit, whereas others are ill and work at the edge of exhaustion; but all of them are terribly deprived, so that a day at the fair ranks as a major event in their lives. Some marry, but they can hardly be said to have homes, because both girl and husband will have to work long hours in the mill, and there will be no energy left for home. In this smothered life there always remains the dimension of inwardness, where the secret heart lives:

There are days when nothing can touch you. If you are just a mill girl in a Southern cotton mill it doesn't matter. Something lives inside you that looks and sees. What does anything matter to you? It is queer about such days. The machinery in the mill gets on your nerves terribly some days, but on such days it doesn't. On such days you are far away from people. It's odd, sometimes then you are most attractive to them.[3]

A great deal of this part of the story flows in and out of the thoughts of the girls, in this manner.

Part Three presents Ethel, the town librarian, who has always lived on the edge of life, feeling that she is missing the great experiences; firm and formidable, she frightens the people she would like to attract; she does not find the love for which she yearns. All is misunderstanding until, after a disappointing affair one evening with Red Oliver, she marries an older man — for security. Her life has been, then, a struggle for expression and love which she has never found, and we leave her trapped.

The last part returns to Red Oliver, shows him, as a result of working in the mills, drawn to the poor people who are enslaved by the machine, reveals his confused thoughts about communism, and has him, at the end, uselessly and almost accidentally killed by an officer of the state militia. The book plays with the idea of communism, but I think without conviction — and certainly without much persuasiveness. Passages like the following reveal Anderson's fundamental sympathy with the working masses, his belief that there is in them more essential human goodness than in their exploiters:

The point was . . . that you have to work in a place to know. People on the outside didn't know. They couldn't. You feel things.

People from the outside don't know how you feel. You have got to work in a place to know. You have got to be there through long hours, day after day, year after year. You've got to be there at work when you aren't well, when your head aches.

Here is the primitivist echo, the notion of man struggling for selfhood but lacking the means of expression. Thinking of such suppressed and inarticulate people, Red Oliver exclaims, "Oh, hell, it's true. Those who are always getting it in the neck are the nicest people. I wonder why." But although the people are good, it appears doubtful whether communist agitation will lead to anything but more misery. These speculations are turned over so often in the mind of the leading character that they create the impression of volitional paralysis: everything is so uncertain, so balanced between alternatives, that action when it comes springs from whim or accident rather than reason, and the results are tragic or futile. Red Oliver is among a group of strikers, but he is not one of them; yet his anger at the moment is such that when the officer of the militia announces that he will shoot the first man who dares to step forward onto the bridge, Red steps forward and is shot. Through the mind of the man shot and the man shooting runs the same thought: "What the hell . . . I'm a silly ass."

The technique of impressionism leads into (as it springs from) the belief that reality is illusory and phantasmagoric. The impressionistic technique of *Beyond Desire* has made this idea finally dominate the book. The minds of the characters are detached from reality; they grope always without ever finding themselves or defining their relation to society. Red Oliver's death is a grisly mistake, for Red acts in confusion and anger. It accomplishes nothing; it does not serve to focus a revolutionary spirit.

Thus the impact of the method which Anderson developed for his short stories has carried over into his novel and imposed upon it an effect which I suspect he did not intend. It is not necessary to labor this point through other books, although it would be instructive to see how impressionism dominated *Dark Laughter*. Let us see how a similar pattern of loose, groping, baffled inquiry appears in *Kit Brandon*.

Kit Brandon (1936) combines Anderson's themes of discovery and social protest into a loosely chronological-associational-auto-biographical narrative of a girl who comes "up" from a southern hill farm to a mill town where she works until the yearning to escape is satisfied by her marrying the worthless son of a big-time bootlegger. For a time she spends money greedily, indulging her flair for clothes and becoming a stylish figure. Then she separates from her husband and, partly as a sort of compensation to his father and partly for excitement, becomes a driver of liquor cars, racing across state lines, dodging federal agents, acting as decoy. From this life she escapes, too, when the bootlegging gang is broken up and its members jailed. The book ends with Kit having eluded the chase, a warm young woman of thirty, stimulated to go into a way of life, whatever it might be, that would not isolate her from society as her illegal rum-running had done. "There might be some one other puzzled and baffled young one with whom she could make a real partnership in living." [4]

This thin thread of narrative emerges piecemeal as Kit confides to the author. It comes out with no particular shape. Rather the emphasis is on two or three themes that are reiterated tiresomely through the girl's rambling discourse. One is the old Anderson theme of discovery: an utterly unsophisticated, illiterate young girl comes down from the hills and begins to know life through the society of the mill in which she works. Naturalistic primitivism saturates this "discovery," for Kit is presented as having finer sensibilities and a more decent heart than the rich people by whom she is exploited. Through Kit's personal development Anderson works in the theme of isolation, dwelling constantly on the loneliness, the spiritual poverty, the yearning and groping of young people who do not have the intellectual equipment to communicate with each other or the financial and social status to work their way into the great grasping hypocritical world of American opulence. Kit's situation as a rum-driver becomes a symbol of this isolation. Going by night from town to town, living under aliases, spending days in hotel rooms with nothing to do but read and look out at the people on the streets, she represents the plight of the individual in a society given over to the soul-hardening rapacities of American industrial materialism. The following passages of reverie show how this theme is presented (hiatus dots are in the text):

She had a terrible need . . . it growing in her . . . of something . . . a relationship . . . some man or some woman, to whom she could feel close. Just at that time she had . . . it was she felt the strongest thing in her . . . the hunger to give.

Loneliness.

The loneliness, so pronounced in Kit at that time, was not so unlike the loneliness of many Americans.

Loneliness of the radical in a capitalistic society, of the man who wants to fight it, who does feel in himself a kind of social call . . .

Immediately the thing called "respectability" gone. Such a one, a Eugene Debs for example, may be the most gentle of men. He becomes in the public mind something dangerous, is pictured as Kit had been pictured, as a dangerous one.

. . . The life of the artist in any society.

. . . Life of the labor leader and for that matter loneliness also of the lives of successful Americans, even the very rich, the leaders of a capitalistic society.

And so on, through other applications that so isolated a person as Kit Brandon, with her meager background, would not be able to make.

But the question here is not so much that Kit would not be capable of this order of abstraction, but that the method in which this and a hundred other passages are presented displays an end-point of naturalistic unform. It is experience recorded without commentary, without adequate selection, and without the saving grace of being organically related to an action. It is indeed related to an action, but as I have said it is a very thin thread of narrative, and when it has worked itself out enough has not happened to justify the amount of idle reverie accompanying it. The pretense of completeness — the appearance of giving all the unselected facts — which I have elsewhere identified as the secret of successful naturalism, has here become what it pretended. Here indeed we have a random and repetitious gathering of reverie that seems to say again and again, "This is the way life feels. How dreary and cheated it is!" Only once or twice during the book does it take the shape of a statement like the following: "What a queer mixed-up thing life was, people always being driven here and there by forces they themselves couldn't understand, some being hurt, sold-out by life, others apparently lifted up." This could be a quotation from *Sister Carrie*, but whereas it is an idea that is woven into the form of that novel, it enters without breathing life into the body of *Kit Brandon*. The early ideal of appearing to give a complete circumstantial account of an area of reality has been replaced by the unhappy fact of random and uninteresting repetition. The massive documentation of *An American Tragedy* is sustained and informed by an idea; here the vague themes of loneliness, discovery, and inhibition appear in dozens of static reveries.

Nor does the form here do anything with Anderson's later theme of social protest. The naturalist-primitivist assumption that the underprivileged are essentially kinder and wiser than their exploiters is not made credible by reiteration alone; but the action that would dramatize this idea is not here. What has happened to Anderson's later books closely resembles what appears in the three latest novels of James T. Farrell about Bernard Clare (or Carr), although the differences are as illuminating as the similarities.

X

James T. Farrell: Aspects of Telling the Whole Truth

THE work of James T. Farrell offers a remarkable study in the process by which form or technique controls content. He began writing in a convention of selection (to be described presently) which undertook to present the whole truth more fully and precisely than previous novelists had done but which had the unexpected effect, in a few years, of leading Farrell to take a different view of his subject matter from what he had had at starting. In writing about certain aspects of modern life he not only purged himself of his bitterness but also achieved a different conception of his material. What he began by assailing he ended by defending. He thus in a sense wrote himself inside out, and the process reveals something about the implications and consequences of attempting to fulfill the naturalistic goal of telling the whole truth.

～ ～

In his great *Studs Lonigan* trilogy [1] Farrell wrote of the Chicago South Side with a conscious and conscientious naturalism. He presented a character and revealed his destiny in the closest possible (so it seemed at the time) relation to the social, economic, and spiritual conditions in which he lived. The presentation is ostensibly objective; certainly it satisfies the literary canons of objectivity. The point of view is controlled and consistent. But the attitude that appears in almost every page is the author's cold, furious loathing of the spiritual barrenness of Studs' life. The values of school, playground, church, and home are revealed in their naked poverty. Studs does not reach beyond them, and he exhibits the terrible spectacle of humanity wasted. If one read only the *Studs Lonigan* trilogy, he would lay it down, I believe, with the conviction that its dominant emotion was concentrated despair and disgust for the conditions that dwarfed and then blighted Studs' spirit. *Studs* is magnificent writing. It is naturalistic in the tradition of Dreiser, with its careful accumulation of detail, its pretense of naïveté, its obvious inclusion of the reader in the tragic agon — for here as in *An American Tragedy* the reader is made aware that the forces which blight the growth of Studs' spirit are not fatal but social: the reader cannot stay outside of the conflict. Whereas the emotions aroused by classical tragedy are pity and terror, the emotions aroused by such naturalistic tragedies as this are pity and guilt. The Greek and Shakespearean tragedy exhilarates, the modern depresses.

Yet depressing as it is, the *Studs Lonigan* trilogy owes much of its power and unity to its tragic form. Studs' consciousness, his personality, and his economic status are three strands of a life that moves as it ends, in waste. The tragic form is not marked by a great ethical issue and a critical choice, but by the relentless dissipation of energy, idealism, and intelligence in the futile and purposeless activities of a young man who does not know what to do with his life.

In *Young Lonigan* (1932) it is shown that Studs yearns with the fervent idealism of youth for a good life. He has undefined aspirations, which come nearest to definition in his love for Lucy Scanlan and in certain tentative responses he has to church ritual and to the beauty of nature. The concrete ambitions upon which he can focus, however, are the idea of being a tough guy, a gang leader, and of growing up to be a lawyer, a politician, or a workman getting his pay on Saturday night and going out, independent, to drink beer with the guys. The code of his friends is never give a sucker an even break, never allow oneself a noble thought, never express pity or sympathy or charity or respect — for these are signs of weakness and will inevitably subject one to ridicule and even physical persecution. In the parochial school the boys are rebellious and the nuns and fathers are obtuse and tyrannical. Here begins the boredom, the stultifying emptiness of spirit that grows through the trilogy in Studs. At home Studs is subjected to his mother's shrill clamoring for him to be a priest and to his father's nagging discipline. His parents have ideals of success and respectability but they have no ability to make goodness desirable, and so all their advice takes the form of scolding, which accounts for Studs' conviction that home is a place to sleep and get away from as much of the rest of the time as possible.

Ashamed of his rare impulses toward beauty and goodness, ignorant of any single creative outlet, Studs turns to drink, brutality, and sex. The tough guy can express himself by ganging up on a Jew or a Protestant, breaking a window, or robbing a store. Every night the gang roams the streets, dawdles in the poolroom, or stands on the corner looking at the girls. And always the tough "goofing" goes on — hard talk to show that one has neither softness nor tolerance. The dominant notes of this life are boredom and frustration. Violence as a form of self-expression palls; it can satisfy only while it increases in intensity; and so the limit is very soon reached where violence and filth provide no relief from boredom. Studs passes before us time after time in a dull twilight reverie of sexual desire. He is increasingly aware as the years pass that he has missed his chance to amount to something or to do any of the things that important people do, and his waking consciousness is dominated by a weary, bitter sense of defeat.

The foil that sets off this bitterness is his memory of Lucy Scanlan. Lucy was pure beauty and goodness, and Lucy liked Studs; but the tough guy was violently shy before a nice girl, and if he mastered his shyness for a moment he was still unable to talk to her in respectable language. One of the profound insights in Farrell's books is the knowledge that communion between individuals demands a medium. Whether it be politics, art, creative work, literary background, or social conventions or traditions — or all these together — both friendship and love communicate through shared experience. One may go even further and say that they grow and live through shared experience. Even love cannot sustain itself and must be nourished by common interests and activities. All of Studs' loves and friendships are exactly as poor, as thin, as unsatisfying as the meager and tawdry content of his mind. His relation with Lucy goes no further than a couple of walks and one beautiful scene in which she and Studs sit in a tree in the park, singing and swinging their legs and enjoying the sunshine. This glimpse of bliss stays with Studs for the rest of his life. It alone embodies the vague search for goodness that haunts his defeat.

The story of Studs' dreary life, which ends when, at about thirty, he contracts pneumonia from lying drunk in a gutter, need not be rehearsed in greater detail. Farrell has conveyed a sense of Studs as a real and sympathetic personality, an individual perfectly capable of a good life who achieves only the status of a minor tough guy and feels that he is always on the outside looking in. He has shown the sources of Studs' mind and accounted for the terrible poverty of his intellectual and emotional life. The work is dominated by a tone of furious irony which rises occasionally to shrill denunciation (when we accompany Studs to a movie) or sinks to repulsion when we assist at a drunken brawl that ends with a brutal rape. Paradoxically, the bitterness of tone is justified by the profusion of evidence, for whereas bitterness usually evokes suspicion that the writer is giving a distorted picture, here the detail is so rich, so almost tediously exhaustive, that it justifies this tone, which brings to it a certain aesthetic relief.

It is noteworthy that the naturalistic form of this work does not involve the assumption that a strict pattern of cause and effect is being worked out step by step, in the rigidly "experimental" manner of Zola, before our eyes. Farrell's naturalism is descriptive rather than explicitly deterministic insofar as it appears in the form of the novel. We are not, in short, persuaded that Studs must on that particular night of his life have contracted pneumonia or that the forces behind any single incident in the work are scientifically or systematically demonstrated. Farrell is not interested in this sort of pattern. What he does make entirely convincing is that we are in possession of all the elements that go into Studs' life, so that we have a complete understanding of his mind and character and so that the events of his career are made probable. Different things could have happened to Studs just as probably, but barring extraordinary accidents we feel that what did happen was perfectly typical. Typical and probable but not inevitable. This is why I say the naturalism is descriptive rather than formally deterministic.

I have already attempted to account for the tone of this work. The violent sense of outrage derives from the other half of the divided stream of transcendentalism — from the idealism which assumes the dignity of man and the inherent right of every individual to self-development and social justice. Because of this tone and the assumptions which accompany it, *Studs Lonigan* is a reproach to every American who reads it.

Part of the tragic effect of *Studs* comes from the fact that Studs is always on the edge of the action. Just as he feels that the big opportunities are always passing him by, so he is never the toughest guy in his gang, never does the dirtiest deeds, never achieves the extremes of depravity and cynicism that are evinced by the characters who carry the action. The wildest drinking, raping, and destroying are not performed by Studs himself. The really depraved ones are part of the environment in which Studs moves. This quality of watching, of drifting, and of being led into evil because there are no influences to lead him into good attracts the tragic sense of waste, the emotions of pity and fear, to Studs in a way that might not occur if he were the leader in evil. We can deplore the forces which fail to lead and inspire Studs and the forces which debauch him. But what of the really vile fellows? Are we to understand that at heart they are no tougher than Studs? Are we to believe that they too are tragic figures? Perhaps, but in the process of "accounting" for Studs' fall the writer has to make his cronies appear absolutely vile; he has to give them a drive toward evil which operates like a force in nature. What I believe all this shows is how the introduction of ethical values — values

244

derived from the transcendental tradition — controls the form and consequently the effect of the *Studs Lonigan* trilogy. The result is another version of the tragic form of Norris's *Vandover and the Brute*. Whereas Vandover struggled against the weakness in his own character, and failed, Studs struggles very feebly against evil companions and likewise fails. Farrell's tragedy therefore approaches the qualities of melodrama.

After the *Studs Lonigan* trilogy and *Gas-House McGinty* (1934) Farrell turned to a different slice of the same kind of life. He turned to a four-volume study of the childhood, the family life, and the young manhood of Danny O'Neill,[2] who finally gets to the University of Chicago and promises to escape — as the author, who has never hesitated to acknowledge the autobiographical elements in this work, himself escaped to a literary career and a different life. Danny O'Neill comes from about the same milieu as Studs — he plays in the same neighborhood and would like to be one of Studs' gang instead of being bullied because he is a few years younger than they. Danny's family is not spiritually or culturally superior to Studs', nor are Danny's boyhood thoughts and ideals very much nobler; but they are a little more successfully directed. Danny has a spark of ambition, he is subject to constant friction at home and in school, and somehow he continues to study and grow until he is firmly able to criticize the world from which he has come.

Similarities of style, setting, detail, and general tone, however, do not conceal differences between these books and the *Studs* books which make their total effect entirely different. The reader is constantly among the thoughts of Studs, although he does not identify himself with Studs. But he does become identified with Danny, and he therefore does not see in the environment a controlling force. Danny's family, likewise, presented with much fuller and much harsher detail than Studs', become people who are interesting in and for themselves. In a sense they are wasted humanity, but in a more immediate sense they have personal qualities which are not accountable to the environment. They are all alive and kicking. They are loved and hated by the author, and to Danny they appear to possess an independent, nay a willful perversity: as characters and as people they take the bit in their teeth and run. The blighting environment is still acknowledged. Close attention is given to the effect of the Church on Danny's mother, who year after year slips so much money surreptitiously into its swollen coffers that the O'Neill family never have enough of anything and live like pigs.

But the author has again and again taken sides with these people against America. Values of integrity and fortitude and courage begin to emerge. The cold fury of the *Studs* trilogy is now tempered with what appears to be admiration. One gets the impression that the emancipated author looks with no little wonder upon the dogged persistence of those who never are able to rise above their milieu. He has maintained that they have more guts and integrity than carloads of liberals and intellectuals who jump from left to right, from isolationism to interventionism, at the slightest prickings of social change. Thus the spiritual barrenness which is the main concern of the *Studs* trilogy is now still hated, yes, but also defended, admired, and even set up as having virtues of integrity rare in the flabby and corrupt capitalistic world above these people.

It is impossible within my limits to do justice to the variety and abundance of human insights in this two-thousand-page work. It takes Danny from the time when he is a little boy to his college days. It gives an almost incredibly detailed picture of the family soul, of childhood and adolescent activities, and of the society in which these lives have their setting. Danny's father, Jim O'Neill, does not earn enough to support all of his children, and so Danny is taken to live with his grandmother O'Flaherty and his aunt Margaret in a household that is largely supported by his uncle Al O'Flaherty, a traveling shoe salesman. Danny thus from the beginning is torn between love, pride, and shame. At the O'Flahertys' he must listen to constant abuse of his parents. When he goes to his parents' (a few blocks away) for a visit he is ashamed of them and also tortured by guilt because he enjoys a better life at the O'Flahertys'. And he is ashamed of his shame. At church, in school, bullying and being bullied, stealing, playing baseball, going to shows and penny arcades, slowly growing through the torments of childhood into the tortures of adolescence and manhood, Danny lives through the agonies of frustration, embarrassment, shame, and, as he approaches maturity, pity, guilt, and finally indignation against the American society that fosters such spiritual starvation.

The old grandmother is the most amusing figure in the books. Illiterate, mean, shrill, truculent, vindictive, profane, and sanctimonious beyond belief, she has the power again and again to embarrass her whole family by her ridiculous pride and her violent efforts to defend them where they do not want to be defended. She picks a quarrel with the most innocent bystander and screams like a witch. Her ignorance is equaled only by her evil and superstitious piety. In her home there is rarely a quiet hour; Danny lives between extremes of murderous hate and slobbering sentiment. This is the surface; but the longer Danny lives the more he becomes attached to the old harpy. From time to time she is presented in reverie of her youth in Ireland, when she was beautiful and desired; and this evocation of the pathos of nostalgia invests her with dignity. She becomes a strong and simple person who has been uprooted and transported to a brassy new world of commerce and gadgets. If her piety is repulsive, one gathers the impression that in a simpler life it would be admirable. Her cruel vituperation of Jim O'Neill, who cannot support his family, rises to poetic heights and thus gains a kind of wild grandeur. At her death, in the fourth volume, our hearts are wrung, for something has passed for which the cheap modern world can have no substitute.

Uncle Al, the shoe salesman, is the pitiful epitome of 100 per cent Americanism. He recites all the maxims of bigotry and conservatism, the confident old saws about supply and demand, Protestants, communism, and the value of education. Al loves Danny with all the intensity his starved heart can summon. He gives him advice which Danny ignores; he sees in Danny the promise of his own frustrated ambitions. Most of all — and most pathetic — he imagines developing between him and Danny a relation of love, trust, and communion such as he has always dreamed of and never known. But as Danny grows up he finds Al's advice platitudinous, his mind empty, his enthusiasms boring, and he shrinks from his company. And then toward the end of the series attitudes of guilt, pity, and admiration are associated with Al. His limitations become strengths. What at first appeared as narrowness of outlook now seems the stubborn determination of a limited man to do good as he knows it. What at first appeared as the timidity of a man caught in a rut which he did not have enterprise enough to get out of now seems to be self-sacrifice and love of family. The violent rages do not appear so often. Al's single-minded devotion to his family stands out against the general background of an America full of vacillating intellectuals. We are led to consider the vast difference between lip-service and action: Al acts by what light he has; the sophisticated world talks and talks and commits itself to nothing.

Another unforgettable character, drawn with pity and repulsion, is Danny's aunt Margaret. In Farrell's books women deteriorate less gracefully than men. Drink, scolding, and piety, sloppy dependence alternating with screaming independence, fatuous chastity with revolting promiscuity, rudeness with cowardice — these qualities make of home a hell. Margaret loves a prosperous businessman who loves her, leaves her, and after sending her money for a time withdraws completely. Margaret meanwhile takes to drink and self-pity. With a different set of circumstances, Margaret might have made a respectable wife; but she is so undisciplined, so vapid, so nasty that the reader cannot feel any considerable sense of waste. Occasionally he does, to be sure, but the image of Margaret as a "respectable" housewife dispels it quickly.

The most effective and moving passages in these volumes, nevertheless, are those which render in one way or another the waste of human potential and the poverty of human relationships among people whose ignorance, insecurity, and emotional maladjustment prevent them from attaining the dignity of which they are presumably capable.

If this statement appears to be a direct contradiction of what I have written about Farrell's defending these people against America and endowing them with "virtues of privation" (i.e., integrity, loyalty, fortitude, and faith) beside which the idle rich look cheap and silly, I can only say that this paradox is in the books and that it defines my sense of their somewhat confused total effect. I would also urge that such an effect cannot be functionally related to naturalism, for it does not proceed necessarily from any of its premises or theories. The effect derives rather from the author's relation to his materials. I see him performing at once acts of penance, of denunciation, and of purgation. He is purging himself through these books of the pent-up exasperations and frustrations of his childhood. He is denouncing the nation and the social system which he deems guilty of the waste of these and millions of other lives. He is doing penance for his own early impatience, his failure of sympathy, his inability to know his father.

Through the Danny O'Neill tetralogy the purgation has been effected; having effected it Farrell has discovered that his own traumata do not differ in essence from those of hundreds of other people who have achieved workable adjustments; and so now he can return a third time to the same materials and treat them another way. The boy whose childhood was blighted by his family's stupidity and crudeness is now seen as not greatly different from thousands of other boys who struggled through unhappy years to security and confidence in themselves. In a new preface to *Studs Lonigan* Farrell explains that Studs was not a "hard guy" but a typical youth from a lower-middle-class family.[3] He does not wish the reader to look down upon Studs but to see that he is presented more realistically than most writers present their characters. Penance has been done, too, and so there is no longer the dammed-up tide of indignation and exasperation with the family and the shame that went with them.

Now if the expression of penance, purgation, and denunciation have rendered the effect of the Danny O'Neill books ambiguous, it should be possible to begin again — to give a complete, objective, and unconfused account of how a young writer fights his way through doubts, discouragements, and indifference to the full realization and recognition of his powers. *Bernard Clare* [4] is the beginning of a third enterprise in autobiography. It is a third look at the material that went into the two earlier works. Bernard has come to New York, at the age of twenty-one, to defy his parents and be a writer. His thoughts move in a narrow orbit of girls, diffidence, scorn, the desire to be a writer, and hatred of all organized business. The novel shows Bernard trying to impress a girl in the New York Public Library; deeply but fruitlessly moved at the execution of Sacco and Vanzetti; at work for United Cigar, where he despises his co-workers and puts out the absolute minimum of effort; engaged in an affair with a married woman whom he tortures with his own scruples; selling advertising in Queens and, again, working only a fraction of the required hours; and finally living in the Y.M.C.A. and attempting to confuse the uplift of that organization by asking cynical questions. Bernard is callow, desperate, earnest, contemptible, unscrupulous. He lives with shyness and desire every waking hour, and when he escapes from these pangs he suffers fearful doubts of the means by which he does so. No emotion or idea possesses him to the point of freeing him from tormented self-consciousness. I know of no character in fiction farther removed from the ideal of personal integration, no one who "thinks with the blood" less than Bernard.

Bernard's thoughts are forever tied to the immediate situation in which he finds himself, and the method of Farrell's writing is to present Bernard's thoughts as he reacts to what he sees. If he is to meditate on the danger of failing and subsequently becoming a worthless bum, it will be because (and when) he is approached in the park by a pitiful old drunk who boasts of his talent. If he despises business, it is when he is listening to businessmen talking business. When Sacco and Vanzetti are executed, Bernard goes to Union Square and is caught up in a surge of proletarian defiance. This constant dependence of thought upon concrete situation keeps the novel rigorously concerned with the personality of the protagonist. It is a source of strength because it is so concrete and immediate; it is impossible for the reader to doubt that what he is reading about is real. The only question is whether experience is properly represented when measured out thus piece by piece. One insight may mean more in a man's life than a thousand hours of reverie or depression.

Viewed in the same scale, Bernard is less admirable than Danny and even than Studs. He is more narrowly self-centered, more contentious, more supercilious, more arrogant, less imaginative. Yet this volume indicates that Bernard is destined to amount to something in the literary world, and the subsequent volumes take him further toward success. The narrowness of outlook, the tendency to ride a single interminable groove of reverie, which were given as evidences of spiritual sterility in Studs, now appear as normal qualities of the questing spirit — the growing pains of all men. In this shifting of perspective the very qualities that were by implication deplored in Studs are now defended in Bernard. "Here," Farrell seems to say, "is what people are really like. Bernard is the way a young man actually is today. He is narrow, self-centered, confined by his fears and doubts. And if you consider him dull, barren, and contemptible you are merely admitting that you prefer a fanciful and idealized image of man to the Real Thing."

Here a very significant shift in the intention of a major naturalist appears. It is a shift in the novelist's conception of truth and in his notion of the purpose of naturalistic writing. The world which he began by denouncing he now proposes to accept and explore, watching the actual so closely that he brings to bear upon it no discernible force of the ideal. Let us see how this new intention affects the conventions of fiction. Bernard wants to write, if we are to judge by the facts given, in order to be able to sneer at Babbitry. Does this make Bernard contemptible, or does it reveal to the reader that most writers' (and therefore most people's) motives are "lower" than we like to suppose? I suspect that neither is true, that Farrell, impelled by the same sense of guilt that leads him in all his books to emphasize the appalling waste of time, energy, and talent which is characteristic of all men, is actually dealing with the ignoble motives of his own experience. We all acknowledge Thoreau's sentence, "I never knew, and never shall know, a worse man than myself," as a just verdict. Whitman makes the same confession ("The wolf, the snake, the hog, not wanting in me") in order to establish contact with Everyman. Do we not all despise ourselves? Do we not all waste our talents and debase the purity of our better selves? But do we get at truth by exposing the hog and the snake in ourselves? Is man fairly represented by a literal account of everything he thinks and does? If Bernard Clare is to become a successful writer, he will have had qualities which are not revealed in this novel. If he is to be just a cheap fourflusher and heel, for all his inner torments, then we are misled by the constant suggestion that he is an important person.

The ironic fact is that every reader of *Bernard Clare* will be able to identify beneath his own respectable exterior impulses and thoughts considerably more vicious than Bernard is credited with — and yet I believe he will consider himself essentially superior to Bernard. This paradoxical situation derives, as I have suggested, from the fact that characterization in the novel has always been highly artificial, representational, conventionalized, selective, and symbolic. According to the convention, characters in novels are not photographed, nor are their lives transcribed factually, with full accounts of every meal eaten and bodily function performed. But these facts are not denied just because they are not dwelt upon. Writers have sought to represent the reality of their characters by dealing with traits, motives, and qualities that are several degrees more interesting, worthy, and able than those of the actual people they represent. We all know this, or we should not dare, for example, to condemn Hamlet's mother as morally insensate — since most of us have on occasion acted more ignobly than she. Farrell has wrenched this convention several degrees in the direction of complete literal reportage, but he has not gone all the way by any means, and the result is an ambiguity: with reference to the convention Bernard is a despicable worm, but with reference to actuality he is "better" than the average pious citizen. In terms of the convention Bernard has an inordinate proportion of unbeautiful qualities, and the reader is too likely to ask whether all this conscientious description of his thoughts is worth his attention — and why the ideal image of Man is so dim in his person.[5] To this Farrell would apparently answer that he is getting closer to the truth than writers have generally done. In terms of actuality Bernard has only a moderate share of vicious tendencies, but in terms of actuality has he enough ideal qualities to make him worth our time? The effect of Farrell's method, in short, is to make his hero appear worse than he "really" (!) is.

Art has always idealized its materials. It has done so, I suppose, because man lives so constantly with his lower nature that he wants, in art, to study his rare best self in patterns of beauty and virtue. This is the source of the convention to which I have referred. It is also true that this convention has always spread a virus of delusion and hypocrisy for which it has been treated by the perennial ministrations of literary radicals, whether in characterization or metrics. The convention was pretty inane when the early naturalists swung into action, but they were working with the convention as well as on it. Let it not be supposed that they were attempting to transfer the bare and stinking actuality of life into the novel.

Farrell writes on after the early assault of his cohorts has succeeded in greatly modifying the convention in the direction of actuality. He is no longer in the context of c. 1930 whence his magnificent *Studs Lonigan* emerged; and to dwell upon Bernard's "lower" nature is to slip into the ambiguity of anachronism, of pushing against something that is no longer there in the same form to push against. Writers today are abundantly aware of the hoggish and snakelike elements that Anthony Trollope barely brushed. With Trollope the convention was perhaps drawing, graciously and exquisitely, somewhat far from actuality. But the James Cains and the John O'Haras have changed all that, and in doing so they have made this aspect of Farrell's naturalistic method supererogatory. The assumption I see in *Bernard Clare* is that this material is important because it is *true*; I believe that Farrell is one of our important writers, but the truths for which I value him are still his insights into the ideal of Man and its struggle for realization and fulfillment — truths which emerge from his books almost in spite of the dogged banality of his style and his masochistic kneading of the gray dough of life.

～ ～

To recapitulate: between *Studs Lonigan* and *Bernard Clare*, Farrell has inverted himself in two ways. In the first place, with each book he has developed a more literal and exhaustive presentation of the facts of life and the quality of thought. Where he began by representing the boredom and limitedness of Studs' outlook, he has come to the point where he gives a much fuller account of the tedious and self-centered reveries of Bernard Clare. He has extended the convention of representation, by which all novelists select and indicate without ever pretending to give the true (and boring) proportion of creative thinking to dull reverie, until his latest manner comes closer to being transcription than representation. Thus the personality of Bernard Clare is less attractive than that of Studs. At the same time, in the second place, Farrell has been constantly modifying his conception of what is admirable. What he first set down as a picture of Studs' appalling spiritual barrenness he has come to defend as a reasonable account of the mind of a typical young American — and he has gone on in the direction of literalness in describing Bernard Clare until a promising writer appears tedious, selfish, and almost contemptible.

The tone of Mr. Farrell's three major works has evolved in a continuing organic relation to their structures. In *Studs Lonigan* the tone of indignation and contempt accompanies the formal tragic structure of the protagonist's disintegration under the impact of his environment; the writer is definitely outside of this work. In the Danny O'Neill books the tone wavers ambiguously, as we have seen, between indignation and defensiveness; the writer is alternately inside and outside of his action; and the structure involves little more than a chronological succession of situations and impressions which could end at any point where the author chose to stop writing. In *Bernard Clare* the tone is far more nearly objective; the writer is pretty consistently inside of his action watching the world through Bernard's eyes, presenting Bernard's mind and personality without judgment other than what I have described as the assumption that Bernard is typical of questing youth; the structure again is merely a chronology of situations and impressions. There is no action beyond the suggestion of self-discovery, and this we must consider somewhat further.

The characterization of Bernard Clare reveals certain very modern ideas about personality which have always been present in Mr. Farrell's work. The tragedy of Studs Lonigan is that he has no moral center, no ethical focus. He never achieves that sense of "moral certainty of self" which marks a fulfilled and effective personality. And this semi-vacuum which is Studs does not ever notably affect anyone. Modern society is responsible for this depersonalizing of personality. Our schools, far from deploring it, stress doing rather than being. An active child cannot pine; if he acts in and with a group he need not even think, for he participates in a mass life and a mass mind. Modern educational theory produces, intentionally, this dissolving of the self in the group. It is organized for the mythical average child, and it is thrown into defensive disorder by the unusual one who makes his little classmates feel inferior. (Recent educational forums on the superior child underline the point.) The world must appear different to this sort of consciousness from the way it appears to a focused personality. Judging from the way one hears them talk, events happen to these children. The world is a spectacle in which they are not ethically involved. Life is like a day at Coney Island. You visit the fun-houses, take the rides, and perhaps you hit a jackpot or meet the girl of your dreams. It can be interesting, dangerous, or dull; you never know till it happens, for you are doing nothing to control your destiny. This is of course an extreme statement of the case against modern man. It would be nearer the truth to say that this is the pattern against which modern men have to rebel if they are to become *persons* — and many do. Bernard Clare is completely unintegrated, but he does have in extraordinary measure the impulse to rebel, and he is forever trying to find himself, to define his own character against the pattern of gray stupidities in the lives around him. There is an ethical impulse in his rebelliousness, but Bernard is too utterly self-centered to care about anything so abstract as a value. He cares only about himself.

A symposium entitled *Naturalism and the Human Spirit*, published in 1947 and containing essays by such distinguished contemporary philosophers and critics as John Dewey, Sidney Hook, and Eliseo Vivas, contains many passages in which the writers attempt to formulate a statement that will retain naturalism's attack on supernaturalism without denying the practical freedom of the will. I say practical because I do not see in these passages statements of ontological or epistemological positions that define the naturalistic cosmos. What I do see is a constantly reiterated identification of naturalism with scientific method. The naturalist sees the world not in timeless abstractions but as a succession of concrete problems. Such problems constitute reality. The naturalist proposes to approach them with an open-minded and dispassionate use of available concrete data. Thus he will discover himself and the world as he responds to the problems which successively present themselves to him. The inference I draw is that the good life will emerge in proportion to the scientific method employed. There is also the implication here that action is more productive than contemplation, that problems which are in theory insoluble dissolve when submitted to the pressure of concrete action. The opposition involved in any theoretical formulation of the problem of will versus determinism disappears under the impact of action. Do not look back to explain how and why something occurred; look forward to discover what lies in the future and can be known only through action.

These formulations reflect a stage in the development of naturalistic theory which can be identified in the evolving forms of Farrell's novels. The first stage assumed perfect determinism, reduced will to a fiction and thought to a chemical reaction; it found its most nearly perfect formal expressions in clinical studies of disease and degeneration and in tragedies of environment where the hapless protagonist was destroyed by the social and economic pressures of his milieu. The second stage followed when these very limited forms were exhausted and when it became increasingly apparent that it was in actual fact quite impossible to demonstrate in a novel a scientific, experimental sequence of causes and effects. The second stage is descriptively naturalistic; it describes the stream of consciousness, or it describes the mind and the experience of a Studs Lonigan in a way that makes what happens to him appear typical and probable. So far as I can see, however, this stage of naturalism, if it does not use the simple tragic form of *Studs*, is either structurally formless or else derives its structure from other sources than naturalistic theory. Most modern psychological novels, if they do not take shape around an act of violence and its violent consequences, lack the structural definition which has been traditional in the novel. We are no longer sure where the novel stops and personal history or reportage begins. The third stage, which eschews abstractions in favor of problem solving, must perforce exist in the flux of its own explorations.

I believe Farrell's *Bernard Clare* can be interpreted as an application of this latest formulation of naturalistic theory. Bernard's past is not presented as an inevitable, law-bound continuum. Rather his present is seen as a threshold to the problems of the future. Bernard finds his way into this future. He *makes* himself by his response to the series of problems with which he is confronted. This statement may be an accurate account of Bernard's relation to his world, but I do not see in it a description of a very effective form for the novel. The writer may indeed present Bernard groping through problem after problem, but in Farrell's style the application of this thesis does not constitute an illuminating organization of reality — except insofar as it is illuminating to see how personalities emerge when they grow without values, without moral certainty of self, and without the conception of personal responsibility.

XI

Later Trends in Form: Steinbeck, Hemingway, Dos Passos

IF NATURALISM takes Anderson and Farrell into cul-de-sacs of banality and repetitiousness, where the forms of pure theoretical naturalism have indeed triumphed over the shaping hand of the artist, John Steinbeck has never gone just this way because he has never relinquished his interest in form or allowed it to be controlled by the naturalistic patterns which have been examined earlier in this study. The two great elements of American naturalism — spirit and fact, the demands of the heart and the demands of the mind — are Steinbeck's constant preoccupation; they form the poles of his thought in almost every one of his novels; but they are never united in an Emersonian pattern of oneness where fact is the symbol and expression of spirit and the union of science and mysticism is acknowledged as natural and inescapable. In Steinbeck's work these principles exist in tension, appearing to pull in opposite directions, and the writer deals with them as if he were confused and doubtful and somewhat surprised to see them emerging from a single phase of experience, as they repeatedly do. It is a surprise and a climax when a blundering Okie like Tom Joad perceives that his spirit is one with all Spirit; is it matter for interest that "the boys" in *Cannery Row* live at an opposite extreme from the scientist, with his music and his research, and at the same time find themselves temperamentally closer to him than to anyone else they know; it is likewise remarkable that the communist and the doctor in *In Dubious Battle* have comparable aims and are able to talk with each other about the plight of man. These oppositions show that Steinbeck is everywhere seeking, if not to re-unite, at least to reconcile the divided stream of transcendentalism — but that he sees its parts in dramatic conflict. The forms of his novels depend, however, not alone upon these dramatic oppositions (although these are indeed crucial in the structure of his books) but also upon the conscious imitation of a number of well-established traditional forms. Steinbeck's naturalism is neither mechanistic, nor clinical, nor descriptive; rather it is dramatic and exploratory. The forms of his novels are patterned, as I shall show, on conventional types; his naturalism figures as a set of conflicting ideas in them. It is not a new way, for him, of arranging reality or of dealing with causation or personality.

Thus we see in novel after novel a belief in science, a firm belief in material causation, a belief in the spontaneous goodness of simple men, and a radical distrust of commerce, industry, the business outlook, and conventional piety and morality. The latter he finds either fraudulent or irrelevant to the fundamental problems of men — except insofar as they interfere. These ideas seem to pull Steinbeck in various directions: toward science, toward brotherhood, and less clearly toward transcendentalism and revolution. His ideals draw him to naturalistic primitivism and toward mysticism; his despair at the inhumanities of commercialism pulls him toward the opposing extremes of retreat and revolution. His forms do not embody these forces; rather they are conventional genre-forms that permit his characters to express and to move about among these ideas.

The *Cup of Gold* (1929) is an adventure story patterned after the quest for the Holy Grail. In *To a God Unknown* (1933), which deals with a farmer whose devotion to his land becomes a mystical pagan fertility cult that leads to suicide when his crops fail, the form is that of chronicle, appropriate for the presentation of a myth. The counterpoint of mysticism and absorption in natural process here first strikes the note that rings through the later works.

In *Tortilla Flat* (1935) we turn to a mock epic. Danny and the other *paisanos* of Monterey live a wild life of irresponsible gaiety, as happy as they are poor, until they find treasure. Then come greed and fear and drink and finally a mock-epical disaster in which the hero is destroyed in a general debacle. The rollicking independence of these *paisanos*, their poverty, their touching poetic enthusiasms are calls of a spirit free from the drudging materialism of conventional American life. But, alas, Danny and his friends are not finally proof against the demands of the devil of materialism, for although they will not work for money they will gladly take and use it when it comes to them free; and since their use of it is not disciplined by puritanical thrift and responsibility, or by a typical businessman acquisitiveness, they cannot use it without being destroyed by it. Here again there is double counterpoint: the unspoiled *paisanos* are ignorant and miserable even while they are gay — for the demands of spirit are not fully met within the limitations imposed on them by their ignorance and consequent poverty. And when the money comes they have the source of power without the means to control it, and they run wild. Steinbeck is thus in effect lamenting the division of the American transcendental ideal into a condition where knowledge and spirit (power and love) are nowhere properly joined. Because it is not exactly feasible to defy the whole massed array of American materialism with a handful of barefoot *paisanos*, Steinbeck draws the action in mock-epic tone — but the grim idea is not far under the rowdy surface, and Steinbeck's sympathy is clearly with the simple, goodhearted people who are not equipped to cope with evil.

The form of *In Dubious Battle* (1936) is sharply dramatic, building a conflict between the communist organizer who is dominated by an idea so completely that he has lost his sense of the value of the individual and the simple, pathetic goodness of the fruit pickers whom he "organizes" into strikes, starvation, bloodshed, and defeat. The fruit growers, with their deputies and their guns, are set in dramatic opposition to the pickers, who are loyal and generous. And in a sort of counterpoint there stands opposed to the heartless (or misguided) communist a doctor who tends the sick and injured and comments wisely and tenderly upon the dubious battle as he observes it. The intellectual pattern here is too rich to be simply formulated, but we can identify the issues of love (or sharing) versus greed where the true and false attitudes toward matter appear, and of dispassionate benevolence (the doctor) versus misguided idealism (the organizer) where the true and false expressions of spirit appear. In this book Steinbeck obviously believes in the tender wisdom of the scientist and the warm hearts of the people. The people are good but weak; the doctor is wise but a condition of his wisdom is nonparticipation. The conflict is not satisfactorily resolved because the battle is dubious. That is, it does not appear in 1936 that love and intelligence are winning over greed and bigotry; whereas the violent force of communism that has undertaken to act in the interests of the people becomes as destructive as the rapacity of the fruit growers. The dialectic of the situation does not work into a new synthesis but remains in tension, for the antithesis of communism is not valid for America, and the antitheses of love and wisdom are not yet powerful enough to prevail.

In Dubious Battle evolves in a closely knit action as the strike mounts in stubbornness and the reprisals of the owners mount in violence. The strike fails because the force of the owners is superior to the force of the strikers, but, as I have suggested, the issue is not pointed in favor of the stronger order and discipline which the communist would impose upon the workers. The communist's values receive their *dramatic* evaluation in the scene where the old communist, Mac, uses the body of his young friend and convert to arouse the spirit of the strikers. He appears to have no feeling for the humanity of his dead friend. Such impersonality, one feels, outrages the sense of brotherhood, the transcendental dream of the dignity of man, without which social reform becomes meaningless. This idea (penetrating indeed for a radical in 1936!) finds significant expression in the note of inconclusiveness which closes the book. The dramatic form has enabled Steinbeck to present an issue, to elaborate some of its ideological implications, and to pass in the end a judgment. He demonstrates that the battle is fruitless because neither side is right. The love and brotherhood of the workers must be implemented by something closer to the American grain than communism if it is to come into its own and unify the American Dream of a full life for all.

The doctor in the story regards all forms of human warfare as "diseases" of society that periodically destroy its effectiveness. He thinks that mankind would preserve itself if it could eliminate these terrible plagues of violence. But his speculations do not lead him to moral zeal or commitment to action, so that he lacks the power without which his thought is ineffective. This constant separation of power and wisdom seems to be the great puzzle to Steinbeck. It is a version of the flaw in creation that philosophers call the Problem of Evil. It is to be solved by some sort of rational idealism which grasps the *meaning* of the physical universe. Here is a transcendental-naturalistic outlook which does not control the form of Steinbeck's novel so much as appear in it. The form is a conventional dramatic opposition of groups of people, and the action seems controlled by intention and choice rather than by forces superior to the wills of the individuals involved. All modern writing with any degree of sophistication of course acknowledges the forces that limit individual freedom. In this area Steinbeck is not unusual. Beyond mechanism and determinism structurally, he discusses as it were in dramatic form the problems that arise from the divided stream of transcendentalism.

Of Mice and Men (1937) is a script for a cinema, a scenario of a little well-made drama. The title suggests that the best laid plans of mice and men gang aft agley, and the idea is quite explicitly naturalistic. The leading characters of this story, George and Lennie, are little better than mice in the maze of modern life. Loyal, foolish, weak, yet possessed of physical power to destroy themselves, they are the People. They are spirit and power inchoate, mixed in chaos rather than fused in form. Lennie's feeble-mindedness symbolizes the helplessness of the folk in a commercial society; perhaps in a larger frame it symbolizes the bewilderment of man in a mindless cosmos. The bond between him and George is not strong enough to let them succeed in the modern world.

The Grapes of Wrath (1939) presents the same issues in the form of epic. The great movement of the Okies across the dustbowl and into the Promised Land of California suggests the biblical analogy of the Chosen People fleeing into Israel. The story is shaped in heroic dimensions, and like the great epics of the past it is laid out over the face of the nation whose struggle it depicts. America struggling with the Depression, struggling for very life, is epic. The Joads are heroes specified among a whole people at war, hurling themselves against the armies of finance and fear. The conflict is not personal but national — which is the essence of the epic spirit. The cross-play of the major themes of Steinbeck's naturalism appears as before: in the people are love, brotherhood, integrity; in the exploiting classes fear, power, suspicion, violence. And in counterpoint speak the ideal forms of these elements: although the people are inadequately equipped to triumph through love, Casy, the Okie preacher, utters thoroughly transcendental statements of the perfection and universality of spirit, and Tom Joad toward the end of the story speaks the same language; whereas the interchapters constitute the author's running commentary on science and material power misused. These chapters say again and again that the fruits of invention and industry need not be human waste and social desolation. The epic search of the Joads overland, a symbol of quest, may indicate the proportions of the effort that will have to be made before any solution to the problem of abundance and desolation is reached. No solution is reached in the book: the climactic incident of Rose of Sharon, having lost her own baby, suckling a starving stranger, indicates that Steinbeck finds his answer in love rather than in revolution. The need for the interchapters, however, reveals that the author's acceptance of a transcendental idea has not carried over into significant form: the themes of quest and struggle and the exposition of the capitalist dilemma of scarcity and "overproduction" are not structurally unified.

The idealistic union of science and mysticism is the theme and the problem of *Sea of Cortez* (1941). This later minor work is a collaboration with E. F. Ricketts, a marine biologist who undoubtedly inspired the figure of "Doc" in *Cannery Row*. *Sea of Cortez* is the record of an expedition to the Gulf of Lower California to observe and collect the flora and fauna of its teeming waters. Mingled with descriptions of sea life are accounts of the ideas and speculations which arose from their scientific findings and from the discussions in which they engaged. These two levels of activity come to stand for the realities of nature and spirit, which have their fusion in human experience. This point is made fairly early in the book, when Steinbeck explicitly declares the identity of the self and what it knows by having an Indian muse, "Of course it will rain tonight, I don't know why. Something in me tells me I will rain tonight. Of course, I am the whole thing, now that I think about it. I ought to know when I will rain." [1]

Such speculations lead Steinbeck to present a concept of Being as a mystical allness that may be felt or intuitively known, somewhat as one is aware of one's environment, without being fully understood. Everything one does understand scientifically adds to one's sense that the total plan, though perfect, is somehow unknowable:

> In such a pattern, causality would be merely a name for something that exists only in our partial and biased mental reconstructions. The pattern which it indexes, however, would be real, but not intellectually apperceivable because the pattern goes everywhere and is everything and cannot be encompassed by finite mind or by anything short of life — which it is . . .[2]

The essence of this pattern is in the gaps between what we can know — gaps between species, gaps between kinds of knowledge, gaps in our calculations:

> The differential is the true universal, the true catalyst, the cosmic solvent. Any investigation carried far enough will bring to light these residua, or rather will leave them still unassailable as Emerson remarked a hundred years ago in "The Oversoul" — will run into the brick wall of the *impossibility* of perfection while at the same time insisting on the *validity* of perfection. Anomalies especially testify to that framework; they are the commonest intellectual vehicles for breaking through; all are solvable in the sense that any *one* is understandable, but that one leads with the power of n to still more and deeper anomalies.[3]

Here then we end with a mystery which is nevertheless meaningful and designed; and the quantum of Planck becomes a generalized philosophical principle. Steinbeck speaks, indeed, of the "universality of quanta," [4] by which he means the unbridgeable gaps or the impossible calculations that appear at the terminal point of any investigation. In this system nature and spirit are expressions of the same whole, and "the truth of the mind and the way mind is must be an index of things, the way things are." [5] These conclusions, presented speculatively in this volume, make a fascinating preamble to Steinbeck's next novel.

Cannery Row (1945) resembles in tone and spirit *Tortilla Flat*, but whereas I have called the latter a mock epic I should call the former a farce. It is the story of a group of self-determined social outcasts — "the boys," they are called — who loaf by their wits on the outskirts of a California town, inhabiting a deserted house which serves as office and binder of their fellowship. Their irresponsible doings are presented farcically and with gusto. What these doings seem to mean is that formal society is a mechanical stupidity, an outrage to the free spirit, an absurd waste of life which must be defied by the cunning "misfits" and resourceful loafers who make a glory of having neither goal nor purpose in their lives.

This genial irresponsibility is balanced by the wholly admirable figure of a scientist who, although equally independent of formal society, does have a purpose. "Doc," a marine biologist, lives in the same town a life of utter unconventionality and devotion to science. The "boys" discover that he is like them, that he can understand and help them, and that his life embraces values which they can wholly admire if not emulate. Thus emerge, more or less fused, the two great strands of Steinbeck's transcendental naturalism: the belief in the unfettered human spirit, and the belief that exact scientific knowledge will bring us to inmost truths. Both strands appear with noteworthy differences from what they were a generation earlier. The unfettered human spirit of the boys is not socially active, whereas the liberating value of Doc's science consists in its being a way of life rather than a key or an answer

to the riddle of the universe. Doc's life has form because it is controlled in devotion to an ideal. The boys are admirable because
they are spontaneous and because they take joy in the simple
physical pleasures of life.

The story, which I have called a farce, comes to a climax when
these boys invade Doc's house and in a night of wild irresponsible
drunkenness reduce it to a shambles. What does this mean? I believe it shows that Steinbeck is not as irresponsible himself as he
has often been considered. He has been blamed for presenting
his boys as if they were exemplary citizens; reviewers of *Cannery
Row* wanted to know what would happen to America if the boys
were taken as examples. But the way they destroy the possessions of
their good friend who trusts them shows that mere defiance of accepted standards and values does not make a way of life. The boys
represent only half the answer. Doc's quiet expeditions to the sea-
side to collect specimens illustrate the devoted rather than the
irresponsible escape from society.

The Wayward Bus (1947) was received coldly and has not been
widely read; its relative failure can be laid, I believe, to the fact
that it presents a naïve version of that tension in Steinbeck's
thought that has been so interesting because so typical of the
American dilemma. According to the epigraph, a quotation from
Everyman, the work is a "morall playe"; but every serious work
of fiction is in some sense a morall playe because all deal with the
representative as well as the particular. This novel bears a strong
formal resemblance to *The Canterbury Tales* — where of course
the element of morall playe is ubiquitous — for it introduces a
number of American pilgrims on a bus trip, the trials, surprises,
and conflicts of which allow them to reveal themselves and to test
the values which they have absorbed from our culture against the
native strength of the Mexican-American driver, Juan. Juan is the
strong one. The spoiled wives, intellectual girls, rapacious businessmen, misers, and girls who live on men all learn from Juan
as they discover that their needs which have been frustrated and
exacerbated by American commercialism could be clarified and
in several instances satisfied through the agency of his life; its

integrity, competence, and moral certainty of self evince a spiritual organization that rootless Americans do not have.

The naïveté of this novel, which as I have said has prevented its being favorably received, appears in the fact that Juan's personal superiority is not justified. He comes from Mexico; he is a good mechanic; he is a good lover; he knows what he wants; he has contempt for aimless Americans; he yearns sometimes for the fidelity of his semiprimitive forebears. He is, in short, set up before us as a noble savage who can repair a bus and haul it out of a hole better than a typical American can do. There is something phoney in this sort of primitivism, for neither Juan's Mexican-Catholic roots nor his mechanical competence go deep enough to account for his superiority to the group of travelers.

Tortilla Flat and *Cannery Row* are comic (i.e., mock epic and farce) presentations of the conflict between the demands of matter and the demands of spirit. Whereas *Tortilla Flat* makes a mock epic of the destruction of the corrupted *paisanos*, *Cannery Row* brings in an early flash of Steinbeck's solution, namely, science. His scientist is neither footless like "the boys" nor sordidly materialistic like those whose major goal is money. He is a local outcast with larger affiliations to the worlds of knowledge and spirit. Steinbeck's third use of the same sort of situation in *The Pearl* (1947) is a serious parable. Wealth brings misery to the poor Indian pearl diver. The misery indeed precedes the wealth, for Kino is beleaguered by thieves and murderers who would wrest his enormous pearl from him. The only actual prosperity he knows is the feverish generosity of those who seek to dupe him. After terrible hardship and the loss of his baby, Kino and his wife return to the simple life by the sea, but they have been brayed in the crucible of the world and burned black by its evil. They are bewildered and sad but hardly wiser. Kino does hurl the great pearl back into the sea, as his wife had tried to do earlier, but this is an act of desperate withdrawal from the world that has hurt them. The parable seems to suggest both that Kino is better off as a primitive and that he is defeated because he does not have the knowledge of civilized men which enables them to trick and

267

destroy him. It says that wealth is the root of all evil. But on the other hand it says that knowledge is power and power over the material world is good. And it says there is strength in simplicity. But Kino's strength fails through ignorance: the pure heart is not enough, just as it was not enough for the fruit pickers of *In Dubious Battle*. *The Pearl* has the quiet strength of its hero, Kino, and in this respect is impressive; but the simple symbolism of the parable cannot resolve the great contradictions of its themes. Once again we see that Steinbeck's naturalistic themes have not been finally welded, in significant form, into that marriage of spirit and matter by science that Steinbeck so obviously yearns for.

Steinbeck's use of traditional forms appears in the parables with which he sets forth the theme of more than one of his novels. In *The Grapes of Wrath* there is the parable of the tortoise crossing the highway. Knocked by a car, carried off by Tom Joad, beaten by sun and wind, he is the People; he struggles on indomitably, and he probably in the end reaches his destination. This is the story of *The Grapes of Wrath*. *Cannery Row* contains a charming chapter about a gopher who builds a beautiful home on a perfect site, where there are no cats and no traps and perfect drainage, but where, alas, he waits in vain for a mate to appear, and so finally has to leave his paradise and go seek a mate where there are traps and other dangers. This is the story of *Cannery Row*: you can't eat your cake and have it; you can't enjoy the luxuries of civilization without paying for them. *The Wayward Bus* has a scene in which a disgustingly drunk woman tries to kill a fly, in her store, and succeeds only in breaking dishes and destroying food. The fly, expertly evading, is described in metaphors of the airplane. The fly symbolizes the efficiency and integration of Juan; whereas the drunken woman typifies individuals disorganized and debauched by our commercial society. This is the substance of *The Wayward Bus*. The drunken woman, furthermore, is Juan's wife; she of course symbolizes the commercial world from which he cannot free himself.

I assemble these animal fables because they epitomize Steinbeck's typical mixture of naturalistic idea with conventional form. The form merely *illustrates* the idea with a sort of analogy. It does not represent the successful embodiment and interaction of the forces from which the idea grows. This statement does not only describe Steinbeck; to a degree it describes the presence of naturalistic ideas in a great deal of contemporary fiction: naturalistic ideas and attitudes are everywhere now, but they rarely control the form as the early naturalists attempted to make them do. In many contemporary novels naturalistic ideas have prevented the use of ethical-dramatic motivation and structure and have left the novelist with nothing in the way of form but a loose chronological stringing-together of experience. This has gone on to the point where the line between the novel and the journalistic autobiography has nearly disappeared. A truly significant form would solve symbolically the problem of the tension — at present unresolved — between the ideal and the material, the demands of spirit and the cold force of matter, the dream of brotherhood and the instrument of science. It would, that is, if this were possible.

If the test of a philosophy is whether it can be imaginatively incarnated in works of art, the formal looseness of so much contemporary fiction would seem to indicate that naturalism cannot achieve the coherence and integrity that go with a completely acceptable criticism of life. Or it may merely indicate that naturalism lost its grip before it took a real hold, that modern man has been baffled by the findings of science and by his inability to assimilate them and has therefore turned away from them toward either the growing religiosity or the defeated questing of existentialism which have dominated the period from 1930 to the present. A striking example of the sort of formless search that I have mentioned is Harold Robbins's *Never Love a Stranger*, a "novel" in which the lack of center appears not only in the loose accumulation of the action but also in the character of the hero, who toward the end of his chronicle remarks:

But what about me? I had never turned to look inside myself. What about me. Of all the people I knew, I knew myself least of all. Why did I do things? What did I want? Why was I content to drift, never really searching for an answer to myself? I wondered. What did I want? Money? Love? Friends? Respect? I searched through my mind for the answer, but none was forthcoming.

I had read a lot while I lived with Marianne. She had quite a few books, and I had devoured them — some good, some bad — but the answer wasn't in them. What did people think about me? What was there in me that they liked? Why did they take me into their homes and hearts when I had so little to give in return? [6]

Another such chronicle is *Knock on Any Door*, by Willard Motley, which on a somewhat larger canvas depicts the vicious life of a character without character, a personality without any knowledge of himself. We are told that his instincts are not bad, and we see that crime and vice attract him because he has not been properly educated; but because he is not a personality with an ethical center his story is a tract, or a case history, with sociological implications but without the form and insight that make art. Steinbeck has advanced beyond mechanistic naturalism to the point where he has recognized the two halves of the divided stream of American transcendentalism. His conventional forms have provided means for illustrating his ideas (which are for the most part questions) but they have not permitted him to embody the forces with which his ideas deal.

～ ～

The categories which have been set forth for the analysis of naturalism do not apply very effectively to the work of Ernest Hemingway. The themes, motifs, and techniques of naturalism can all be identified in his work, it is true, but one must be content to acknowledge that Hemingway is not contained by them. He triumphs in the end over the great naturalistic breach which I have described in this volume. His reintegration of spirit and matter, of the demands of science and idealism, in *For Whom the Bell Tolls*, culminates a career which in its earlier phases exemplifies the division of these principles. His early works struggle and protest continually against the fact that modern public morality, having lost touch with the facts of life, reveals a corrupt and despicable travesty of idealism. In them the very concept of idealism is eschewed because it has been so badly mauled that Hemingway will have nothing to do with it, while he concentrates on establishing certain definite, tangible, basic *areas* of experience that he can treat without being contaminated by the prevailing hypocrisy of his time. These areas — love, sex, violence, fear, death, and certain scrupulously presented versions of human intercourse — define Hemingway's search for what is concretely real and can therefore be presented in terms of actual — we might almost say physical — experience. The values in these early works are generally negative. Positive values are presented with a diffidence that approaches aversion.

Although it is true that Hemingway eschews "ideals" and "values" in favor of concrete and actual experience in his early writings, it is obvious that this program is motivated by ideals and values which appear perhaps not in but certainly between the lines in everything he writes. A typical early story is "Big Two-Hearted River" in which the leading character goes out to a strong river and expertly catches a pair of fine trout. The story, scrupulously objective, is alive with gusto for things skillfully done. The character knows just where in the river to expect the best trout to strike; he is equipped with precisely the right tackle; he has and he enjoys the possession of a quick eye and firm muscles. The thrill of fighting the big fish he hooks is so great that it makes his shoulders ache and his hands tremble. His excitement when a great trout breaks his line is so intense that he has to climb out of the stream and rest on the bank. It becomes so strong, presently, that he stops with just two big fish for supper. Here is a summit of well-being, for the fisher is at once enjoying a pure and satisfying physical experience and the sense of being clean and free from the confusions and hypocrisies of society. The experience is presented as a sort of catharsis in which the man cleanses and liberates his simple capacities and physical drives by using them exclusively. Yet the story is dark with fear and tension, too, under the studied objectivity of the description, for the man is trying almost desperately to regain the physical composure that he enjoyed before his nerves were shattered in the war. This need makes the fishing a serious image of life as well as the practice of a sportsman's skill; it is the tension and fear under the surface that give the story its extraordinary power. With Hemingway there is always present an extra dimension and intensity of meaning because every simple physical fact is loaded with significances.

In "The Capital of the World" we are shown what it takes to make a bullfighter. After the matadors and picadores have gone home, two waiters in a Madrid restaurant make beautiful veronicas and reboleras with their aprons. The thing needed, the older tells the younger, is not skill but courage; and to convince his young friend of this fact he fastens two sharp knives to a chair and pretends to be a charging bull. Young Paco on the third pass moves in too close, his femoral artery is severed by the sharp knife, and he dies in a few minutes, still "full of illusions." The incident brings out the confused values of the sordid world of whores and broken-down bullfighters in which Paco lives, and it takes us at the end to the inescapable fact of death which is still real even in a world full of illusions.

Death and violence are the substance of *Death in the Afternoon* (1932) where the art of bullfighting unites technique and danger, pattern and peril, beauty and terror. The art which takes the matador to the very brink of death with every pass finds its meaning in the danger and invests with nobility a life otherwise dull and sordid. Indeed it is significant that the bullfighters are men without focus or meaning — or are intolerably vain and arrogant — except when their lives take form in the bull ring. Here is one way that Hemingway embodies an idea that appears constantly in his work. The chaos of life takes shape where technique and peril are fused in some sort of purposeful activity. The peril is essential: without it technique is, to Hemingway, frivolous. (Any waiter in Madrid can do perfect veronicas with an apron.) This idea, accompanying his "naturalistic" attack on conventional values, is an affirmation of humanity against an alien universe. It is significant that this affirmation does not deny that the cosmos is without meaning or purpose and does not affirm any participation of the supernatural in human affairs. Hemingway's affirmation is highly pragmatic: the tonic and discipline of danger glow in his lines. This discipline is necessary because, as he tells in this famous passage from *A Farewell to Arms,* the old values have been corrupted until they are worse than dirty words:

I was always embarrassed by the words sacred, glorious, and sacrifice and the expression in vain. We had heard them sometimes standing in the rain almost out of earshot, so that only the shouted words came through, and had read them, on proclamations that were slapped up by billposters over other proclamations, now for a long time, and I had seen nothing sacred, and the things that were glorious had no glory and the sacrifices were like the stock-yards at Chicago if nothing was done with the meat except to bury it. There were many words that you could not stand to hear and finally only the names of places had dignity . . . Abstract words such as glory, honor, courage, or hallow were obscene beside the concrete names of villages . . .[7]

Morality is an aspect of action. In *Green Hills of Africa* Hemingway says, "I know only that what is moral is what you feel good after." Lady Brett, in *The Sun Also Rises,* having done a decent thing, comments, "I feel rather good, you know. I feel rather set up." And, being a little drunk, she elaborates as she would not have done sober, "It's sort of what we have instead of God."

Hemingway's pursuit of concrete experience uncorrupted by the shams and hypocrisies of society takes him into other attempts to escape the constrictions of "normal" life. One of these is the concept of the idyl. It appears in *The Sun Also Rises* when Mike and his friend go up into the Spanish hills on a fishing trip. There for a while they are refreshed and liberated in a simple contact with nature. They are reduced to simple activities and simple needs, and their personal relations are correspondingly purified. The idyl takes place in a hospital in *A Farwell to Arms,* where the wounded hero and his nurse are isolated from the world and completely absorbed in their love. In *To Have and Have Not* the hero, Henry Morgan, is the good, direct, earthy, perfectly honest man, and he is *therefore* driven into what our society makes a life of crime. Henry Morgan has too much integrity and gusto to be able to conform. So he runs rum into Florida in his boat. He lives with danger and skill, taking the day's events as they come, sexually attuned to his wife, courageous and vital. His life itself is the idyl, presented in contrast to the follies and frustrations of the corrupt and wealthy women for whom he daily risks it; but his defiance links him to that society: his service enables it to defy the laws which it has enacted as pious gestures, as nods toward a morality which it does not intend to practice, as expiatory scourging for sins which it does not intend to forgo. It is therefore almost inevitable that the agent of its repentance should suffer the peril and the punishment that it deserves. Henry Morgan's needs as an individual make him the scapegoat of the society which he means to defy.

Between the needs of the individual and the demands of society (or nature) there is a perpetual contest in which the individual is destroyed in direct proportion to the "nobility" of his needs or the purity of his impulses. There is no problem or contest for the individual who has become completely identified with his milieu; those partially assimilated to cant and humbug are merely discontented; whereas those whose spiritual demands are greatest find themselves in positions where they are in conflict with both the physical and the social environment. This contest controls the form of most of Hemingway's work. In *The Sun Also Rises* Jake has, to begin with, suffered a wound in the war which has destroyed his sexual powers. This emasculation (if that is what it is) is symbolic of what the modern world has done to its people. The Lady Brett, who loves Jake, is by that love also cut off from fulfillment. And so the book moves in a comic frame of search and frustration *after* the main contest has been resolved by this defeat of the leading characters. A significant though minor expression of the same theme appears in the plight of the young bullfighter whose prowess is threatened by greed, lust, and vanity. Lady Brett, "seeking reality," is his undoing, until she makes herself feel "good" by renouncing her intention of marrying him.

The theme of involvement and conflict dominates *A Farewell to Arms*. It is explicitly stated in several famous passages. The protagonist, for example, speculates on what happens to people who allow themselves to become involved emotionally or committed to a person or a cause:

If people bring so much courage to this world the world has to kill them to break them, so of course it kills them. The world breaks every one and afterward many are strong at the broken places. But those that will not break it kills. It kills the very good and the very gentle and the very brave impartially. If you are none of these you can be sure it will kill you too but there will be no special hurry.[8]

Although involvement brings hurt, it is impossible not to become involved, for to remain forever apart is to deny one's most urgent needs. The conflict between individual needs and social demands is matched by the contest between feeling man and unfeeling universe, and between the spirit of the individual and his biological limitations. Catherine's death in childbirth at the end of *A Farewell to Arms* represents the unpredictable and, apparently, uncontrollable power of biological environment over the human spirit. Her love for Henry, which was the most private and personal thing in her life, brings upon her this destructive force. Not every loving woman must die in childbirth, but Hemingway makes his point that no one is proof against the fatal and arbitrary onslaughts of this mindless universe — onslaughts which are more savage against the good, the gentle, and the brave. Henry acknowledges this plight when he says, "You always feel trapped biologically."

Nick Adams in "The Killers" represents a simple version of involvement or what might as well be called the discovery of evil. He finds that nothing can be done for Ole Andreson, who has got in trouble with the underworld and knows that he must sooner or later pay the price by being shot down in cold blood. Nick would like to help, and he would like not to know that such things can happen. He can do neither. Henry Morgan, in *To Have and Have Not*, living in defiance of society, is nevertheless caught in the end and killed in a fight with gunmen. Outside of society, he nevertheless lives on it through his rum-running, and its evil finally reaches out for him. Thus the strong suffer. Another fine story,

"The Snows of Kilimanjaro," reveals the thoughts of a dying man who has betrayed his abilities and his awareness of man's plight, for the sensual and material attractions of our society. He has done so because the disillusion of the post-World War I era has made it easy for him to capitalize on his charm and personality and make the idle rich support him. Like Henry Morgan, he has been destroyed by the thing he despised. Rich society has consumed him, let him betray his vision, and left him to die with no truths expressed in the stories he was capable of writing.

The style of these stories and novels is keyed to the various levels of naturalistic thought which they express. When the intention is to catch some of the few physical, tangible realities that the disillusioned man may trust, the style is bare. Even the subordinate clause is eschewed, with the effect of eliminating all complexities that may be traced to the human mind and therefore may not exist in the pure nature of things. (This assumption is of course a romantic pretense — a metaphor of integrity, like Robinson Jeffers's admiration of hawks and stones, but it is a powerful symbol too.) The opening lines of *A Farewell to Arms* are representative of this mode. When the characters experience heightened emotion, Hemingway often reveals only their outward physical reactions; but when he goes into the mind of a character, he slips into a stream-of-consciousness technique that renders the flavor of intense emotion still without forcing him to use the abstractions he distrusts.

The great change in Hemingway's work came with *For Whom the Bell Tolls* (1940), the most explicit, sustained, and triumphant reunion of its divided stream that American naturalism has seen. The story of Robert Jordan is the story of an intellectual, radical, atheistical, naturalistic American who finds that in order to save one's life one may have to lose it. Robert Jordan leaves his sophisticated security as an American teacher of English and goes to Spain to fight, to love, to understand, and finally to die for the antifascist cause in the Civil War. In this novel Hemingway makes the connection between material conditions and spiritual insight toward which he has been reaching in all of his earlier works. The Spanish people teach him that integrity is wholeness, that in integrity the demands of the heart and the demands of material satisfaction are fused in good living. It is significant that Hemingway should discover this transcendental fusion not, for example, in American regionalism but in the primitive integrity of the Spanish peasant. Of the earth earthy, he walks on the inelastic plank of famine, and his emotions arise from the core of humanity. His thinking is of a piece with his very existence, for he has no place to flee, no refuge, no sanctuary, no escape. When he opposes the fascists he does so with his whole self. His commitment is complete, irrevocable, fatal — an act of the whole man.

Jordan, the American intellectual, finds with these Spanish peasants fighting for their lives the condition for his act of total commitment. With them he is enabled to achieve an almost complete integrity because he is on a losing side which he has joined voluntarily and from which he could presumably escape. Thus, so far as any person is ever free, he is in a situation of his own choosing, and in it the demands of spirit and the demands of physical reality are welded into inseparable unity.

Hemingway's style undergoes changes that reflect the new spiritual commitments of this book. In the earlier novels and stories Hemingway limits himself to simple sentences or to sentences in which simple statements are connected by *and's* or *but's*. This self-imposed limitation is an aspect of his statement that he will not be taken in by the hypocrisies of our society; he will not bother with tenuous complexities when his particular aim is to cut through conventional cant and get down to some few basic experiences which a man can have and talk about without feeling soiled. But having served a long apprenticeship in this rigorous school, the writer now in *For Whom the Bell Tolls* uses the complex and the compound-complex sentence freely, saying in his manner-of-saying that now he dares handle subtleties and complexities of thought because they are complexities which he has earned for himself. He has not taken them over ready-made from the public store; he has earned them one by one and now he is entitled to test and weigh them at whatever length he chooses.

The form of this novel depends upon the artificial but effective pattern of a military skirmish — it could not be called a campaign or even a maneuver — of four days' duration. In the embrace of violence and death the characters discover and reveal themselves and the novel vibrates with power and life. Its center — the attempt to defend a position and protect a retreat from the fascists — gives meaning and focus to the entire lives of the people involved. Robert Jordan, having blown the bridge which the fascists needed for their attack, has his leg broken when his horse is shot and falls on him. Left behind on the slope of the gorge, he will kill one or two more fascists before he dies:

Robert Jordan saw them there on the slope, close to him now, and below he saw the road and the bridge and the long lines of vehicles below it. He was completely integrated now and he took a good long look at everything. Then he looked up at the sky. There were big white clouds in it. He touched the palm of his hand against the pine needles where he lay and he touched the bark of the pine trunk that he lay behind.

The form of naturalistic novels has traditionally depended upon external cycles of disease, justice, or economic activity, and the cycle provided by war responds perfectly to the demands of a tradition which, presumably eschewing the forms of dramatic-ethical conflict and denouement, needs a movement and shape provided by forces other than the decisions and choices of the characters. The Spanish War further serves the needs of the idealistic half of the divided stream of transcendentalism because it provides a situation in which the part reveals the whole: here the single incident is a pattern of all incidents in which men fight for the higher values of brotherhood and justice. "No man is an island" says the epigraph. The bell tolls for us too. The unity of the incident and the universal is thus affirmed and demonstrated. With the tragic ending and the completed task which brings integration and understanding to Robert Jordan as he is about to die, there is no looseness of form or shapeless accumulation of details. The microcosm appears further in the love of the hero for Maria, a Spanish girl who has been raped and almost driven insane by the fascists. She is restored by her love for Jordan; and he finds with her an emotional counterpart to the spiritual fulfillment that comes to him during the action. He makes her leave him at the end by saying, over and over, "Thou will go now, rabbit. But I go with thee. As long as there is one of us there is both of us."

Techniques of stream of consciousness and impressionism, which make the late novels of Sherwood Anderson so formless, contribute greatly to the power and depth of *For Whom the Bell Tolls*, for its thematic and formal unity are only enriched by any detail of thought or reverie in the leading characters. It is the relevance of all such detail, indeed, that contributes powerfully to the novel's effect of seeming to render the whole life and soul of each character and to show that the meaning of a life embraces its total world.

Having achieved his unity, Hemingway has used it in one bad and one good book. In *Across the River and into the Trees* (1950), he works back through the terrors of World War I, through the heroism of World War II, and prepares to die as a tough old fighter loving a perfect young girl. In *The Old Man and the Sea* (1952) he writes a symbolic account of his old argument: that a man must have a skill which he practices perfectly in the presence of great danger. The Old Man in this superb story catches a huge marlin which is eaten up before he can get it back to land; but he has lived greatly during his two-day contest with the fish and the sharks, and he is ready for new encounters at the end. They will be tragic, embodying his knowledge of himself and the world, and he will have always new and harder challenges from a nature that is endlessly resourceful in defeating her bravest challengers. Here nature and spirit are fused in a formal pattern composed of human skill and the natural challenge or obstacle to which it is keyed. The skill achieves substance and life as a dance, a ritual, or a sport, the unpredictable natural element becoming the medium in which the skill finds expression, form, and significance.

In the bullfight of earlier stories the fusion is forced and ritualistic; Hemingway demands that the matador come dangerously close to the horns, for the ritual has meaning only if it is made very real by the imminence of death. With the old fisherman the ceremony is purer; he has to fish to live. Between the perils of starvation and death at sea he enacts a ritual more basic than the bullfighter's and therefore more noble. In the supreme challenge of the enormous marlin he wins; and then he loses his catch to the sharks. The rich symbol grows through the action into a picture of man's life. His spirit can find substance and expression — which is to say existence itself — only in a more or less fatal involvement with natural forces which will some day triumph over him. In these precarious conditions life has its beauty because it has form — and the form must be tragic. Here, with a somewhat different medium from that of *For Whom the Bell Tolls*, we find the same final integration of nature and spirit.

～ ～

Although I deal with him briefly, John Dos Passos is a tremendously significant figure in the development of naturalism, particularly as an end-point in the evolution of naturalistic forms. We have looked at many of the ways in which the writer struggles to force his materialistic philosophy into a fictional structure that will represent it adequately while it permits him also to explore his characters; and we have seen one form after another discarded because it has brought obvious inconsistencies or taken the vitality and inwardness away from the characters. Dos Passos is a culmination and an end-point of the dark matter-dominated trends which have been explored in this volume; he has written almost as if he intended to carry these tendencies to their extremest possibility.

His early structure embodies and demonstrates the fractured lives and fractured values of the twentieth century. He writes a kaleidoscope, a pattern that always changes and never repeats because the possible combinations and permutations are endless; and this structure perfectly states its meaning because it is its meaning. It is a picture of chaos, a blind, formless, struggling, frantic world moving in so many directions at once that it would be impossible for anyone to imagine an intelligent control of its energies. In this whirling chaos the characters work on their destinies — they do not work them out — and the reader is interested in the quality of their experiences as he shares the energy and variety of their lives. Here is a perfect naturalistic form, in which the envelope of chaos contains, physically and metaphorically, the busy volitions of the individuals who move back and forth to weave its web. This form renders a picture of chaos: there is no suggestion that any event is demonstrated as inevitable because the picture does not consider a purposeful form in the world. That premise is not apparent.

In *Manhattan Transfer* (1925) Dos Passos is just leaning toward these effects. The title suggests the form, which is a sort of musical chairs. Characters appear and are described to the point where the reader begins to see them as people, only to be set aside while other characters are introduced and partially developed. As new people are introduced, the earlier ones fade into the background, and some of them disappear, so that there seem always to be about the same number involved in the game. In another figure, it is as if a wave passed over Manhattan, carrying three or four characters across the island and picking up half-a-dozen others whom it abandons successively as it picks up still others in its path.

The central characters, Jimmy Herf and Ellen Thatcher, have a hard time of it, whereas others become big-time mobsters, politicians, businessmen, and operators. The effect of the continual shift of scene and character is to fix them in a series of positions; we have to accept these positions as evidence of their fates, but we cannot follow in detail the steps by which they came to be. Here is clearly a device that eliminates the will and shows the characters riding along on or under the wave of time and event that sweeps over the city. Psychologically, it depicts persons who are not persons but a succession of reactions to stimuli. The fragmented presentation suggests that life is not integrated by purpose or order, that it is a flow of sensation, that man is controlled by his basic physical responses. Since we do not like to think of ourselves in such purely physiological and mechanistic terms, the effect of the book is bewilderment.

It cannot be accident that many of the characters have father fixations. At the bottom of this totem is Bud, from Cooperstown, who has killed his father with a hoe in revenge for many beatings with a chain, and fled to New York. Ellen has a full-scale Oedipus complex; she drifts from man to man and does not "love anybody for long unless they're dead." Hovering in the background is her father with whom she had a relation so close as almost to displace the mother whom they both rejected. Jimmy Herf, too, breaks away from a widowed mother who oppresses him with her morbid devotion. Ellen for a while is a beautiful and successful actress, married to a homosexual, while Jimmy watches her with dog-like devotion from a distance. After a divorce, and a couple of her affairs have dwindled away, she marries Jimmy and has a child; but then Jimmy loses his job, and when Ellen goes back to work she drifts into a new affair with an old friend. Presently she divorces Jimmy to marry this rising politician, and Jimmy stumbles off somewhere into the country. Harried people waver from disillusion to despair; the very successful are not much less desperate than the failures. Nobody seems able to help or to care about others. Starvation, abortion, crooked finance, hijacking, money panics, and general aimlessness fill this portrait of a city, and the tone is as grim as it is sensational. The idealism of the American Dream is present as indignation and bitterness at the conditions which have thwarted that Dream, but this is so only if the reader deduces it from the ironic juxtapositions and from the overtones of Dos Passos' language, which shows the city always incredibly bright and polished, while its lives are dull and morally sterile. Traditional values may be scorned, both by the characters and their author, but there is no feeling here that science has the answer. A mad world of finance, sex, crime, and personal search is not a background against which the idea of scientific progress glows brightly.

Manhattan Transfer went through numerous editions in a few years after its publication. It owes a very great deal to Joyce's *Ulysses*, from which it takes the method of showing the life of a city by flash after flash of incident and personal experience. Dos Passos is more sentimentally aware of his people than Joyce is: he shows their agonies and fears and defeats in passages of considerable force—as when Ellen is preparing herself to accept George Baldwin, for security, after she has set Jimmy Herf aside:

> She had made up her mind. It seemed as if she had set the photograph of herself in her own place, forever frozen into a single gesture. . . . Beyond the plates, the ivory pink lamp, the broken pieces of bread, his face above the blank shirtfront jerked and nodded; the flush grew on his cheeks; his nose caught the light now on one side, now on the other, his taut lips moved eloquently over his yellow teeth. Ellen felt herself sitting with her ankles crossed, rigid as a porcelain figure under her clothes, everything about her seemed to be growing hard and enameled, the air blue-streaked with cigarettesmoke, was turning to glass. His wooden face of a marionette waggled senselessly in front of her.[9]

He is also sampling a larger city than Joyce's Dublin, over several years (centering at about 1920) rather than a single day. Although *Ulysses* is tremendously complex, its Dublin is snug and intimately familiar, whereas Dos Passos' Manhattan is a screaming turmoil of machines and people—a clouded vortex in which the characters are arrested for poignant moments and then disappear again into the whirling background. Yet there is an improbable amount of interplay among them; nearly every character crosses the paths of several of the others or even becomes more or less involved with them, and since they come from all parts of the country and move from Greenwich Village to Uptown, so much interplay has a special effect. It suggests that the form of this novel is consciously made to embody and express its naturalistic philosophy. Joyce, who is neither cold nor sentimental in *Ulysses*, had much more to say and a much more intimate control of his material. Aimlessness, whirl, and coincidence, expressed in the form of *Manhattan Transfer*, do not add up to a novel that says much, although its frantic picture is vivid and sensational. What it says is that social and personal chaos weaves a pattern that is no pattern but rather an unstopping movement—back and forth, in and out, up and down—whether it be in transit, sex, business, or life. It is a movement of agony, of a society in its death throes.

In spite of these conclusions, the technique of *Manhattan Transfer* is inconspicuous beside that of the trilogy *U.S.A.* (1937), composed of three huge novels, *The 42nd Parallel* (1930), *Nineteen Nineteen* (1932), and *The Big Money* (1936). In these novels Dos Passos has extended his method of projecting the kaleidoscope to the point where he fashions his pattern out of three elaborately contrived elements which interrupt and supplement the central narratives — the Newsreel, the Camera Eye, and the Biography. With this invention he seeks to find styles that are appropriate to the various types of material treated and that in blending give the effect of variousness, energy, and turmoil that we saw in a simpler way in *Manhattan Transfer*.

The body of the trilogy is devoted to the careers of a dozen representative people through the years from about the turn of this century to the big money days of the twenties. The first novel approaches World War I, the second deals largely with civilian activities during the war, in New York and Paris, the third explores the big money boom after the war. There is no central character in *U.S.A.* Each novel deals with about four of the dozen, and there is a slight carry-over from one novel to the next. In *The 42nd Parallel* the main characters are Mac McCreary, son of a laborer, who struggles through the labor movement, joins and leaves the I.W.W. in the Northwest, and ends by living with a Mexican girl and comfortably selling radical books from their shop; J. Ward Moorehouse, from Delaware, who marries wealthy women, rises through business and public relations into politics, where he pompously mediates between capital and labor with the purpose of keeping the latter in line, and has a long platonic relation with Eleanor Stoddard, who is a frigid, frustrated, artistic, ambitious bitch from Chicago, comes to New York, where she prospers as an interior decorator, has an important position in the Red Cross in Paris (this is in the second volume), and finally marries a Russian prince; and Janey Williams, mousey and fearful, who becomes the devoted secretary of J. Ward Moorehouse.

Nineteen Nineteen adds the career of Janey's brother, Joe Williams, an ignorant bloke trying to get along, who joins the Navy, deserts, and brawls his way purposelessly through the action; Richard Ellsworth Savage, cultured and personable, who somehow drifts down into opportunism and debasement of his literary talents in J. Ward Moorehouse's employment, a kind of unhappy playboy; Eveline Hutchins, daughter of a Chicago minister who terrifies her, seduced by a Mexican painter, who joins Eleanor Stoddard for a while as interior decorator, goes with her to Paris, is jilted by the man she loves, has a brief affair with Moorehouse and another with a soldier named Paul, and later dies from a lethal dose of sleeping pills; and Daughter, a wild Texas tomboy who has a gay and frantic life spending her father's money and running from men, traveling abroad after the war, who transfers the early frustrated passion that has been the cause of her restlessness to Dick Savage, and who dies, pregnant and rejected by him, in an airplane crash.

The Big Money almost has a central character, Charley Anderson, aviator and war ace, who goes into business manufacturing airplanes and is on the way to riches when he is caught up in the fever of market speculation that takes his money as fast as he can make it. An airplane crash puts him out of circulation and he loses his part in the business; his drinking and gambling increase, and he dies in Florida after an automobile accident when he tried to beat a train to a crossing, going eighty-five miles an hour. Charley's is the grittiest and most desperate story in the whole trilogy. There are also Mary French, a spectacled student, drab and miserable, who devotes herself to Reform; and Margo Dowling, who works her busy, heartless way through a number of men to a fat contract in Hollywood.

These interweaving careers (all the characters know some of the others at one time or another) are given in larger segments than those in *Manhattan Transfer*; but always with a clinical detachment that makes them seem like figures on a screen compelled by drives the inwardness of which we never know, until finally we come to the conclusion that all their drives are instinctive or compulsive. The total effect is much like the strident chaos of the first novel.

The three devices which interrupt the central narratives and "formalize" the chaos depicted represent the ultimate stylistic expressiveness of the naturalistic movement. The Newsreel introduces a section with bits of headlines, advertisements, feature articles, and phrases of news, interwoven with lines of poetry which presumably represent some of the emotions — usually popular and sentimental — being experienced at the time. Superficially, it represents a world of fraud and sophistication, violence and treachery; it is a backdrop of hysteria behind which the serious business of society, if such it can be called, is concealed; for high finance and international relations continue to control the world while the public is engaged with sentiment and sensation.

The Biographies — there are twenty-five of them scattered through the three volumes — are condensed records of typical public figures of the time, from the fields of business, politics, technology, labor, and the arts. Such figures as Carnegie, Hearst, Insull, Rudolph Valentino, Isadora Duncan, William Jennings Bryan, and Eugene Debs constitute a sampling of specific figures who dominate the stage and also move the properties and scenes of our time. They are set forth ironically and bitterly, for the businessmen are greedy and unscrupulous, the entertainers are victims of their public as well as panders to its lusts and vanities, the liberal politicians are confused by their ambitions and the inadequacies of their idealism, and the efficiency expert (F. W. Taylor) is an inhuman machine who dies with a stop watch in his hand. If these are the public heroes, the images of greatness which they portray for the common man — through the jittery glittering Newsreel — show why "our storybook democracy" has not come true. The one figure presented by Dos Passos with a devotion approaching reverence is Thorstein Veblen, the lonely and satiric analyst of leisure-class conduct and the sabotage of efficiency by rapacious business, who could not fit into our academic world and who died leaving the request that his ashes be scattered into the sea and no monument or memorial of any sort be erected to his name.

The Camera Eye is Dos Passos' subjective and rather poetic commentary on this world. It occurs fifty-one times through the trilogy, revealing the character, interests, and life history of the artist — how he came out of Virginia, went to school abroad and at

Harvard, drove an ambulance during the war, was disillusioned by the Versailles Treaty and the rampage of materialism which followed it, and lived as a newspaper reporter and radical through the big money days of the early twenties. He is an oversensitive and fastidious intellectual, recoiling from the grubby masses and yet seeing in them the backbone and heart of the America which the great sweep of his novel shows being corrupted, debauched, and enslaved by the forces of commercial rapacity. He sees America through the lens of a poetic tradition — Whitman, Sandburg, perhaps Hart Crane — which impels him to identify the physical elements of our nation with the dream of greatness and individual realization that it has always embodied for the transcendentalist.

Here the characteristics I have attributed to American idealism when it breaks away from its scientific discipline and control — of unfocused idealism and uncontrolled protest — become increasingly evident in the notions that virtue is in the people, waste is the natural expression of the exploiters, and wealth is in a long-term conspiracy to sabotage labor and destroy our resources. It is perhaps not extravagant to identify the perfectly expressive form of this work with the final division of the great stream of American idealism. The form expresses a chaos; it is a fractured world pictured in a novel fractured into four parts through four styles from four points of view. This division of the subject combines with the range and variety of the materials treated to give the impression that nothing can be done because the problem is too complex to take hold of. It can be watched in the frantic samples that Dos Passos gives us, but we get no sense of comprehensible process that might be analyzed and controlled by the application of scientific method, because it is, finally, a *moral* deterioration that Dos Passos depicts. Thus with the radical writer we come full circle to the conservative position.

The point can be illustrated by samples of the Camera Eye taken from *The Big Money*: returning from Europe,

throat tightens when the redstacked steamer churning the faintlyheaving slatecolored swell swerves shaking in a long greenmarbled curve past the red lightship.

spine stiffens with the remembered chill of the offshore Atlantic
and the jag of framehouses in the west above the invisible land
and spiderweb rollercoasters and the chewinggum towers of Coney
and the freighters with their stacks way aft and the blur beyond
Sandy Hook [10]

and the vision spreads over the nation, to

the whine and shriek of the buzzsaw and the tipsy smell of
raw lumber and straggling through slagheaps through fireweed
through wasted woodlands the shantytowns the shantytowns [11]

He refuses a profitable job because he cannot become part of the
exploiting machine, talks with other seekers in Greenwich Village,
listens skeptically to orators in Union Square, identifies himself
in Whitmanesque fashion with hunters and adventurers in the
West, and toward the end makes a pilgrimage to Plymouth to hear
about Sacco and Vanzetti.

pencil scrawls in my notebook the scraps of recollection the
broken halfphrases the effort to intersect word with word to dove-
tail clause with clause to rebuild out of mangled memories un-
shakably (Oh Pontius Pilate) the truth . . .
. . . how can I make them feel how our fathers our uncles haters
of oppression came to this coast   how say   Don't let them scare
you   how make them feel who are your oppressors America
rebuild the ruined words worn slimy in the mouths of lawyers
districtattorneys collegepresidents judges   without the old words
the immigrants haters of oppression brought to Plymouth how
can you know who are your betrayers America [12]

And the final cry of denunciation:

they have clubbed us off the streets   they are stronger   they
are rich   they hire and fire the politicians the newspapereditors
the old judges . . . America will not forget her betrayers . . .
America our nation has been beaten by strangers who have
bought the laws and fenced off the meadows and cut down the
woods for pulp and turned our pleasant cities into slums and
sweated the wealth out of our people . . .
we stand defeated America [13]

The trouble here is that the indictment has been torn loose from
the facts. People are not virtuous because they are poor. If we
choose to be sentimental about trees, it was the poor pioneer who

cut down and burned the hardwood forests over half a continent, a fearful waste, whereas the big corporations that cut the pulp-wood conserve their trees carefully and have over the decades increased their reserves beyond the nation's needs. The prairies were gulched by the poor farming and overgrazing of the pioneers, too, long before they were fenced and restored and protected by the avaricious big money farmers.

Particularly significant of this division and confusion is the fact that most of the central characters are sexually frigid, inhibited, deprived, or frustrated. Margo Dowling is unfeeling; Janey is terrified of sex; Eleanor Stoddard is apparently quite frigid; Daughter is confused and repressed, and her sudden passion for Dick Savage causes her destruction; Mary French is completely inhibited and neurotic. Where the sexual life is presumed to be satisfactory, Dos Passos ignores it, but with the others a substantial preoccupation of the author is to explore the fears, the desolation, and the guilty aimlessness which he relates to the sense of being unloved. This preoccupation gives the book a pervasive dreariness which combines with the fact that people seem always to be smoky, grimy, gritty, and tired to make a desolation that is, ultimately, wholly subjective. It is a literary effect contrived by careful selection of detail and control of language.

It is true that the possessors of great wealth and power have abused both, and yet he has loaded the dice so heavily in favor of the common man that the reader is skeptical when Dos Passos is most earnest. His idealism has lost its hold on fact. The result, as usual, shows the facts (in the stream of materialism) as grim, dark, and uncontrollable, whereas the optimism of spirit is dissipated in fierce but unreliable indignation. The form of this trilogy is a perfect embodiment of this division between nature and spirit: the main blocks of the narrative portray characters groping in a hopeless jungle of sensation and instinct, whereas the Camera Eye cries its somewhat irresponsible protest against the retreat from the American Dream, denouncing the wrong culprit as often as the right one.

XII

Some Contemporary Consequences
of Naturalism

ROMANTICISM has been defined by Lionel Trilling as the movement to "secularize the spiritual" which, he says, prevailed through the nineteenth century and continues to dominate the twentieth. We are still devoted to the enterprise of realizing in the daily world of experience the blessings and beatitudes that were formerly associated with a divine dispensation. Transcendentalism is an aspect of romanticism to which this definition particularly applies. Seeing nature as the symbol and incarnation of spirit, the transcendentalist fused the secular and the spiritual. For him, science and intuition were equally fruitful ways to realize man's aspirations in the tangible present. Naturalism, as I have sought to show, flows with this great modern stream. Its inspiration is the conviction that scientific knowledge can release man from superstition, from fear, from the tyranny of tradition, from physical ailments, and from poverty — release him into an era of personal enrichment and fulfillment beyond anything the world has seen.

The prophetic visions of Shelley, the despair of Manfred, the frantic defiance of Ahab, however bitter, magnify a vision of man to the superhuman. The human agony cries out to the farthest reaches of mind and proclaims its supreme destiny. Man's vision of good and evil measures his greatness, for in these romantic terms man thinks Himself against the universe. The effect is not very different whether like Ahab he defies God, like Hardy denounces him, or like Zola and Norris identifies himself, emotionally, with the social and natural cataclysm that he portrays in the naturalistic novel. The force and scope of such novels express their meanings with a roar that drowns out the statements of abstract theory that appear in them. We may speculate whether they are optimistic or pessimistic, but their shouts of wrath and glory we cannot fail to hear.

Zola's language abounds with images of eating and smelling that express his physical gusto and his total participation in the reality that he treats in his work. Such extension becomes an expansion of author and reader, by a sort of physical mysticism, into superman and god. The line from Wordsworth's and Emerson's transcendental emphasis on a Spirit, whose dwelling is the light of setting suns/ And the round ocean and the living air, to Whitman's inversion of the same ideas, by which spirit becomes the expression or essence of material things, on to this physical gusto of Zola and the thundering invocations of Norris in *The Octupus*, to Dreiser's probing of inscrutable "chemic" forces linking man and nature in cosmic mysteries — this romantic line is strong and unbroken.

～　～

Naturalism has its roots in the Renaissance birth of science and secularism. The Enlightenment contributes its emphasis on reason and on the essential goodness of human nature. The Romantic period converts these theories into a religion of nature and man. And the Victorian age adds the ingredient of humanitarianism which gives the romantic passion of naturalism its social reference. When we first see it taking literary shape in the late nineteenth century, the essence of naturalism seems to be its emphasis on process in organic rather than purely mechanical terms; that is, people and society are seen as growing and developing, for good or bad, rather than merely functioning mechanically and statically.

Its pervasive concern with the organic accounts for its attention to monsters, maniacs, degenerates, and social ulcers; the malfunctioning of the social organism is so obviously like a disease that the connection did not require explanation. The enthusiasm with which writers followed Zola into the world of aberrations, lesions, deformities, and social decay expressed their optimism and exuberance. In this atmosphere there should be no question of "pessimistic determinism," for the grimmest demonstrations of cause and effect in the destruction of an individual by a disease or of a society by its cancers of poverty and injustice were presented as triumphant proof that ills existed, that such ills could be diagnosed and cured, and that scientific knowledge was therefore the potential salvation of mankind. The confusions of form that came because it was so difficult to unite determinism and moral idealism in a literary structure; the growing fear that man was trapped rather than liberated by the findings of science; the loss of faith in man revealed by contemporary authoritarianism, social orthodoxy, brain-washing, "social engineering," and the deterioration of our educational system toward its focus on "life adjustment" and mediocrity — these are all consequences which the American Dream did not include or foresee.

The naturalistic movement was contemporary with the great modern change from Newtonian to relativity physics. The former described a world of constant entities, both physical and moral, in which both physical and moral events could be described in terms of their stable elements. Thus the laws of the conservation of mass and energy express the same large frame of reference as the use of stable personal "traits" like courage, loyalty, industry, thrift, and pride in the discussion of man. (We need not argue here whether either one is the cause of the other; the important fact is that the physical and the moral frames of reference correspond.)

The movement from Newtonian to relativity physics is typified by the movement from phrenology to psychiatry. Relativity physics dissolves the stable entities of the old order. Matter and energy are now known to be forms of the same whole. If this discovery seemed at first to be a scientific proof of transcendentalism (as was repeatedly affirmed by the physicists), it came all too quickly to moral relativism and confusion. Values today are as relative as matter. Just as any solid is transparent (or even gaseous) to a being who vibrates at a certain rate, so moral values are aspects of time, condition, adjustment, and culture. The Big Lie and the hydrogen bomb are children of the same "philosophy."

The romantic assault on superstition, tradition, and bigotry was sustained by zeal, awe, delight, and anger. The quality of plenitude which is one of the criteria of the romantic spirit achieves a second flowering, after the Victorian drought, in the naturalistic spirit. One can imagine no term that misses this spirit more completely than the label "pessimistic determinism." Wild, flamboyant, and extravagant, naturalism burned its way through one form after another like a prairie fire, dazzling, powerful, and destructive. Because it consumed the materials that nourished it, it continually reached into new terrains, until today the embers of its dying passage glow almost wherever we look. We see particularly how the search for form, which has been a central problem of this book, has eventuated. The naturalistic drive has in fact consumed the new materials which it originally offered the novelist. As a liberating force it began with a great explosion, a blowing to smithereens of the compact old ethical, orthodox order, which scattered fires in a dozen directions. These new fires, as we have seen, were used for light and heat by novelist after novelist, and one by one they burned out.

Frederic and Garland could not use them — the heat was too fierce. Norris really just played with the fires, the romanticism of Zola becoming with him more a mannerism than a conviction by the end of his short literary life, although the expression of plenitude through a feeling for natural dynamism in his work is of the essence of naturalism. With London the personal protest with its attendant vanity always defeated the shaping mind; socialism, supermen, and survival made a sentimental slush. Churchill understood the new ideas but could not abandon the old romantic storytelling forms that would not accommodate them. Dreiser's wonder and pity had become old-fashioned and clumsy in *The Bulwark* and *The Stoic*. James Farrell's pursuit of grim reality has lost its force by the Bernard Carr series. The later novelists like Hemingway, Steinbeck, and Dos Passos have been indefatigable experimenters with form: Dos Passos buries himself in it; Hemingway alone recognizes what he is doing when he pursues ethical values in a naturalistic jungle; Steinbeck has compromised with sentiment and sensation until the distance from the hard if limited integrity of *In Dubious Battle* to the maundering of *Sweet Thursday* and the fatuity of *East of Eden* is a descent painful to contemplate.

I have remarked several times on the fact that the early zeal and confidence of naturalism lost their force, as the twentieth century passed, because science constantly found new limitations to man's freedom. Freudian psychology showed the mind to be largely controlled by drives buried in the subconscious. Statistics, economics, and sociology multiplied evidences of environmental forces that overshadow the will. And at least three other factors have contributed to this trend.

For one thing, wars and depressions and growing populations have steadily increased the individual's insecurity to the point where, as we entered the forties, the drive for security began to supplant the old Dream of equality, justice, and a richer life for all. It was no longer just science that discovered limitations rather than opened doors; it was the changing personal psychology of people who found the world too big and complicated to manage. We are told every day that radio and the airplane have reduced the size of the world, and the implication is that now that we can travel rapidly over the earth we should be able to see all man's problems in global perspectives and solve them with master plans. But the thoughtful observer knows that the world of experience, the world of problems, the world which impinges upon the individual's mind and conditions its attitudes is immeasurably more vast and complex than it was only fifty years ago. Its vastness daunts the zeal and idealism of all but the boldest spirits. The sharp fellow today looks at his TV, keeps up with his installment payments, and does not get himself involved with any cause that might lead a prospective employer or buyer to consider him "unsound."

Our thunderous mid-century prosperity adds to the trend in a second way. The year 1956 saw a national income in the United States nearly twelve times as great as that of 1933. People in the fifties have been so busy earning and spending this money that they have little time even to think about making a better world. Many of them, indeed, are confident that the better world is here, while others hide their fears and bewilderment in frantic activities of steadily diminishing creative value. The voice of protest has faded to a whisper — or a neurotic whine. "Americanism" and loyalty are joined in a booming tumult of self-praise, while European attacks on our materialism make us even more unwilling to criticize ourselves.

Another element contributing to this trend is the moral relativism which seems to derive from the century's preoccupation with depth psychology. The key word in this context is adjustment. All the way from the primary school to the analyst's couch, the emphasis is on helping the individual to get along happily with his fellows, his limitations, and his half-buried fears. Adjustment and self-expression are now prime values, having displaced the old moral absolutes that gave early naturalism its fire. The high school student who explains his failure of an examination by saying that he was feeling hostile to his mother that morning and the college students who seriously endorse religion because it helps them "adjust" to their limitations represent a psychological reorientation away from the American Dream that could hardly be more extreme. (Yet with all this we have never been so maladjusted. Mental illness increases alarmingly. Psychiatry booms.)

When science has brought us to a moral relativism that substitutes therapy for personal responsibility, the last trickle of the stream of idealism has disappeared, and the divided stream of naturalism has lost a vital half of itself. As the sustaining moral sentiment of transcendentalism thus disappears, leaving us alone with statistics, therapy, moral relativism, adjustment, and security as the shibboleths of our social comment, presided over by the processors, the public relations experts, and the propagandists, a new value-drive gathers force, for man cannot live by pure science. Today the romantic faith in nature is being replaced by existentialism (for the sophisticated) and the return to orthodox Christianity (for those who are less desperate or perhaps less adventuresome).

Perhaps the strongest evidence I have seen of this change in the intellectual climate is the fact that where the idealism of the earlier naturalists is not specifically stated it is missed often by even the most intelligent of young readers. The early Hemingway, particularly of *The Sun Also Rises*, is not taken seriously. Jake and Brett and their friends are regarded as professional escapists and thrill-seekers who drink to be smart. Their moral earnestness is not felt. The almost desperate care of their drinking, the ritual of their self-control are missed. Crane's *Red Badge of Courage* has recently been reinterpreted as portraying spiritual crisis and absolution in a pattern of Christian symbolism and reference. Such an extreme aberration is possible only to a reader who does not participate in Crane's passionate idealistic indignation with the hypocrisies of traditional public morality. Contemporary moral relativism is color-blind to the bright red flame of Crane's earnestness, and so it can read patterns into his work that would never occur to one who felt the immediate shock of his true colors.

The novel today reflects these trends in tone and subject matter. There are elements of idealism in *Point of No Return, Executive Suite, The Hucksters, The Great Man,* and *The Man in the Grey Flannel Suit,* but they are carefully trimmed, represented generally in terms of nostalgic memories of childhood rather than revolt against the fundamental ills of our world, and accommodated to Exurbanite problems of keeping up with taxes, alcoholism, time-payments, and above all holding one's job. The crisis in these novels is not personal but typical; their expert reportage mixes glamour and sociology, presents the individual as obviously a product of his milieu, and accepts this world of conformity and surfaces with a bit of scorn and a great deal of complacency.

The element of reportage, at worst, dissolves the form of the novel to a shapeless blob, a scrapple of facts rather than an articulated and meaningful action. Returning to a larger perspective for a moment, I should like to suggest a parallel between some other fictional forms and some of the trends in religion that obtain today. With reportage barren, the old ethical choice structure displaced, and the obvious naturalistic forms of social cycle and clinical study exhausted, novelists have turned to the artificial and contrived use of myths and literary monuments of antiquity to impose a kind of form on their subjects. Joyce's *Ulysses* is the most obvious and influential example. Frederick Buechner's *A Long Day's Dying* (1950) is a modern story woven about and into the myth of Philomela. Allegory in Kafka, Mann, Norman Mailer (*Barbary Shore*, 1951), and Mark Schorer (*The Wars of Love*, 1954) serves the same function of giving structure and holding the line against reportage. It is possible to discern the same motivation behind the growing interest in religious formalism of our time. Intellectuals have repeatedly said that, being without purpose or belief, they sought out religious instruction in order to enter into a disciplined pattern that would shape their lives. It is the conscious and therefore somewhat artificial search for form that marks these two enterprises as evidences of the same condition — a condition ultimately attributable to literary and philosophical naturalism.

As naturalism uses up, one by one, the forms described in Chapter I, it spreads out so far that it covers the whole literary landscape — but very thinly. Its themes of sensationalism, violence, and intimate sexual disclosures have become commonplaces, and few would question the gain thereby of honesty and truth. Unfortunately, although restrictions and taboos are a very severe block to the serious writer, the removal of them does not guarantee any improvement in the quality of the novel. Every novelist selects and organizes his material in the terms permitted by whatever convention he employs. When the convention is stretched further and further toward the shape of actuality it may burst or — as we have seen in the case of James T. Farrell — turn inside out and contradict its original intentions. The movement toward stark actuality is therefore fraught with various dangers and is not automatically a benefit to the novel.

It flows off, indeed, in a number of different streams toward what appears (in gloomy moments) to be a drying up of the novel:

For example, the grim naturalistic tragedy loses its power as soon as the writer ceases to believe that his dark picture of human waste is in effect a beacon for progress. From the glowing enthusiasm of Zola's depiction of a homicidal maniac in *La Bête Humaine* to the hopeless chronicle of despair in Motley's *Knock on Any Door* we see the course of determinism as the fire of scientific ardor dies out to the cold desolation of uncontrollable fact, where there is bitterness without hope. Psychology increasingly influences novelists to represent certain neurotic patterns as almost universal; and when everybody is bound in an Oedipus complex the knowledge of it becomes an accepted condition of life rather than an opening door. Psychiatry, it has been aptly said, makes all characters one character. Violence which was fraught with excitement, discovery, and defiance in early naturalistic fiction, now abounds in the novel as a sensational end in itself; the hard-boiled detective story is a genre made of this isolated aspect of naturalism. The interest in documentation which originally embodied the scientific zeal to know has slipped — again, by losing its idealism — into the reportage of information about trades, crafts, careers, and places which seems today (if one is to judge by the advertising) to attract novel buyers more than the penetration of character or the exploration of an ethical problem, which used to be the heart of the novel.

The knowledge which in theory brings power has, in our century, brought forth vistas of man's inhumanity so appalling as almost to paralyze the happy idealism of 1900. We have seen millions murdered in concentration camps; worse, we have seen the survivors of these nightmares awake to a postwar world that has no place for them. We have come to terms with fascism in Spain, Portugal, and Latin America and with the political and social indecencies of many other nations. So much to be done, while the evils mount faster than the cures; small wonder that Americans pull the covers over their heads and escape into their chromium-plated dreams. We are now indeed a part of the great world, and we sense that our unique position in it cannot be maintained indefinitely; but with so much of evil and injustice elsewhere the average individual inclines to take what he has and not ask too many questions.

It may have something to do with this spiritual condition that a writer like Nelson Algren is drawn to write so warmly and sympathetically of the ruined lives of bums and addicts in *The Man with the Golden Arm* and *A Walk on the Wild Side*. The first of these books, particularly, seems to declare that admirable human qualities have little — or perhaps a negative — bearing on social status and that the poetry of human relations appears most richly where people are stripped down to the core of survival and have no strength or use for complicated emotions. Living on the barest edge of physical survival, his people simply have no use for vanity, sanctimoniousness, or prestige; being free and pure, their loves and affections are beautiful. Now this point of view is very like that of the early Hemingway. The heart of his early work is his attempt to get down to experiences and emotions that are clean in a world that has been contaminated by hypocrisy and false sentiment. He too finds that the clean emotions must be the simple ones — hunger, fear, sex, despair — near the bone of life, where the contamination has not begun, and where the individual can know that what he feels is true.

The difference between these two writers shows what has happened in a generation. Hemingway conveys a tremendous sense of serious commitment to life; he is, through his characters, looking for answers, trying to know himself, seeking integrity and directness, in short, finding where the life of man signifies. He is serious and therefore indignant about society. Algren seems to have given up even the pretense that society could be improved or purified. For him it has become a jungle of viciousness and injustice beyond reclamation; only the waifs and strays merit attention because only they are capable of tender and beautiful feelings. One may be deeply moved by *The Man with the Golden Arm* but must, I believe, finally regard it as irresponsible and inaccurate — a sentimental contrivance that has little to do with reality but rather explores a cul-de-sac in the author's imagination. Algren's subject matter, considered alone, would seem to be firmly in the naturalistic tradition; but his total attitude toward it is not so at all. He represents the stream of transcendentalism divided and indeed separated, with the idealistic branch turned into tenderness and sentiment (as in the recent works of Steinbeck) which soften the hard surfaces of his world without endowing them with that hope which in the vision of the American Dream saw Nature glowing with Spirit, with meaning, and with life.

The tension established by naturalism between the idea of freedom and the recognition of law has continued to trouble all our novelists, who have obscured, rejected, evaded, or faced it, according to their several bents. I have remarked in Chapter IV that Faulkner has consistently recognized the dark subconscious scars and fears that drive his people. Indeed almost no important Faulkner character is without his terrible agonies of spirit. Think of Quentin, Caddy, Jason, Joe Christmas, Sutphen, Hightower, Anse, Jewel, Darl Bundren, and a dozen others. And yet these characters are all taken quite seriously by their creator; he does not condescend or patronize; he does not parade them as cases; he does not pretend that a timely lecture to the parents or mental hygiene classes in school would have prevented their sufferings. Faulkner does not see psychic malignancies, as the early naturalists did, but rather growth under normal conditions.

In taking these tormented people seriously he endows them with tragic freedom which permits them to work on (not work out) their fates under the narrow limits available to man. The many discoveries of depth psychology that Faulkner employs are treated as basic conditions of life, which man can only face with his free will and intelligence. Thus for him naturalism has widened the sphere of human sensibility and experience — to use Wordsworth's phrase — without altering the idea of man inherited through the Great Tradition. Lesser writers contrive somehow to evade the full tragic condition of life, as if they dared not do otherwise. Psychological penetration, spectatorship, devotion to reportage of the passing business and social parade, and humor give subjects to writers who choose not to deal with the ultimate problems of living. If naturalism originally promised a way for the courageous solution of mankind's problems, it has become a means of evasion and escape for an enormous segment of the mid-century world.

The struggle to win a degree of self-control and creative achievement through one's fears and the world's hostility is Hemingway's central subject. His creative life has been an effort to use his agonies and so master them — and he has succeeded impressively. Faulkner and Hemingway are not seriously concerned with the supernatural, and in this respect they are naturalists; but they assume both freedom and responsibility as basic conditions of life. In this they have, I believe, completely and profoundly resolved the confusions and cross-purposes that were brought into modern fiction by naturalism. But theirs is an accomplishment of which only the most gifted, serious, and courageous writers are capable.

NOTES AND INDEX

Notes

[1] See Chapter VI.

[2] A quasi-political grouping of left-center-right will orient us among the major critical approaches to naturalism that are current. The right wing is conservative and "pessimistic"; the left stresses social progress; the center tries to reconcile the extremes.

The right wing is represented by Harry Hartwick, *The Foreground of American Fiction* (New York, 1934); he maintains that the determinism of the naturalists was so pessimistic that they conceived of nature as a vast, horrible, indifferent mechanism, a "contrivance of wheels within wheels; man is a 'piece of fate' caught in the machinery of Nature . . . Man's only duty is to discharge his energies and die, at the same time expressing his individuality as best he can." (Pp. 17–18.) Naturalism, he says, destroyed religious faith and inspired literature the conviction that might is right, that "men should court the simple atavistic behavior of children and savages, who have not yet been corrupted by ideas." (Pp. 18–19.) Here we see the simplest false correlation between the treatment of sordid or brutal characters in a novel and the author's own moral position. Actually it reveals a great interest in ideas on the part of the author when he attempts to dramatize the "struggle for existence" in a novel of violence. Jack London, for example, is a novelist of ideas, intensely *interested* in the "atavistic behavior of children and savages" and frontiersmen; but he does not advocate mindless violence. An equally extreme right-wing position appears in Oscar Cargill, *Intellectual America* (New York, 1941). Mr. Cargill concludes that naturalism is pessimistic determinism (a phrase he uses repeatedly), according to which failure and degeneracy are the natural ends of man, who is helpless to better his condition; no naturalistic work, he says, can show any hope for man or any ideas about social reform. If it has an affirmative note, it is not naturalistic. His entire structure of theory rests on the single point that determinism eliminates human freedom.

The extreme left-wing position appears in George W. Meyer's "The Original Social Purpose of the Naturalistic Novel," *Sewanee Review*, October 1942. Mr. Meyer argues from Zola's statement in *Le Roman Expérimentale* that science will find the truth that will set men free; if this is Zola's belief, then no genuine naturalistic novel can evince any pessimistic determinism. Mr. Meyer goes a step further to accept Zola's distinction between fatalism and determinism: Zola said the latter was optimistic, because it could be used by the scientist as the instrument for controlling nature, and therefore Mr. Meyer concludes that a deterministic novel must be optimistic and progressive. Mr. Meyer shows that Mr. Cargill is in error when he labels the philosophy of naturalism "pessimistic," but he too is in error when he insists that the naturalistic novel must be "optimistic." Mr. Meyer's error is not serious, because in its larger social context even a depressing novel like *An American Tragedy* communicates, as I have said, the conviction that social ills can be cured by the will of man — and there is buoyant enthusiasm apparent everywhere in Zola's gloomiest works. But in theory, at least, it is not possible to distinguish between that for which God is responsible and that for which "man is at least partly responsible." (P. 6.) To separate fatalism from determinism is to deny the "monism of the cosmos" which is the foundation rock of naturalistic theory. In *theory*, Zola recognizes neither God nor the human will — only law. And law is neither optimistic nor pessimistic.

³ Meyer, *op. cit.*, p. 7.

CHAPTER II

¹ *Mes Haines* (Paris, 1866; ed. 1869), pp. 71–72.

² See *Le Roman Expérimentale* (Paris, 1880), pp. 220–226, where Zola explains that Taine made a science of what Sainte-Beuve performed in sheer virtuosity. I speak of the "experimental novel" when referring to the 20-volume Rougon-Macquart series, and to *Le Roman Expérimentale* when referring to Zola's collection of essays, published in 1880, that explain and defend his program.

³ "Je n'aurai à faire ici qu'un travail d'adaptation, car la méthode expérimentale a été établie avec une force et une clarté merveilleuses par Claude Bernard, dans son *Introduction à l'étude de la médecine expérimentale*. Ce livre, d'un savant dont l'autorité est décisive, va me servir de base solide. Je trouverai là toute la question traitée, et je me bornerai, comme arguments irréfutables, à donner les citations qui me seront nécessaires. Ce ne sera donc qu'une compilation de textes; car je compte, sur tous les points, me retrancher derrière Claude Bernard. Le plus souvent, il me suffira de remplacer le mot 'médecin' par le mot 'romancier,' pour rendre ma pensée claire et lui apporter la rigueur d'une vérité scientifique.

"Ce qui a déterminé mon choix et l'a arrêté sur l'*Introduction*, c'est que précisément la médecine, aux yeux d'un grand nombre, est encore un art, comme le roman. Claude Bernard a, toute sa vie, cherché et combattu pour faire entrer la médecine dans une voie scientifique. Nous assistons là aux balbutiements d'une science se dégageant peu à peu de l'empirisme pour se fixer dans la vérité, grâce à la méthode expérimentale. Claude Bernard démontre que cette méthode appliquée dans l'étude des corps bruts, dans la chimie et dans la physique, doit l'être également dans l'étude des corps vivants, en physiologie et en médecine. Je vais tâcher de prouver à mon tour que, si la méthode expérimentale conduit à la connaissance de la vie physique, elle doit conduire aussi à la connaissance de la vie passionnelle et intellectuelle. Ce n'est là qu'une question de degrés dans la même voie, de la chimie à la physiologie, puis de la physiologie à l'anthropologie et à la sociologie. Le roman expérimentale est au bout." (*Le Roman Expérimentale*, pp. 1–2.)

⁴ "J'ai voulu étudier des tempéraments et non des caractères. Là est le livre entier . . . Les amours de mes deux héros sont le contentement d'un besoin; le meurtre qu'ils commettent est une conséquence de leur adultère. Enfin ce que j'ai été obligé d'appeler leurs remords consiste en un simple désordre organique. Mon but a été un but scientifique avant tout. Qu'on lise le roman avec soin, on verra que chaque chapitre est l'étude d'un cas curieux de physiologie."

⁵ "Il est indifférent que le fait générateur soit reconnu comme absolument vrai; ce sera surtout une hypothèse scientifique empruntée aux traités médicaux. Mais lorsque ce fait sera posé, lorsque je l'aurai accepté comme un axiome, on deduire mathématiquement tout le volume. Prendre avant tout une tendance philosophique non pour l'étaler mais pour donner une suite à mes livres. La meilleure serait le matérialisme, je veux dire la croyance à des forces sur lesquelles je n'aurai jamais besoin de m'expliquer." (Quoted in Pierre Martino *Le Naturalisme Français* (Paris, 1923), p. 30.)

⁶ "Quand les temps auront marché, quand on possédera les lois, il n'y aura plus qu'à agir sur les individus et sur les milieux, si l'on veut arriver au meilleur état social. C'est ainsi que nous faisons de la sociologie pratique et que notre besogne aide aux sciences politiques et économiques. Je ne sais pas, je le répète, de travail plus noble ni d'une application plus large. Être maître du bien et du mal, régler la vie, régler la société, résoudre à la longue tous les problèmes du socialisme, apporter surtout des bases solides à la justice en résolvant par l'expérience les questions de criminalité, n'est-ce pas là être les ouvriers les plus utiles et les plus moraux du travail humain?" (*Le Roman Expérimentale*, p. 24.)

⁷ "Je veux expliquer comment une famille, un petit groupe d'êtres, se comporte dans une société, en s'épanouissant pour donner naissance à dix, vingt individus, qui paraissent, au premier coup d'oeil, profundément dissemblables, mais que l'analyse montre intimement liés les uns aux autres. L'hérédité a ses lois, comme la pesanteur.

"Je tâcherai de suivre, en résolvant la double question des tempéraments et des milieux, le fil qui conduit mathématiquement d'un homme à un autre homme. Et quand je tiendrai tous les fils, quand j'aurai entre les mains tout un groupe social, je ferai voir ce groupe à l'oeuvre, comme acteur d'une époque historique.

"Les Rougon-Macquart, le groupe, la famille que je me propose d'étudier, a pour caractéristique le débordement des appétits, le large soulèvement de notre âge, qui se rue aux jouissances. Physiologiquement, ils sont la lente succession des accidents nerveux et sanguins qui se déclarent dans une race, à la suite d'une première lésion organique. Historiquement, ils partent du peuple, ils s'irradient dans toute la société contemporaine, ils montent à toutes les situations . . . et ils racontent ainsi le second Empire à l'aide de leurs drames individuels." (*La Fortune des Rougon* (Paris, 1871), Preface.)

⁸ "Vois donc, dans l'hérédité directe, les élections: celle de la mère, Silvère, Lisa, Désirée, Jacques, Louiset, toi-même; celle du père, Sidonie, François, Gervaise, Octave, Jacques-Louis. Puis, ce sont les trois cas de mélange: par soudure, Ursule, Aristide, Anna, Victor; par dissémination, Maxime, Serge, Étienne; par fusion, Antoine, Eugène, Claude. J'ai dû même spécifier un quatrième cas très remarquable, le mélange équilibré, Pierre et Pauline. Et les variétés s'établissent, l'élection de la mère par exemple va souvent avec la ressemblance physique du père; ou c'est le contraire qui a lieu; de même que,

dans le mélange, la prédominance physique et morale appartient à un facteur ou à l'autre, selon les circonstances . . . Ensuite, voici l'hérédité indirecte, celle des collatéraux: je n'en ai qu'un exemple bien établi, la ressemblance physique frappante d'Octave Mouret avec son oncle Eugène Rougon. Je n'ai aussi qu'un exemple de l'hérédité par influence: Anna, la fille de Gervaise et de Coupeau, ressemblait étonnamment, surtout dans son enfance, à Lantier, le premier amant de sa mère, comme s'il avait imprégné celle-ci à jamais . . . Mais où je suis très riche, c'est pour l'hérédité en retour: les trois cas les plus beaux, Marthe, Jeanne et Charles, ressemblant à Tante Dide, la ressemblance sautant ainsi une, deux, et trois générations. L'aventure est sûrement exceptionnelle, car je ne crois guère à l'atavisme; il me semble que les éléments nouveaux apportés par les conjoints, les accidents et la variété infinie des mélanges doivent très rapidement effacer les caractères particuliers, de façon à ramener l'individu au type général." (*Le Docteur Pascal* (Paris, 1893; ed. 1915), pp. 116–117.)

[9] "Et Gervaise Macquart arrivait avec ses quatre enfants, Gervaise bancale, jolie et travailleuse, que son amant Lantier jetait sur le pavé des faubourgs, où elle faisait la rencontre du zingueur Coupeau, le bon ouvrier pas noceur qu'elle épousait, si heureuse d'abord, ayant trois ouvrières dans sa boutique de blanchisseuse, coulant ensuite avec son mari à l'inévitable déchéance du milieu, lui peu à peu conquis par l'alcool, possédé jusqu'à la folie furieuse et à la mort, elle-même pervertie, devenue fainéante, achevée par le retour de Lantier, au milieu de la tranquille ignominie d'un ménage à trois, dès lors victime pitoyable de la misère complice, qui finissait de la tuer un soir, le ventre vide." (*Ibid.*, p. 123.)

[10] "Étienne, à son tour, chassé, perdu, arrivait au pays noir par une nuit glacée de mars, descendait dans le puits vorace, aimait la triste Catherine qu'un brutal lui volait, vivait avec les mineurs leur vie morne de misère et de basse promiscuité, jusqu'au jour où la faim, soufflant la révolte, promenait au travers de la plaine rase le peuple hurlant des misérables qui voulait du pain, dans les écroulements et les incendies, sous la menace de la troupe dont les fusils partaient tout seuls, terrible convulsion annonçant la fin d'un monde, sang vengeur des Maheu qui se lèverait plus tard, Alzire morte de faim, Maheu tué d'une balle, Zacherie tué d'un coup de grisou, Catherine restée sous la terre, la Maheude survivant seule, pleurant ses morts, redescendant au fond de la mine pour gagner ses trente sous, pendant qu' Étienne, le chef battu de la bande, hanté des revendications futures, s'en allait par un tiède matin d'avril, en écoutant la sourde poussée du monde nouveau, dont la germination allait bientôt faire éclater la terre." (*Ibid.*, pp. 124–125.)

[11] "Oui, notre famille pourrait, aujourd'hui, suffire d'exemple à la science, dont l'espoir est de fixer un jour, mathématiquement, les lois des accidents nerveux et sanguins qui se déclarent dans une race, à la suite d'une première lésion organique, et qui déterminent, selon les milieux, chez chacun des individus de cette race, les sentiments, les désirs, les passions, toutes, les manifestations humaines, naturelles et instinctives, dont les produits prennent les noms de vertus et de vices." (*Ibid.*, p. 127.)

[12] "Je te répète que tous les cas héréditaires s'y rencontrent. Je n'ai eu, pour fixer ma théorie, qu'à la baser sur l'ensemble de ces faits . . . Enfin, ce qui est merveilleux, c'est qu'on touche là du doigt comment des créatures, nées de la même souche, peuvent paraître radicalement différentes, tout en n'étant que les modifications logiques des ancêtres communs . . . C'est l'hérédité, la vie

même qui pond des imbéciles, des fous, des criminels et des grands hommes."
(*Ibid.*, p. 132.)

¹³ *Une Campagne* (Paris, 1880), p. 135.

¹⁴ "Dans cette union intime, la réalité de la scène et la personnalité du romancier ne sont plus distinctes. Quels sont les détails absolument vrais, quels sont
les détails inventés? C'est ce qu'il serait très difficile de dire. Ce qu'il y a de certain, c'est que la réalité a été le point de départ, la force d'impulsion qui a
lancé puissamment le romancier; il a continué ensuite la réalité, il a étendu
la scène dans le même sens, en lui donnant une vie spéciale et qui lui est propre
uniquement à lui, Alphonse Daudet.

"Tout le mécanisme de l'originalité est là, dans cette expression personnelle
du monde réel qui nous entoure." (*Le Roman Expérimentale*, p. 215.)

¹⁵ "Seulement, la question de méthode et la question de rhétorique sont
distinctes. Et le naturalisme, je le dis encore, consiste uniquement dans la
méthode expérimentale, dans l'observation et l'expérience appliquées à la lit-
térature. . . . Si l'on veut avoir mon opinion bien nette, c'est qu'on donne
aujourd'hui une prépondérance exagérée à la forme. . . . Au fond, j'estime
que la méthode atteint la forme elle même, qu'un langage n'est qu'une logique,
une construction naturelle et scientifique. Celui qui écrira le mieux ne sera
pas celui qui galopera le plus follement parmi les hypothèses, mais celui qui
marchera droit au milieu des vérités." (*Le Roman Expérimentale*, p. 46.)

CHAPTER III

¹ *Seth's Brother's Wife: A Study of Life in the Greater New York* (New
York, 1887), pp. 32–33.

² *The Damnation of Theron Ware: or Illumination* (New York, 1896), pp.
42–43.

³ *Ibid.*, pp. 477–480.

⁴ *Crumbling Idols* (New York, 1894), pp. 52 and 77.

⁵ See *Roadside Meetings* (New York, 1931), p. 70 and *passim*.

⁶ *Crumbling Idols*, p. 101.

⁷ *Ibid.*, p. 28.

⁸ *Jason Edwards: An Average Man* (Boston, 1892), p. 58.

⁹ *Rose of Dutcher's Coolly* (New York, 1895), p. 36.

CHAPTER IV

¹ Kirkland, in *Zury: The Meanest Man in Spring County* (1887), began with
harsh frontier poverty and turned to romance as soon as he had established his
setting. This story does endow the heroine with an illegitimate child, but the
unique experience which took her virtue and made her a mother was so coyly
suggested that I did not realize what had occurred until I read the sequel to
Zury. Henry Blake Fuller, in *The Cliff-Dwellers* (1893) and *With the Procession*
(1895), deals with Chicago business and society realistically, skeptically, but
with so much of ironic reservation on the one hand and sentimental romance
on the other that the adumbration of naturalism is faint indeed. Boyesen's
The Mammon of Unrighteousness (1891) makes similar explorations of manners and morals assailed by materialistic ambitions.

² *Maggie: A Girl of the Streets* (New York, 1892) was published under the
pseudonym Charles Johnston. The only complete edition of Crane's prose and
poetry is *The Works of Stephen Crane*, ed. Wilson Follett (New York, 1925–
1926), in 12 volumes. His letters have not been collected.

³ In *The Monster and Other Stories* (New York, 1899).

⁴ *The Red Badge of Courage* (New York, 1895).

⁵ *The Monster and Other Stories* (New York, 1899).

⁶ *The Open Boat and Other Tales of Adventure* (New York, 1898).

CHAPTER V

¹ See *Martin Eden* (1909); *John Barleycorn* (1913); and the life by Charmian London, *The Book of Jack London*, 2 vols. (New York, 1921) — a book which does not conflict with the autobiographical statements in London's fictions and indeed seems often to be based upon them for the period of London's life before his marriage in 1905 to the authoress.

² See *John Barleycorn* and the accounts in *The Book of Jack London*, I, 99–109.

³ *The Book of Jack London*, II, 72. "Serling" should read "Sterling."

⁴ *Ibid.*, I, 286.

⁵ *Ibid.*, I, 297.

⁶ *Ibid.*, I, facing p. 304.

⁷ *Ibid.*, I, 313. In an early story London writes, "He was without sin. He could not, by the very nature of things, have been anything else than he was. He had not made himself, and for his making he was not responsible. Yet we treated him as a free agent and held him personally responsible for all that he was and that he should have been. As a result, our treatment of him was as terrible as he was himself terrible." (*The Human Drift* (New York, 1917), p. 40.)

⁸ *The Book of Jack London*, I, 297–298. London would have been hard put to it to prove these statements.

⁹ *Revolution and Other Essays* (New York, 1910), p. 12.

¹⁰ Harry Hartwick, *The Foreground of American Fiction* (New York, 1934), pp. 17–18.

¹¹ This notion of the will to live or to struggle for power, which is here presented as the basis of Nietzsche's philosophy, has, as the reader will recall, been presented a few pages earlier as the rationale of the conduct of the ruthless frontier brute. As the last paragraphs of this section explain, the Nietzschean ideal of the superman (misguided though it may be) is an ideal of perfected manhood which will exalt the whole race to a better life. No such ideal of progress inspires the "brute."

¹² See H. L. Mencken, *The Philosophy of Friedrich Nietzsche* (New York, 1908), pp. 103ff. Also Leo Berg, *The Superman in Modern Literature* (London, 1915); B. de Casseres, *The Superman in America*, University of Washington Chapbooks, number 30 (Seattle, 1929); and W. H. Wright, *What Nietzsche Taught* (New York, 1917).

¹³ *Philosophy of Nietzsche*, pp. 112–113.

¹⁴ See de Casseres, *The Superman in America*, p. 15. *The Reader's Guide* between 1897 and 1907 lists thirty articles on Nietzsche — only three a year. Shaw's *Man and Superman* (1905), Mencken's *Philosophy of Friedrich Nietzsche* (1908), and James Huneker's *Egoists: A Book of Supermen* (1909) brought the word and many of Nietzsche's ideas into this country and before the eyes of the popular reader. Nietzsche's works were not generally accessible in translation at the turn of the century, although a number of them had been translated. M. A. Mugge, *Friedrich Nietzsche: His Life and Work* (London, 1908), contains an extensive bibliography in which are listed the following English

editions: *The Case of Wagner*, tr. Thomas Common (London, 1896, 1899; contains *The Twilight of the Idols* and *The Antichrist*); *Thus Spake Zarathustra: A Book for All and None*, tr. Alexander Tille (London, 1896, 1899); *A Genealogy of Morals, Poems*, tr. W. A. Haussmann and John Gray (London, 1897, 1899); *The Dawn of Day*, tr. Johanna Volz (London, 1903); *Beyond Good and Evil*, tr. Helen Zimmern (London, 1907); *Human, All-Too-Human*, Chapters I–III, tr. A. Harvey (Chicago, 1908). The first complete translation of Nietzsche's works, edited by Oscar Levy, appeared in 1909–1914. Toward 1910 other books appeared, such as J. M. Kennedy, *The Quintessence of Nietzsche* (New York, 1910); and Anthony M. Ludovici, *Nietzsche and Art* (Boston, 1912).

[15] L. S. Friedland, "Jack London as Titan," *Dial*, LXII (January 25, 1917), 51.

[16] "Primordialism and Some Recent Books," *Bookman*, XXX (November 1909), 278. Here is a shrewd recognition of London's concern with his own manliness.

[17] *Book of Jack London*, I, 384.

[18] *A Daughter of the Snows* (ed. London, 1908), pp. 201–202. There is no complete edition of London's works.

[19] *Ibid.*, p. 148. Later Corliss explicitly states the materialistic philosophy of living life for the sake of what can be enjoyed on earth, since nothing afterwards is certain; see pp. 220–221.

[20] *The Call of the Wild* (New York, 1903; ed. 1912), p. 43.

[21] See page 98 above.

[22] *Ibid.*, pp. 198–199. There is some confusion here in presenting Buck's oldest "racial memory" as a state of companionship with man. If such were the case, his "atavism" surely would not draw him away from man. It is further uncertain why Buck should begin to go wild just when he has found a man whom he loves with his whole nature. And of course no attempt is made by London to explain the reason for Buck's "return to type" or for his power and intelligence and courage. His atavism, likewise, is something we experience vicariously rather than something we understand. Racial memory is the subject of *Before Adam* (1907), in which the hero dreams of his prehistoric life as one of the cave folk. These cave folk carry on a struggle for existence with the more primitive tree folk and the more civilized fire-people who have bows and arrows. As usual with London, the story is seen through the eyes of one of the strugglers.

[23] *The Book of Jack London*, II, 49–50.

[24] *The Sea-Wolf* (New York, 1904; ed. 1915), p. 19.

[25] *Ibid.*, p. 50. This is the attitude toward evolution often taken by one who is closely involved with the struggle. Darwin and Spencer could see evolution as a law of progress. London's deviation from their beliefs is a measure of his deviation from those of Nietzsche — always in the direction of brutality and the preoccupation with physical aspects of the struggle for existence. London probably did not know Nietzsche's works when he wrote *The Sea-Wolf*.

[26] The reader's sense of waste in the life of Wolf is what causes his sympathy for him. As Humphrey exclaims, "Why is it that you have not done great things in this world? With the power that is yours you might have risen to any height. Unpossessed of conscience or moral instinct, you might have mastered the world, broken it to your hand. And yet here you are . . . living an obscure and sordid existence." (*Ibid.*, p. 99.)

[27] This use of disease seems to have something in common with the French naturalistic tradition. The French naturalists had given considerable time to

clinical studies of degeneration (see Chapters I–II). Norris's first novel, *Vandover and the Brute*, traced the progress of a mental or nervous failing that finally destroyed its bearer. *Germinie Lacerteux* (1865) traced a similar mental and physical breakdown. London may well have been influenced by this tradition, for although people die of "brain fever" in earlier novels, that obscure malady is never made the object of special consideration within the novel — it is usually employed to facilitate hasty exits.

[28] Readers have always responded to the spectacle of a "superman" grandly asserting himself. Beckford's *Vathek* depends for its appeal on precisely this sort of spectacle, as does much heroic literature. London told the story of such a brute superman more consistently in *Burning Daylight* (1910); the hero is a tremendous pioneer and gold seeker who at one point rushes into the office of the corporation that is cheating him of his honest earnings and forces the squirming capitalists, at the point of his gun, to give him fair treatment. Burning Daylight (the hero's name) stands for the individual asserting himself against those trusts which London hated all his life. Hence his self-assertion is ethically good and can provide the material for a novel that will not offend the average reader. Wolf Larsen, unfortunately for the novel, had no evil to combat; but among brutal and murderous sailors — with no Humphrey on the scene — he might well have emerged triumphant with no offense to the reader's sensibilities.

[29] Quoted from *The Book of Jack London*, II, 57; the passage dates from after the composition of the novel, probably from the summer of 1905.

[30] Charmian London, *op. cit.*, II, 31–33, tells of Jack's bringing her volumes of Nietzsche in the summer of 1905. He speaks of himself at that time as "getting hold of some of Nietzsche" (II, 31) — and the probable conclusion to be drawn from these rather indefinite statements is that 1905 marks London's *first* acquaintance with Nietzsche's works. Thereafter he mentions him at every opportunity; and it is hard to imagine what besides ignorance could have kept him from speaking of Nietzsche in *The Sea-Wolf*.

CHAPTER VI

[1] Franklin Walker's *Frank Norris: A Biography* (New York, 1932) is the most extensive biographical study of Norris. Ernest L. Marchand's *Frank Norris: A Study* (Stanford University Press, 1942) is the best study of his writings.

[2] Walker, *Frank Norris*, pp. 81–82.

[3] *Ibid.*, p. 59.

[4] *Ibid.*, p. 64.

[5] *Ibid.*, p. 65.

[6] In Volume X of the *Complete Edition of Frank Norris* (New York, 1928). This tale was probably written before Norris had read Zola. Harry Hartwick, *op. cit.*, *passim*, contends that such primitive characters are the logical and characteristic product of the naturalistic philosophy in its purest form.

[7] Walker, *Frank Norris*, pp. 73–75.

[8] *Ibid.*, p. 154.

[9] *Ibid.*, pp. 252–253, quoted from Isaac Marcosson, *Adventures in Interviewing* (New York, 1919), pp. 237–238.

[10] See the chapter so entitled in *The Responsibilities of the Novelist* (New York, 1903), written in 1901–1902.

[11] *Ibid.*, pp. 25–26.

[12] Walker, *Frank Norris*, p. 257.

[13] Ed. 1914, pp. 244–245. This novel was not published during Norris's lifetime. It survived the San Francisco earthquake and was discovered more than ten years after his death, among family effects.

[14] From an unsigned editorial identified and quoted by Walker, *Frank Norris,* p. 83.

[15] *McTeague: A Story of San Francisco* (New York, 1899; ed. 1903), pp. 1–2. I have throughout this chapter quoted accessible editions of the various novels.

[16] *Ibid.,* p. 89. This statement is cast in language which clearly shows the emotional pleasure Norris found in contemplating the mysterious and ineluctable forces defined by the naturalistic philosophy.

[17] Volume III, p. 286, of *The Complete Edition of Frank Norris.*

[18] *Ibid.,* VI, 31.

[19] *The Octopus: A Story of California* (New York, ed. 1935), II, 251.

[20] "The first novel, 'The Octopus,' deals with the war between the wheat grower and the Railroad Trust; the second, 'The Pit,' is the fictitious narrative of a 'deal' in the Chicago wheat pit; while the third, 'The Wolf,' will probably have for its pivotal episode the relieving of a famine in an Old World community." (From the Preface to *The Pit.*)

[21] *Ibid.,* II, 13–14. It is at such points in naturalistic novels that one must distinguish between what a writer intended to do, or says he has done, and what the actual form of the novel shows that he has done. One cannot take for granted Norris's statement in *The Responsibilities of the Novelist* that he was a naturalist and from this deduce that Magnus Derrick is not held morally accountable for his deeds because naturalism by definition excludes moral responsibility. Yet observe a recent reinterpreter of *The Octopus* pursuing exactly this kind of circular logic:

"According to the philosophy of determinism, it is plain that none of the characters in *The Octopus* may be blamed for his contribution to the general socioeconomic disorder in which he exists. It is true that the perverse actions of Magnus Derrick and S. Behrman give to the forces of nature — the wheat and the railroad — the false appearance of deliberate malevolence. But this is not to say that Derrick and Behrman are guilty of deliberate misbehavior [though they are "perverse"]. They cannot be held morally responsible for their unnatural endeavors, because their characters have been determined by environmental factors beyond their control. [How, then, are they "unnatural"?]" G. W. Meyer, "A New Interpretation of *The Octopus,*" *College English,* IV (March 1943), 357.

This article reveals a mixture of ethical and naturalistic thinking similar to that which many critics have discerned in Norris's writings. For example, despite the firm statement just quoted that determinism operates throughout *The Octopus,* Mr. Meyer a page earlier frees the characters from its operation by introducing the element of chance — which is of course the very thing that a consistent determinist denies. He writes, "The fact that chance governs the fate of the majority of the characters in *The Octopus* is established by the two most sensational incidents in the book. It is chance, after all — chance set free by misdirected human action [observe the ethical standards introduced here] — that kills the ranchers at the irrigation ditch. . . . The real tragedy of the irrigation ditch is that men should have given chance such a favorable opportunity to express itself." (*Ibid.,* p. 356.) What is chance? Is it Lurking Evil? The fact is that Norris has not been able to confine himself to the rigidly deterministic philosophy that he wanted to follow, and, as will appear later in the discussion, he never really confined his thinking to pure materialistic determinism.

[22] *Ibid.,* II, 286. Oddly enough, this passage follows right after Shelgrim's explanation that "the Wheat will be carried to feed the people."

[23] *The Pit: A Story of Chicago* (New York, 1903; ed. 1924), pp. 79–81. Norris brings in, quite gratuitously, a description of the food market in similar language: "A land of plenty, the inordinate abundance of the earth itself emptied itself upon the asphalt and cobbles of the quarter. It was the Mouth of the City, and drawn from all directions . . . this glut of crude subsistence was sucked in, as if into a rapacious gullet, to feed the sinews and to nourish the fibres of an immeasurable colossus." (Pp. 61–62.) The probable dependence of this picture upon Zola's descriptions of the food market in *Le Ventre de Paris* has been frequently suggested.

CHAPTER VII

[1] Carl Van Doren in *The American Novel* (1940) gives him two pages, crediting him with being "morally strenuous but intellectually belated" (p. 261). He is given little more than a page in Percy Boynton's *Literature and American Life* (1936), where there is no significant comment. Parrington's *Main Currents,* Volume III, has only notes on Churchill. A. H. Quinn, in *American Fiction: An Historical and Critical Survey* (1936), gives five pages mostly to summaries of the main novels. He concludes that Churchill is prolix, lacks constructive ability, is superficial, and "lacks distinction of style" (p. 501). He makes no attempt to deal with the intellectual tensions which affect the form of his novels. F. T. Cooper, "Some Represenative American Story Tellers: XII — Winston Churchill," *Bookman,* XXI (May 1910), has given the most extended account of Churchill's work that I know. Some of his very judicious remarks are quoted below. The present chapter is based on my longer study of Churchill, *The Romantic Compromise in the Novels of Winston Churchill,* University of Michigan Contributions in Modern Philology, No. 18 (1951).

[2] "It is only when a moment . . . like *this* comes that the quality of what we have lived seems so tarnished, that the atmosphere which we ourselves have helped to make is so sordid. When I think of the intrigues, and divorces, the self-indulgences, — when I think of my own marriage . . . Can we just seize happiness? Will it not elude us just as much as though we believed firmly in the ten commandments? . . . What I'm afraid of is that the world isn't made that way — for you — for me. We're permitted to seize those other things because they're just baubles, we've both found out how worthless they are. And the worst of it is they've made me a coward, Hugh. It isn't that I couldn't do without them, I've come to depend on them in another way. It's because they give me a certain *protection,* — do you see? — they've come to stand in the place of the real convictions we've lost. And — well, we've taken the baubles, can we reach out our hands and take — *this*? Won't we be punished for it, frightfully punished?" (*A Far Country,* p. 381.)

[3] *The Dwelling-Place of Light* (New York, 1917), p. 13.

[4] The owners of the mill "were fond of him, grateful to him, treating him with a frank camaraderie that had in it not the slightest touch of condescension, but Ditmar would have been the first to recognize that there were limits to the intimacy. . . . At an early age, and quite unconsciously, he had accepted property as the ruling power of the universe, and when family was added thereto the combination was nothing less than divine." *Ibid.,* p. 27.

⁵ P. 139. Here he speaks as a scientific materialist. Again, "Was she in love with Ditmar? The question was distasteful, she avoided it, for enough of the tatters of orthodox Christianity clung to her to cause her to feel shame when she contemplated the feelings he aroused in her. It was when she asked herself what his intentions were that her resentment burned, pride and a sense of her own value convinced her that he had deeply insulted her in not offering marriage . . . on the other hand, if he had done so, a profound, self-respecting and moral instinct in her would, in her present mood, have led her to refuse. She felt a fine scorn for the woman who, under the circumstances, would insist upon a bond and all a man's worldly goods in return for that which it was her privilege to give freely; while the notion of servility, of economic dependence . . . repelled her far more than the possibility of social ruin. This she did not contemplate at all . . ." Here is a passage in which the reader must admire the balanced interpretation of the status of love and social relations in the modern world. No more realistic presentation of the sexual question could be asked; we are not put off with moral tags; Janet's inhibitions are to be expected from one of her temperament and environment. I find, however, some difficulty in reconciling Janet's passion for Ditmar with her instinct against marrying him. To the priggish Victorian there may be an antipathy between "lust" and love, but for a freer modern spirit we should expect them to fuse — especially when Janet is nubile and Ditmar unattached.

⁶ "It seemed incredible, now, that she had ever deceived herself into thinking that Ditmar meant to marry her, that he loved her enough to make her his wife. . . . In the events of yesterday, which she pitilessly reviewed, she beheld a deliberate and prearranged plan for her betrayal." *Ibid.*, p. 281. The romantic assignation is completely reinterpreted in retrospect.

⁷ Insall, the writer, considers "principles" unimportant when there is practical work to be done. His words discredit the strikers: "He had forced her to use an argument that failed to harmonize, somehow, with Rolfe's poetical apologetics. Stripped of the glamour of these, was not Rolfe's [he is the radical for whom Janet works] doctrine just one of taking, taking? And when the workers were in possession of all, would not they be as badly off as Mrs. Brockle-hurst [an empty rich lady who indulges in charity and liberalism because she has no individual development] or Ditmar? . . . She beheld in Insall one who seemed emancipated from possessions, whose life was so organized as to make them secondary affairs." Here is a truly amazing jump — as if a starving mill worker could, by developing his inner self, be emancipated from possessions as Insall is! As Churchill unwittingly shows, only those who have had possessions for long enough to rise above them — that is, for generations — can rise to the good life. To set this goal up as an answer to the strikers' use of violence is to turn his back on the very problem which he has presented so forcefully in the earlier pages of his novel. For even Ditmar was too "new" to be genteel.

⁸ Notably Yvor Winters, *Primitivism and Decadence: A Study of American Experimental Poetry* (New York, c. 1937); and W. K. Wimsatt, Jr., and M. C. Beardsley, "The Intentional Fallacy," *Sewanee Review*, 54 (July 1946), 3-23.

CHAPTER VIII

¹ *A Book about Myself* (New York, 1922), p. 253. The title has since been changed to *Newspaper Days*.

² *Ibid.*, p. 210.

³ *Ibid.*, p. 140.

[4] *Ibid.*, p. 127. In *The "Genius"* (New York, 1923), p. 104, he wrote: "I stood by the window last night and looked out on the street. The moon was shining and those dead trees were waving in the wind. I saw the moon on that pool of water over in the field. It looked like silver. Oh, Eugene, I wish I were dead." It should be remarked that a good deal of *The "Genius"* is autobiographical.

[5] *A Book about Myself*, p. 451.

[6] *Ibid.*, p. 370.

[7] *Ibid.*, pp. 369–370.

[8] *Ibid.*, p. 198.

[9] *Ibid.*, p. 70. This was in 1891–1892; though written in 1922 it reflects ideas which Dreiser seems to have held steadily from about 1892 on.

[10] *Ibid.*, pp. 457–459.

[11] *Ibid.*, pp. 375, 141, 263, and 344.

[12] *Hey Rub-a-Dub-Dub* (New York, 1919), pp. 157–158. Dreiser's wide and sympathetic vision of life, his willingness to see and think about its sordid side, make one respect him for failing to arrive at a categorical explanation for the meaning of it all. If the philosopher must withdraw into an ivory tower in order to round out his system, the man who deals with the whole moving pathos of life-as-it-is should not be without some admiration. The practice among academic critics of disposing of Dreiser as a "peasant" or a "journalist" who could not think things through is based, if it has a base, upon ignorance of his personal experience.

[13] *A Book about Myself*, p. 326.

[14] *Hey Rub-a-Dub-Dub*, p. 134. This book was written in 1919 and consequently shows evidence of familiarity with the Freudian approach to sex. It may be remarked, however, that Dreiser's attitude toward problems of sex is substantially the same in all his novels from 1900 to 1925.

[15] Joseph W. Beach supports this interpretation of Dreiser's thought: "If I suggest a possible inspiration from the French naturalists, it is because his work is strongly colored by the terminology and deterministic assumptions of nineteenth-century science, which were so strong an element in Zola and his group. But it may have been direct from science, rather than from literature, that Dreiser took his disposition to regard human behavior as one manifestation of animal behavior in general, or even — to use his more frequently recurring term — as a chemical phenomenon." (*Twentieth Century Novel*, pp. 325–326.)

[16] One Wandell, a city editor, "was always calling upon me to imitate Zola's vivid description of the drab and gross and the horrible if I could, assuming that I had read him, which I had not." (*A Book about Myself*, p. 207.) Again: "Be careful how you write that now. All the facts you know, just as far as they will carry you. . . . Write it strong, clear, definite. Get in all the touches of local color you can. And remember Zola and Balzac, my boy, remember Zola and Balzac. Bare facts are what are needed in cases like this, with lots of color as to the scenery or atmosphere, the room, the other people, the street, and all that." (*Ibid.*, p. 211.)

[17] "It is interesting that Dreiser, who is often alleged to have derived from Zola, says here that he never read him, not until after his own first novel, *Sister Carrie*. But in Wandell's presence he dared not admit it." (Dorothy Dudley, *Forgotten Frontiers: Dreiser and the Land of the Free* (New York, 1932), p. 95.)

[18] "Hazard had . . . written a novel entitled *Theo*, which was plainly a bog-fire kindled by those blazing French suns, Zola and Balzac. The scene

was laid in Paris . . . and had much of the atmosphere of Zola's *Nana*, plus the delicious idealism of Balzac's *The Great Man from the Provinces* . . . It seemed intensely beautiful to me at the time, this book, with its frank pictures of raw, greedy, sensual human nature, and its open pictures of self-indulgence and vice." (*A Book about Myself*, p. 126.) This work "was the opening wedge for me into the realm of realism . . . the book made a great impression on me!" (*Ibid.*, pp. 131–133.) Unfortunately *Theo* was never published.

[19] "For a period of four or five months I ate, slept, dreamed, lived him and his characters and his views and his city. I cannot imagine a greater joy and inspiration than I had in Balzac these Spring and Summer days in Pittsburgh." (*Ibid.*, p. 412.)

[20] *Sister Carrie* (New York, 1900; ed. 1917), p. 362. There is no collected edition of Dreiser's writings.

[21] American reviewers were also offended by its treatment of lives which they deemed too sordid for genteel readers. See Dudley, *Forgotten Frontiers*, p. 186.

[22] *Sister Carrie*, p. 85. The italics are mine.

[23] *Ibid.*, p. 101.

[24] *Ibid.*, p. 362.

[25] The gap between Dreiser's work and the experimental novel of Zola is a wide one, for Dreiser does not make even a pretense of controlling his conditions and discovering truths about the nature of human psychology and physiology. Just where Zola, for example, would theoretically put most emphasis — i.e., on the extraction of laws about human nature — Dreiser is most uncertain and most sure that no certainty can be attained. To him such laws would be fruitless for the very reason that external conditions cannot ever be controlled — a fact of which all his experience had convinced him.

[26] *Jennie Gerhardt* (New York, 1911; ed. 1926), pp. 15–16.

[27] *Ibid.*, pp. 400–401. This passage is notable as the most explicit statement of belief in the novel. It comes from Lester, but it represents Dreiser's own attitude because it is virtually the thesis of his novel.

[28] Quoted in Charmian London, *The Book of Jack London*, 2 vols. (New York, 1921), II, 57.

[29] Stuart P. Sherman, *On Contemporary Literature* (New York, 1917), p. 98.

[30] Dreiser comments as follows upon the "meaning" of life: "I can make no comment on my work or my life that holds either interest or import for me. Nor can I imagine any explanation or interpretation of any life, my own included, that would be either true — or important, if true. Life is to me too much a welter and play of inscrutable forces to permit, in my case at least, any significant comment. One may paint for one's own entertainment, and that of others — perhaps. As I see him the utterly infinitesimal individual weaves among the mysteries a floss-like and wholly meaningless course — if course it be. In short I catch no meaning from all I have seen, and pass quite as I came, confused and dismayed." ("Statements of Belief," *Bookman*, LXVIII (September 1928), 25.)

[31] *The Financier* (New York, 1912; ed. London, 1927), p. 35.

[32] *Ibid.*, p. 140.

[33] *The Titan* (New York, 1914; ed. London, 1928), p. 461.

[34] *Hey Rub-a-Dub-Dub*, p. 89. These ideas, expressed in 1919, show Dreiser touched by the Nietzschean philosophy; they precede his conversion to socialism. Mr. Hartwick, however, goes on to insist that they prove Dreiser to have admired and condoned the behavior of Cowperwood as valuable to society. This cannot be entirely true, for the course of the novels does not show Cowperwood

to have been socially useful. The ethical implications are considered further below.

[35] *Theodore Dreiser* (New York, 1925), p. 78.

[36] *The Financier*, pp. 152–153. "That the modern home is the most beautiful of schemes, when based upon mutual sympathy and understanding between two, need not be questioned. And yet this fact should not necessarily carry with it a condemnation of all love not so fortunate as to find so happy a denouement. Life cannot be put in any mould, and the attempt might as well be abandoned at once."

[37] *Ibid.*, p. 137.

[38] *An American Tragedy*, 2 vols. (New York, 1925), II, 78–80.

[39] *The Stoic* (New York, 1947), p. 113.

CHAPTER IX

[1] *The Sherwood Anderson Reader* (Boston, 1947), p. viii.

[2] *Winesburg, Ohio* (New York, 1919), pp. 4–5. There is no collected edition of Anderson's writings.

[3] *Beyond Desire* (New York, 1932), pp. 92–93.

[4] *Kit Brandon* (New York, 1936), p. 373.

CHAPTER X

[1] *Young Lonigan: A Boyhood in Chicago Streets* (New York, 1932); *The Young Manhood of Studs Lonigan* (New York, 1934); *Judgment Day* (New York, 1935).

[2] *A World I Never Made* (New York, 1936); *No Star is Lost* (New York, 1938); *Father and Son* (New York, 1940); *My Days of Anger* (New York, 1943). *The Face of Time* (New York, 1953) goes back to Danny's early childhood, when he is about five years old.

[3] See *The League of Frightened Philistines, and Other Papers* (New York, 1945), "How *Studs Lonigan* Was Written," pp. 88–89.

[4] *Bernard Clare* (changed to *Bernard Carr*; New York, 1946); *The Road Between* (New York, 1949); *Yet Other Waters* (New York, 1952).

[6] George Snell speaks of the *Studs* saga as "a thousand pages of the most frank and detailed naturalistic writing our literature has ever seen" (*The Shapers of American Fiction 1798–1947* (New York, 1947)), but the description is much more appropriate for *Bernard Clare* and the two subsequent volumes of this later trilogy.

CHAPTER XI

[1] *Sea of Cortez: A Leisurely Journal of Travel and Research*, by John Steinbeck and Edward F. Ricketts (New York, 1941), p. 75.

[2] *Ibid.*, p. 149.

[3] *Ibid.*, p. 150.

[4] *Ibid.*, p. 142.

[5] *Ibid.*, p. 257.

[6] *Never Love a Stranger*, by Harold Robbins (New York, 1948), pp. 311–312.

[7] *A Farewell to Arms* (New York, 1929), p. 196.

[8] *Ibid.*, p. 267.

[9] *Manhattan Transfer* (New York, 1925), p. 375. There is no collected edition of Dos Passos's works.

[10] *U.S.A.* (New York, 1937), III, 26.

[11] *Ibid.*, p. 27.

[12] *Ibid.*, pp. 436–437.

[13] *Ibid.*, pp. 461–464.

Index

qualities, 241; tragic effects, 241, 244, 248, 251, 255; spiritual and ethical barrenness, 241–44, 255; violence, 242, 244, 246, 247; irony, 243; descriptive naturalism, 243, 247, 256–57; melodrama, 245; shift in point of view, 246, 247, 249, 251–54; virtues of privation, 249; autobiographical elements, 249; concreteness, 250–51; characterization and shift in fictional conventions, 251–53; reportage, 252, 257; naturalism identified with scientific method, 256; stages of naturalism, 256–57

Works: *Studs Lonigan* trilogy, 240–45; *Young Lonigan*, 241; *Gas-House McGinty*, 245; Danny O'Neill tetralogy, 245–49; *Bernard Clare* (or *Carr*), 250–56

Fascism, 278, 298, 300

Fate, 21, 25, 26, 27, 29, 73, 85, 182, 240, 255, 280: as force in *Vandover*, 122; and Shakespearian tragedy, 123; naturalism as modern approach to, 124, 125; in *McTeague*, 130; in Churchill, 162, 165; in *Jennie Gerhardt*, 197

Faulkner, William, 64: clinical awareness in, 65; tragic view of, 300–1

Financier, The, 199–206, 211, 318

For Whom the Bell Tolls, 270, 276–78, 280

Forces, social, 48, 197

Forces, deterministic: Zola's attempt to study, 96; in Norris, 117, 130, 139, 141, 145, 147, 149, 153; in Churchill, 157, 164–68, 174, 176. *See also* Determinism, Economics, Materialism

Forces, economic, 197, 257, 278

Form, 35, 37, 42, 55, 82, 186, 239, 245, 269, 270, 278, 280, 283: in Newton's mechanics, 5; search for, 22; in Garland, 55, 59; in London, 111; in Norris, 120, 313; in Churchill, 158, 162, 166, 176–77, 178; in Dreiser, 205, 220; confusions of, 224, 232, 233, 238, 292; in Anderson, 237, 238; in Farrell, 240, 243–44, 257; in Steinbeck, 258, 260, 262; dramatic, 260; in Dos Passos, 289; experimenters in, 294; of novel today, dissolved by reportage,

296; myth used today as basis for, 297. *See also* Structure

Forms of naturalistic fiction, 258: panoramic, 21, 142; not dependent on naturalistic philosophy, 23, 38; Zola's comments on, 43

42nd Parallel, 284

Frederic, Harold: beginnings of naturalism, 45; tone, 45–47, 48, 51; ethical and naturalistic motivation mixed, 47–48, 51–52; idealism, 48; literary technique, 48–49, 52; environment, 45–47, 49, 52

Works: *Seth's Brother's Wife*, 45–49; *The Damnation of Theron Ware*, 49–52

Free Association, 233

Freedom, 17, 69, 262, 277, 294

Freud, Sigmund, psychology of, 225, 294

Frustration, 226, 230, 231: theme of, in Anderson, 228, 232; social and institutional causes of, 232: and privation, 234; in Farrell, 242, 246

Fuller, Henry Blake, 309

Galileo, 5

Garland, Hamlin, 224, 232, 293: life, 53; veritism, 53, 54, 61, 62; genteelism, 53–54, 59, 61, 62, 63; technique inadequate, 54, 59, 61, 62; determinism, 55, 57, 59; tension in sketches, 55

Works: *Jason Edwards*, 53, 57–60; *A Spoil of Office*, 53; *Crumbling Idols*, 53, 54; *Main-Traveled Roads*, 54, 56; *Prairie Folks*, 54; "A Branch Road," 56; "Under the Lion's Paw," 56–57; *Rose of Dutcher's Coolly*, 60–63

Gas-House McGinty, 245

Gates, Lewis E., 115

"Genius," *The*, 205–6, 210, 211

Genteel tradition, 53, 54, 59, 62, 63, 164, 165, 166, 168

Germinal, 21, 23, 36–37, 139–45 *passim*, 150, 154, 201

Gilder, Richard W., 53

"Godliness: A Tale in Four Parts," 227

Godwin, William, 6

Goncourt, Charles and Jules, 31, 312

Vandover and the Brute, 115, 117, 118–
25, 128, 132, 151, 245, 312
Veritism, in Garland, 53–54, 61, 62
Versailles Treaty, 287
Violence, 41, 67–68, 73, 78, 79, 81, 84,
97, 109, 261, 262, 263, 283, 297, 298,
305, 311: as theme of naturalistic fiction, 20; in Norris, 115, 117, 132, 133,
136–38, 143; in Churchill, 171–72,
176; in Crane, 222; in Anderson, 228;
in Farrell, 242, 244, 246, 247, 248,
257; in Hemingway, 278; in Dos
Passos, 286
Vivas, Eliseo, 256

Wakeman, Frederick, 296
Walker, Franklin, 114–15, 117
Wallace, Alfred R., 7
Wallace, Lew, 157
Waste, tragic sense of, 241, 244, 245,
248, 251, 263, 265, 287, 311
Wave, San Francisco, 125
Wayward Bus, The, 266–67
Wedekind, Frank, 86
Whitman, Walt, 231, 252, 287, 291:
sees unity of phenomenal and spir-
itual, 11; and Emerson, 13
Will, 4, 38, 40, 74, 84, 90, 91, 93, 101,
102, 105, 113, 118–24 *passim*, 155,
156, 201, 208, 246, 256, 262, 281, 310:
in Newton's mechanics, 5; under
Spencer, 8; implied in naturalistic

fiction, 18; in recent fiction, 41; in
Nietzsche, 100; in Norris, 128, 130,
134, 136, 142, 145, 153; in Churchill,
173, 177; in Dreiser, 188, 195, 199,
207, 209; paralysis of, 236
"Will to power," 100
Wilson, Sloane, 296
Wimsatt, W. K., Jr., 315
Winesburg, Ohio, 222–32, 234
Winters, Yvor, 315
Wolf, The, 313
Wordsworth, William, 19, 291

Yogi philosophy, 214, 217, 219
Young Lonigan, 241

Zola, Émile, 54, 58, 61, 66, 139, 140,
141, 142, 145, 148, 150, 155, 201, 243,
291, 292, 293, 301, 316: concern with
style, 42–44; experimental program
of, 101, 107; and Norris, 114–17
passim, 125; Dreiser urged to read,
186; romanticism of, 293
Works: *Germinal*, 21, 23, 36–37,
139–45 *passim*, 150, 154, 201; *Le
Roman Expérimentale*, 25, 31ff, 305,
306; *L'Assommoir*, 25, 35–36, 40, 95,
135, 201; *Thérèse Raquin*, 32; *Rougon-Macquart* series, 32–44 *passim*;
La Terre, 140; *La Bête Humaine*,
298; *La Fortune des Rougon*, 307;
Le Docteur Pascal, 307–8; *Nana*, 317